LED ZEPPELIN

Contributors:
Geoff Barton, Mark Blake,
Hugh Fielder, Barney Hoskyns,
Peter Makowski, Ian Ravendale,
Scott Rowley, Mick Wall,
Chris Welch

Fox Chapel
PUBLISHING

Used under license. All rights reserved. This version published by Fox Chapel Publishing Company, Inc., 903 Square Street, Mount Joy, PA 17552.

For more information about the Future plc group, go to http://www.futureplc.com.

ISBN 978-1-4971-0462-4

Library of Congress Control Number: 2024905040

Image on page 81 is credited to Alamy.com: Trinity Mirror.
Image on page 101 is credited to Shutterstock.com: Bruce Alan Bennett

To learn more about the other great books from Fox Chapel Publishing, or to find a retailer near you, call toll-free 800-457-9112 or visit us at *www.FoxChapelPublishing.com.*

We are always looking for talented authors. To submit an idea, please send a brief inquiry to acquisitions@foxchapelpublishing.com.

Printed in China
First printing

LED ZEPPELIN

Table of Contents

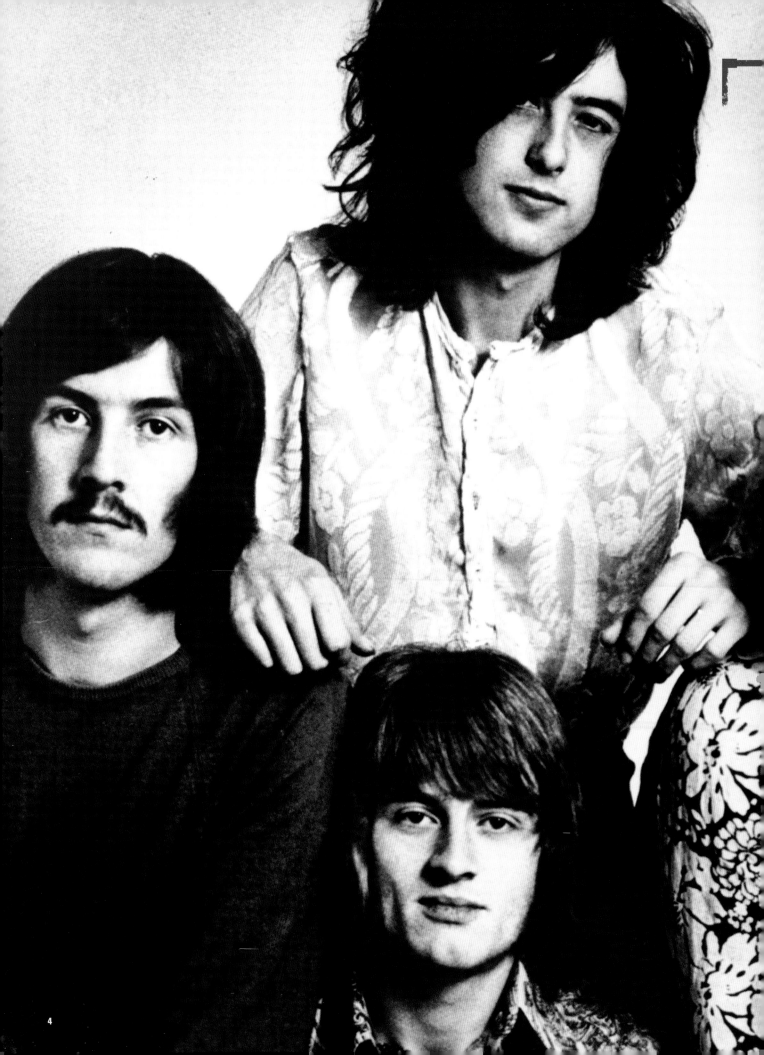

GETTY

Oct 4th 1968

Led Zeppelin's "Secret" UK Debut

When people turned up to a Newcastle ballroom, they expected to see The Yardbirds. Instead, they saw the future of rock.

By: Ian Ravendale

The announcement of a Yardbirds gig at Newcastle's Mayfair Ballroom in October 1968 barely caused a ripple of interest in the Northeast, let alone elsewhere. After a string of Top 10 hits a few years earlier, their career was on a downward slide and they were perilously close to becoming yesterday's men.

What the people of Tyneside didn't know was that the band had actually split up a few months earlier. But rather than cancel a Scandinavian tour, guitarist Jimmy Page had taken the opportunity to relaunch the band with singer Robert Plant, drummer John Bonham, and noted session player John Paul Jones on bass and keyboards.

And so the few dozen people who turned up at the Mayfair for what was supposed to be the first date of The Yardbirds' UK tour were in for a surprise. After sitting through support bands Downtown Faction, the Junco Partners, and New York Public Library (the latter a late replacement for Terry Reid), the audience found themselves confronted with an unfamiliar group. Although they didn't know it, they were witnessing the first British gig by the band that would become Led Zeppelin.

Jimmy Page: We originally thought that by calling ourselves the New Yardbirds we would be able to keep a sort of continuity from the early days of the old group.

Brian Greenaway (Mayfair manager, 1966-71): It all exploded in the 1960s. Friday night we'd often get 2,500 people in. It would be heaving. We had some really big names on, people like The Who.

Revolver: the turning stage at Newcastle's Mayfair Ballroom.

Fraser Suffield (promoter): I promoted a lot of shows in the sixties and early seventies at the Mayfair. I booked the Yardbirds gig in early 1968 via the Sherry-Copeland Agency. The tickets were [about one dollar] to get in. I'll have probably paid around [95 dollars or 127 dollars] for the band.

Bob Sargeant (keyboard player, the Junco Partners): For these Mayfair gigs there would usually be a national band, an up-and-coming national band, and two local supports. The Juncos followed Downtown Faction, New York Public Library followed us, and the New Yardbirds followed them. Terry Reid was on some of the adverts but he didn't play.

Terry Reid: Fantasia and I were on Cream's farewell US tour and couldn't do the gig. We had a lot of juggling around with dates about then.

Tez Stokes (guitarist, New York Public Library): We got the gig the week before the show. We only found out we were supporting The Yardbirds when we got there.

Ray Laidlaw (drummer, Downtown Faction): Downtown Faction were a progressive blues band, and the *Five Live Yardbirds* album had been a huge influence on us. The Yardbirds had changed a lot since then but I was still mildly interested to see them.

Fraser Suffield: I hadn't met The Yardbirds before, so when they arrived I introduced myself. I didn't think, "This isn't the band I booked."

Tez Stokes: We'd met Jimmy Page years before, when he was in Neil Christian's Crusaders. He was a very well-respected guitar player, but very quiet, reserved, and shy. John Paul Jones I met when he was the bass player with the Tony Meehan Band. He stayed with us that night because he had a meeting the next morning with [producer] Mickie Most.

Charlie Foskett (audience member): The day before, I'd taken my Ampeg upright bass into Barrett's music shop in the center of Newcastle to see if they'd be interested in buying it. It was like a stick with a point on one end and machine heads on the other. While I was there, in walks John Paul

Jones. I didn't know who he was, but the shop guys are going, "That's him!" That's him who? They knew him from his session work and that he'd be playing the Mayfair the following day. He had a go with my bass, and starts playing the bass line to "Whole Lotta Love", although of course none of us knew it then. It sounded total rubbish on an upright bass. The strings were a couple of inches off the fretboard, making it really difficult to play. I told him it sounded great. It didn't at all, but I wanted to flog it. He gave me [18 dollars] and left the shop with it under his arm.

Charlie Harcourt (guitarist, the Junco Partners): Before the gig, either the band or their roadie asked if they could borrow our organ. They didn't seem very well prepared. We told them no, they should have brought their own.

Bob Sargeant: I don't remember John Paul Jones playing keyboards that night. That'll be the reason why. I must have been in the bar when they asked, because I'd have said yes.

(l-r) Robert Plant and Jimmy Page in Copenhagen in 1968.

Fraser Suffield: Some bands had rider requirements as long as your arm. The New Yardbirds weren't one of them.

Ray Laidlaw: This was in the days before riders really came in. If you were lucky you might get a crate of beer. All four bands were in the same dressing room, which was a large, disused bar at the side of the stage. We were all milling around, coming and going.

Bob Sargeant: I've got a vague memory of talking to Jimmy at the bar before they went on. He was the only one I spoke to.

Charlie Harcourt: The Mayfair had a revolving stage, so one band would be setting up at the back while the other was performing. When that band finished their set, the stage would turn and the other band would arrive.

Ray Laidlaw: The revolving stage meant you couldn't put your gear onstage until just before you

were about to go on. There wasn't room. The corridors backstage were full of gear.

Charlie Foskett: There wasn't much of a feeling of anticipation before the New Yardbirds went on, although it was crowded around the stage.

Ray Laidlaw: I don't recall the gig being that well attended. The Yardbirds were old news by that point. The Mayfair was a bit like a club, and some people would go no matter who was on.

"A lot of the audience went . . . 'Who's this?' It wasn't The Yardbirds, it was another band."

Charlie Foskett, audience member

Tez Stokes: I stood right at the front and watched. There was hardly anyone there. Some people were sitting in the balcony, looking down.

Bob Sargeant: The bands were expected to be playing when the revolving stage came round. It was usually a 12-bar or something, before they started their set.

Charlie Foskett: Zeppelin weren't playing when the stage came around, they were farting around. Jones was on the left side in front of a silver-fronted Fender Bassman amp. He hit a note and the cloth on the front of the amp wobbled, which I thought was cool. Page posed about with his Les Paul. They weren't using monitors, all of that came later. Bonham was on the floor, on his kit, in front of the riser, which had the amps, waiting for someone to ➤➤

GETTY IMAGES/JORGEN ANGEL/REDFERNS

go, "One, two, three, four." That came pretty quickly.

Bob Sargeant: They were good. Very indicative of what they'd become as Led Zeppelin. I can remember thinking, "Who's that bloke singing?"

Charlie Foskett: A lot of the audience went, "Where's The Yardbirds? Who's this?" It wasn't The Yardbirds, it was another band.

Fraser Suffield: When the band got into it, I thought they were very impressive, with lots of promise.

Charlie Foskett: After five minutes it was, "This is great!" Everybody had forgotten about The Yardbirds. Nobody knew the name Led Zeppelin then, of course, so it was, "Yeah, this is the New Yardbirds!"

Ray Laidlaw: Because they'd only been playing together for a few weeks, they didn't have a presence. When you see a band with feel or atmosphere to them, you come away thinking you've really seen something. I didn't get that with them, because at the time they didn't have it. There was no chemistry.

Charlie Foskett: I thought the band were terrific. The first thing was the energy. Everything was a bunch of riffs. Page's guitar was ripping away. I've heard better soloists, but he was a great showman, a walking skeleton with skin-tight bell-bottom jeans, the hair, and tons of posing.

Ray Laidlaw: I wasn't very impressed with Robert Plant. He was a bit fey. I was more interested in the mechanics of the band. Bonham was pretty damn good. John Paul Jones kept himself in the background, and Jimmy Page was a fantastic player. But the band wasn't finely tuned.

Bob Sargeant: I thought the material they did was similar to what was on Jeff Beck's *Truth* album.

From that UK debut in Newcastle, the only way was up. And up . . .

John Bonham: "pretty damn good," says one audience member.

Ray Laidlaw: Page was basing it on the Jeff Beck Group. He knew how successful they'd been in the US and was using that as his model. I wouldn't be surprised if after each gig he'd go through it with the band: a little more of this, a bit less of that, polish that, drop this number, bring that one in. Like managing a football team.

Bob Sargeant: There was a track on *Truth* called "You Shook Me," with Rod Stewart singing. The New Yardbirds did that number at the Mayfair. They also did "Shapes of Things," the old Yardbirds hit. And they played "Communication Breakdown" and a couple of other songs that turned up on the first Zeppelin album.

Charlie Foskett: I was very much into their overall noise and energy along with the visual thing. They really had their chops together. It was as loud as the gear would allow it to be at that point, and full throttle, including the couple of Yardbirds hits they did. The discerning music lovers were glued to it.

Tez Stokes: Jimmy Page did an extended guitar solo sitting down. The sweat was pouring out of him. As a guitarist myself I was watching very closely, picking up tips. I was very impressed.

Ray Laidlaw: I was thinking that this was the latest version of The Yardbirds, and some of it was really good and some of it wasn't. I didn't go away telling people that The Yardbirds are back and they're fantastic. It was all part of the progressive blues thing that was happening then, where maybe they'd make a couple of albums and that would be it. To me they didn't warrant any more credence than any of the many other John Mayall-influenced bands that were knocking about.

John Porteous (Tyneside record dealer): My friend, the late John Gourley, was Newcastle's top Yardbirds collector. He goes to the Mayfair that Friday night expecting to see the Keith Relf lineup. The band comes on, and he watches three or four numbers. He then goes to the front desk, says the band onstage

aren't The Yardbirds, demands his money back, and leaves. Quite a few others did the same.

Fraser Suffield: I didn't receive any complaints from the Mayfair manager about people wanting their money back. When people were leaving I got no adverse comments about them not being the band they were expecting.

Charlie Foskett: After the last song, it was a case of, "Thank you and goodnight!" The stage revolved and they were off. I did think they had it, and that it could happen for them, given half a chance.

Fraser Suffield: After the gig I went backstage to pay the money to the band themselves. They didn't have a manager with them.

Brian Greenaway: Once a band had been paid they'd be away. They tended not to stay overnight. They'd be in the van and back to London.

Jimmy Page: We realized we were working under false pretenses. The thing had quickly gone beyond where The Yardbirds left off. We all agreed there was no point in retaining the "New Yardbirds" tag, so we decided to change the band's name.

Ray Laidlaw: It only dawned on me three or four months later that Led Zeppelin were the people I'd seen. If they had to stand or fall by the performance that night they probably wouldn't have been signed. It was okay, but not the entity with the mighty presence that Zeppelin became very soon after. ❼

WHAT HAPPENED NEXT?
After several more gigs, Page renamed the band Led Zeppelin. UK university and club dates were followed by a US tour and the release of their eponymous debut album. Downtown Faction evolved into the band Lindisfarne. The Mayfair was demolished in 1999 to make room for a parking lot.

The First Album

As the sixties ended, session supremo **Jimmy Page** put together a band and a plan that would change rock forever—even if it did owe a whole lot to music's past.

By: Mick Wall

In 1969, Chris Welch was the star writer of Melody Maker, then the most influential and prestigious music paper in Britain. He'd been there when Hendrix first set fire to his guitar at the Speakeasy; hung out in the studio while The Who wrestled with Tommy; kept Dylan waiting in reception for an interview while he finished his lunch; driven Rod Stewart home from gigs in the days when Rod was too poor to afford his own wheels. But, Chris says, he had never—ever—heard anything like this. "One of the younger writers brought an early pre-release copy of the album in and played it on the office stereo—and it just leapt out at you! It really did feel like a great leap forward, in terms of the sound you could actually get on a record. And that was just the first track."

Forty years later you can still hear the awe in his voice. But then, 40 years later you can still feel the energy crackling when you play the album he's talking about: the eponymous debut from Led Zeppelin, released in Britain in March 1969. Already available in America since the start of the year, despite attracting some less-than-favorable reviews—notably, from John Mendelssohn in *Rolling Stone*, who damned *Led Zeppelin* as the poor relation to *Truth*, the band offering "little that its twin, the Jeff Beck Group, didn't say as well or better," describing Jimmy Page as "a very limited producer and a writer of weak, unimaginative songs" and characterizing Robert Plant's vocals as "strained and unconvincing shouting." Led Zeppelin's debut album was already on its way to becoming a sizable hit on both sides of the Atlantic, as well as changing the face of rock music completely.

The brainchild of Page, a 24-year-old session guitarist who, somewhat astonishingly, had played on more than half of all the hit singles made in Britain from 1962-66, but who had only recently come to public attention via his late entry into the Yardbirds, the release of the first Zeppelin album could be said to have ushered in the 1970s a year early.

An only child from West London who'd grown up, as he put it, "a loner," Jimmy Page had always gone his own way: leaving school early to play professionally in a band, Neil Christian and the Crusaders; later dropping out of Sutton Art College to become a full-time session player; becoming so successful at that he turned down the chance to replace Eric Clapton in the Yardbirds, then riding high in the charts,

recommending his old school pal Jeff Beck for the job instead. Why endure the endless one-nighters that were then the burden of a touring band of the Yardbirds' stature, when he could earn more money—far more money—doing as many as three sessions a day in London?

Page was the same age, or younger, than the groups whose records he was hired to embellish and improve—from hi-spec artistic fare by Them, the Kinks, Joe Cocker, The Who, and several other notables, to low-rent chart-toppers by Val Doonican, Herman's Hermits, P.J. Proby, and Engelbert Humperdinck. All of which provided a tremendous grounding in an array of different styles—not just musical, but technical, watching producers of the caliber of Mickie Most, Shel Talmy, Joe Meek, and others weave their magic in the studio.

Page's prowess as a guitarist also benefited hugely from an array of often unexpected sources. Not least his obsession with the work of eccentric Scottish genius, Davy Graham, whose groundbreaking album, *The Guitar Player*, demonstrated how to go from folk to jazz to baroque, blues, and even Oriental and Asian music—without sacrificing any of the edgier sounding techniques then making themselves felt in rock. Similarly, other Graham disciples like Bert Jansch and John Renbourn's album *Bert And John* became glued to Page's turntable as he painstakingly worked out the unusual tunings, esoteric fingerings, and strange modal tones.

Page had now begun writing his own songs too. Especially when he found out how much money the writers of hit songs could make. Hired to play on a Burt Bacharach session, Jimmy was flabbergasted to see Burt leaving in a chauffeur-driven Rolls-Royce. The turning point came, however, when the 21-year-old guitarist began an affair with Jackie De Shannon, a successful singer-songwriter from Kentucky who'd written "When You Walk In the Room," a hit for The Searchers. She had then been invited by the Beatles to make a single of her own in London, and Page had been hired to play on the session. They ended up back at her hotel, making love and writing songs together—some of which would get picked up by singers like Marianne Faithfull and P.J. Proby.

It was also during this period that Page recorded a solo single, "She Just Satisfies"— singing with Jackie on backing vocals. It was not a hit, but from now on the session work would pay the bills while Page worked on furthering his career as a songwriter and producer in his own right—as when he and Jeff Beck sat down and started busking up a version of Ravel's "Bolero." This was during the now famous sessions at London's IBC studios in the summer of 1966 that would feature Keith Moon on drums, Nicky Hopkins on keyboards, and session ▸

The Yardbirds with Beck
and Page on guitar?
"It could have been bigger than the Stones," said Page.

"[Together the four of us] had a
collective energy that made this
fifth element . . ."

player John Paul Jones on bass; the same session at which Moony jokingly suggested they form a supergroup and call it Lead Zeppelin (as in lead balloon); an idea they all laughed at but which Jimmy never forgot.

Joining the Yardbirds—as Page did the same year, initially as a temporary replacement for departed bassist Paul Samwell-Smith—had not been part of his cunning plan, more something he did "for fun." But when rhythm guitarist Chris Dreja agreed to take over on bass, allowing Page to forge a fiery new twin-lead-guitar partnership with his old friend Beck, the fun took on a more serious aspect as the musical possibilities opened up before them. "It could have been even better than the Stones," Jimmy recalled. Maybe even more innovative than what Clapton was doing as a soloist in Cream. Could have, would have, should have . . . except for one thing: the self-destructive streak in Jeff that would also unhinge his later career with his own Beck Group. As Jimmy said ruefully, "Jeff's his own worst enemy in that respect."

Within months of Page joining, Beck had bailed out midway through a US tour, complaining of illness, then smashing his guitar in the dressing room and catching a plane to LA where he met up with a girlfriend. Even then, Jimmy thought he could salvage the situation, help take the Yardbirds to the next level. But then there was producer-manager Mickie Most to contend with. Unlike Page, who cared about every last detail, Most treated recording sessions as conveyor belts. "Next!" he'd declare, at the end of a take. "I've never worked like this in my life," Page complained. "Don't worry about it," said Mickie, before counting in the next number.

When the Yardbirds finally fell apart, out on the road in America, where they remained huge long after their star in Britain had faded, Page was enormously frustrated. Having given up an income sizable enough to buy his own boathouse on the Thames, in order to find acclaim with the band, he was determined to keep the show on the road—even if it meant replacing every other member of the band. Hence: the New Yardbirds—formed within weeks of the final Yardbirds show, in July 1968.

Unable to persuade any of his original A-list targets to team up with him—as Aynsley Dunbar, one of the drummers Jimmy initially approached, put it, "the Yardbirds was already sort of old news by then"—a desperate Page finally settled on a lineup comprising old pal from the session world, John Paul Jones, on bass and keyboards, plus two raw recruits from the Midlands, in the shape of 19-year-old vocalist Robert Plant and his drumming pal, John "Bonzo" Bonham, both late of tried-and-failed psychedelic wannabes the Band Of Joy.

It was a close-run thing, though. Before Plant, Page had been considering Chris Farlowe, but he'd just had a huge hit with "Out of Time," which Page, ironically, had played on. Before that there had been talk of Stevie Marriott, but Page went cold on the idea after Small Faces manager Don Arden threatened to "break his fingers." Stevie Winwood was also considered but he wasn't about to quit Traffic to join the New Yardbirds. And so Page turned to Terry Reid, a young gun-for-hire who also baulked at the idea of trying to forge a career in a group where the appendage "New" made them sound suddenly very old.

Fortunately for Page, Reid had a suggestion: a young singer from the Midlands he'd met on the road named Robert Plant. Even so, Page was skeptical. "If he was so good how come I'd never heard of him?" Ultimately, however, Plant was the only decent singer out there that didn't have anything better to do. "I liked Robert," Jimmy would tell me. "He obviously had a great voice and a lot of enthusiasm. But I wasn't sure yet how he was going to be onstage." He added: "The one I was really sure about right from the off was Bonzo." Until then, his inclination had been to offer the gig to Procol Harum drummer B.J. Wilson, who he'd played with on Joe Cocker's monumentally heavy treatment of "With A Little Help From My Friends." But Wilson rated his chances of success with Procol Harum—who'd arrived the year before with the No. 1 "A Whiter Shade of Pale"—as infinitely better than the revival of a band that hadn't had a hit for two years.

Other drummers considered included Dunbar, who had been in the original Jeff Beck Group; Mitch Mitchell, unhappy with Hendrix in the Experience; Bobby

Graham, an old "hooligan" session pal; and Clem Cattini, another session pal. One by one they all turned him down. And so, at new boy Plant's urging, Page had gone to see Bonzo play with Tim Rose at a club in north London. It was July 31, 1968, and, as Page says now, "He did this short, five-minute drum solo and that's when I knew I'd found who I was looking for."

As for Jones, a laconic, professorial figure, even in his early twenties, it wasn't his style to go overboard about anything. He admits now, though, "I sensed something good might be going on with Jimmy." He'd played on Yardbirds records before; worked with Page dozens of times. As he says, "Jimmy promised something a little different from a regular, one-style blues band."

"I jumped at the chance to get him," Page would recall. "Musically he's the best musician of us all. He had a proper training and he has quite brilliant ideas." Page had previously considered Jack Bruce, on the brink of leaving an already disintegrating Cream; Ace Kefford, formerly of the Move, who had also recently auditioned for the Jeff Beck Group; even original Beck bassist Ronnie Wood. "It was pretty obvious they'd probably make it, especially in America," Wood says now. "But I wanted to get back to playing guitar and there was only ever going to be one guitarist in [Page's] group."

On Monday, August 19, the day before Plant's twentieth birthday, a rehearsal was arranged in a small room below a record shop in London's Chinatown. "We ended up playing "The Train Kept A-Rollin'," which had been an old Yardbirds number," recalled Jones. "We ran through it and I thought, is it just me or was that really good?" It wasn't just Jonesy. "It was unforgettable," said Jimmy. "Everybody just freaked. It was like these four individuals, but this collective energy made this fifth element. And that was it. It was there immediately—a thunderbolt, a lightning flash—boosh! Everybody sort of went, 'Wow.'"

The real test, however, would come out on the road, using a three-week tour of Scandinavia to trial run a set list bolted together from old Yardbirds numbers and blues covers—stuff that would, as Page later told me, "allow us to stretch out within that framework. There were lots of areas which they used to call freeform but was just straight improvisation." By the time the tour ended, "I'd already come up with such a mountain of riffs and ideas, because every night we went on there were new things happening."

Twelve days after the tour, Page took his New Yardbirds into Olympic, a popular eight-track studio in Barnes, south London—the same studio the Stones had recently made *Beggars Banquet* in. Concentrating on simply laying down the live set they'd been hammering into shape augmented by a couple of extra tracks, starting with versions of the folk ballad, "Babe I'm Gonna Leave You," and Willie Dixon's "You Shook Me." Page said, "I wanted artistic control in a vice grip because I knew exactly what I wanted to do with these fellows."

Nine days later, after a total of just 30 hours in the studio, the album had been fully recorded, mixed, and was ready to be cut onto a mastered disc. Total cost, including artwork: over two thousand dollars. Even taking into account how experienced and versatile session vets like Page and Jones were—or the fact that all four had proved how well they gelled in the studio when performing as backing band (with Plant on harmonica) on a P.J. Proby session in London, arranged for them by Jones, just prior to that first tour (the track "Jim's Blues," later released on the 1969 Proby album, *Three Week Hero*, is the first studio track to feature all four members of the future Led Zeppelin)—this was extremely fast work.

Opening with the rhythmic battering ram that is "Good Times Bad Times," as Chris Welch says, the immediate impression one got from hearing Led Zeppelin for the first time was one of pure shocking power, its opening salvo summing up everything the name Led Zeppelin would quickly come to represent. A pop song credited to Page, Jones, and Bonham built on a zinging, catchy chorus, explosive drums, and—at exactly the right moment—a flurry of spitting guitar notes, it pointed the way forward for rock music in the seventies, towards heavy duty ➤➤

When the Yardbirds fell apart Page was determined to keep going: even if it meant replacing every member of the band.

"I wanted artistic control
in a vice grip because I knew
exactly what I wanted to do [with Zeppelin]."
—Jimmy Page

The *Truth* hurts: did Page try to out-do the Jeff Beck Group's debut by covering "You Shook Me"?

on the album didn't also take its cue from the work of others, largely without acknowledgement.

Indeed, of the other tracks on the album credited to various band members, all have subsequently had that contention challenged to varying degrees. Beginning with "Babe I'm Gonna Leave You," Page's reworking of a traditional ballad first heard outside contemporary folk circles on a Joan Baez album, although not unjustly credited on the original pressings of Led Zeppelin as a "Traditional" song, "arranged by Jimmy Page." By the time of the 1990 release of the *Remasters* CD box set, the credit had been amended to include A. Bredon, aka American folk singer Anne Bredon, who'd recorded her similar-sounding version over 15 years before.

Similarly, "Black Mountain Side," an acoustic guitar instrumental in the exotic, modal style of Page's earlier Yardbirds-era showcase, "White Summer," down to the percussive accompaniment of the Indian tablas by Viram Jasani. Where "White Summer" had been Page's "interpretation" of Davy Graham's esoteric version of "She Moved Through the Fair" (or more accurately, Graham's reinterpretation of the song as "She Moved Through the Bizarre / Blue Ragga"), with its unique DADGAD tuning—a signature Graham D-modal tuning devised for playing Moroccan music that also proved especially efficacious for ancient modal Irish tunes—"Black Mountain Side" was in fact Page's instrumental version of fellow Graham disciple Bert Jansch's 1966 recording of another traditional Gaelic folk tune titled "Black Waterside"—originally shown to Jansch by Anne Briggs, another Page favorite who had herself been shown the tune by an old folklorist named Bert Lloyd.

As a result, although Jansch's then record company Transatlantic sought legal advice, in consultation with two eminent musicologists and John Mummery QC—one of the most prominent copyright barristers in the UK at the time—it was decided not to pursue an action for royalties against Page and/or Led Zeppelin. As head of Transatlantic, Nat Joseph explained, "It had been reasonably established that there was every chance that Jimmy Page had heard Bert play the piece. However, what could not be proved was that Bert's recording in itself constituted Bert's own copyright, because the basic melody, of course, was traditional."

"My heart just sank when I heard 'You Shook Me,'" says Beck.
"I thought, 'This is a piss-take, it's got to be.'"

riffs and mallet-swinging drums. Its counterpart, meanwhile, on side two, another Page-Jones-Bonham composition titled "Communication Breakdown," with its spiky, downstroke guitar riff and grafting of the ostinato from Eddie Cochran's "Nervous Breakdown," was proto-punk; the sort of sped up, one-chord gunshot the Ramones would turn into a career a decade later. While "Your Time Is Gonna Come," the third of the three originals on the album, is something else again: a wonderfully understated pop song built, in the fashion of the time, around a Bach fugue, played by Jones, then swept into a completely different musical zone by Page's pedal steel guitar—an instrument he had literally picked up in the studio that day and begun to play.

The rest of the album, however, though equally impressive in the scope of its sonic architecture, was quite shamelessly unoriginal in its material, as exemplified by its final track, "How Many More Times"—also credited to Page, Jones, and Bonham but a composition clearly based on several older tunes, primarily "How Many More Years" by Howlin' Wolf, a number which Plant and Bonham had performed in Band of Joy, inserting snatches of Albert King's "The Hunter." The Zeppelin version opened with a bass riff snatched from the Yardbirds' earlier reworking of "Smokestack Lightning," plus more than a passing nod to a mid-sixties version of the same tune by Gary Farr and the T-Bones also retitled "How Many More Times" (and produced by original Yardbirds manager Giorgio Gomelsky). There was even a lick or two appropriated from Jimmy Rodgers' "Kisses Sweeter Than Wine" as well as—bizarrely—a slowed-to-a-crawl take on Beck's solo from the Yardbirds' 1965 pre-Page hit "Shapes of Things." All of which they might have gotten away with if so much else

Nevertheless, crediting "Black Mountain Side" solely to Page seemed a bit rich. It certainly seemed this way to Jansch himself, who told me, "The thing I've noticed about Jimmy whenever we meet now is that he can never look me in the eye. Well, he ripped me off, didn't he?" He smiled. "Or let's just say he learned from me. I wouldn't want to sound impolite." But then, as Page himself admitted, "At one point, I was absolutely obsessed with Bert Jansch. When I first heard [his 1965 debut] album I couldn't believe it. It was so far ahead of what anyone else was doing. No one in America could touch that." Clearly, he was even more taken with Jansch's third album, *Jack Orion*, which contained not only "Black Waterside" but was full of the sort of sinister drones and fierce, stabbing guitar that Page would incorporate into his work throughout his subsequent career in both the Yardbirds and Led Zeppelin.

Even the two acknowledged covers on the Zeppelin album—"I Can't Quit You Baby" and "You Shook Me"—drew accusations of plagiarism. Not through lack of credit this time—both tracks were originally by Willie Dixon and are credited as such on the sleeve, but in the case of the latter, that it was a rip off of the version recently released on the Beck Group's *Truth*. Taken from the same Muddy Waters EP that both Page and Beck had listened to as boyhood friends (the same EP, coincidentally, that contained the track "You Need Love," which would provide Page with yet more "inspiration" when it came to the second Zeppelin album), Jimmy has always claimed it was simply "a coincidence" the same song ended up on both albums; that he hadn't realized Beck had already recorded a version for *Truth*—even though Zeppelin manager Peter Grant (then also working for Beck) had given him an advance copy weeks before its release. Even if it was possible that Page had ➥

Jake Holmes, had been released that summer. Included from it in his set was a witchy ballad entitled "Dazed and Confused." Although acoustic, it included all the signature sounds the Yardbirds—and later Zeppelin—would appropriate into their versions, including the walking bass line, the eerie atmosphere, and the paranoid lyrics: not about a bad acid trip as has long been suggested, says Holmes now, but a real-life love affair that had gone wrong. Watching him perform the song spellbound from the side of the stage that night in 1967 was Yardbirds drummer Jim McCarty and Jimmy Page. McCarty recalls he and Page going out the next day and buying a copy of the Holmes album specifically to hear "Dazed and Confused" again.

Given a new, amped-up arrangement by Page and McCarty, with lyrics only slightly altered by singer Keith Relf, it quickly became a highlight of the Yardbirds' live show. Never recorded except for a John Peel session for Radio 1 in March 1968—a version which sounds almost identical musically to the number Page would take full credit for on the first Zeppelin album, but which on the expanded 2003 remastered CD version of the Yardbirds' *Little Games* album is credited to: "Jake Holmes, arranged by the Yardbirds"—there was never any question in the rest of the band's minds over who the song had been written by. "I was struck by the atmosphere of 'Dazed and Confused,'" said McCarty, "and we decided to do a version. We worked it out together with Jimmy contributing the guitar riffs in the middle."

The only substantial change Page made from the version he'd been performing with the Yardbirds just three months before was his own rewrite of the lyrics, including such darkly misogynistic ruminations as the "soul of a woman" being "created below." Other than that, the song stuck to the original arrangement, up to the bridge, where even then the fret-tapping harked back to Holmes' original. The only other difference of note were the effects Page obtained from sawing a violin bow across the E string on his guitar, creating a startlingly eerie melody full of strange whooping and groaning noises; another trick from his sessions' days. As if to prove just how indiscriminate he was in his "borrowing," Page followed up the bowing section of "Dazed and Confused" with a series of juddering guitar notes lifted wholesale from an obscure Yardbirds' B-side called "Think About It," as happy to be recycling his own ideas as everyone else's.

"I didn't think it was that special," says Jake Holmes now. "But it went over really well, it was our set closer. The kids loved it—as did the Yardbirds, I guess." He says it wasn't until "way later" he first became aware that Page had recorded his own version with Zeppelin—and given it his own songwriting credit. His initial reaction was to be blasé. "I didn't give a s***. At that time I didn't think there was a law about intent. I thought it had to do with the old Tin Pan Alley law that you had to have four bars of exactly the same melody, and that if somebody had taken a riff and changed it just slightly or changed the lyrics that you couldn't sue them. That turned out to be totally misguided."

Over the years, he says, he has "been trying to do something about it. But I've never been able to find [a legal representative] to really push it as hard as it could be pushed. And economically I didn't want to be spending hundreds and thousands of dollars to come up with something that may not work. I'm not starving, and I have a lot of cachet with my kids because all the kids in their school say, 'Your dad wrote 'Dazed and Confused'?? Awesome!' So I'm a cult hero."

In terms of royalties, he just wants "a fair deal. I don't want [Page] to give me full credit for this song. He took it and put it in a direction that I would never have taken it, and it became very successful. So why should I complain? But give me at least half credit on it." The fact that "Dazed and Confused" was destined to become one of Led Zeppelin's great set-piece moments, he astutely points out, "is partly the problem . . . For [Jimmy Page], it's probably more difficult to wrench that song away from him than it would be any other song. And I have tried, you know. I've written letters saying, 'Jesus, man, you don't have to give it all to me. Keep half! Keep two-thirds! Just give me credit for having originated it.' That's the sad part about it. I don't even think it has to do with money. It's not like he needs it. It totally has to do with how intimately he's been connected to it over all these years. He doesn't want people to know." ◆◆

somehow neglected to afford the album even a cursory spin, it seems inconceivable that John Paul Jones would not have mentioned that he had played Hammond organ on the *Truth* version.

The first Jeff Beck knew of his friend Jimmy's decision to record the same track with his new group was when he played it to him. According to Beck, "My heart just sank when I heard "You Shook Me." I looked at him and said: 'Jim, what?' and the tears were coming out with anger. I thought, 'This is a piss-take, it's got to be.' I mean, there's *Truth* still spinning on everybody's turntable, and this turkey's come out with another version."

Years later, Page shrugged when I mentioned it. Beck, he insisted, "was attempting an entirely different thing." And, in fairness, listening to both tracks now, four decades on, what is most striking is the *lack* of similarity between the two tracks. While the Beck version is short and gimmicky, the Zeppelin version is almost three times as long, portentous, with swampy bottleneck guitar more redolent of the original's swooning rhythms, while Page's guitar solo is fluid, haunting, and mysterious, not bitty or showy like Beck's. It's then the thought occurs: Page knew exactly what he was doing. Of course he'd heard the Beck version. This was his hefty retort. That when he played it to Beck he was saying: there you go, Jeff, that's how you do that one. Then probably regretted it when he saw how badly his old friend took it. But if Page wanted to show he was better than Beck by beating him at his own game, it conversely had the opposite effect, making critics feel he was inferior. A feeling that persists in highbrow musical circles to this day.

The most blatant steal on the first Zeppelin album, though, occurred on the track ironically destined to become one of the most closely associated with Jimmy Page: "Dazed and Confused." Although credited solely to Page, the original version of the song had been written by a 28-year-old singer-songwriter named Jake Holmes. Holmes had already tried his hand at various branches of the entertainment industry—from comedy to concept albums—by the time he and his two man acoustic backing band opened for the Yardbirds at the Village Theater in New York's Greenwich Village in August 1967. His solo album, *"The Above Ground Sound" of*

Although credited solely
to Page, the original version of
Dazed and Confused had been written by Jake Holmes.

Led Zeppelin in 1968.

Over the years, Page and Zeppelin's appropriation of other artists' material was to become a longstanding criticism. Rightly so, one might argue, when one considers just how many times they would be accused of it throughout their career. And yet, they are hardly the only guilty ones. David Bowie ripped off the Rolling Stones for "Rebel Rebel"; the Stones ripped off Bo Diddley for "Not Fade Away." And let's not even start on the bands that have subsequently ripped off Zeppelin. It was also partly the era. The Yardbirds were equally guilty. Tracks like "Drinking Muddy Water"—attributed to Dreja, MCarty, Page, and Relf—was an obvious rewrite of the Muddy Waters' tune "Rolling and Tunbling." But then Waters' version was itself a patchwork of several earlier blues numbers. The same went for the aptly titled "Stealing, Stealing," a song originally by Will Shade's Memphis Jug Band, but with the Yardbirds again listed as authors.

One could argue that with the folk and blues traditions based almost entirely on tunes handed down over generations, each passing bringing its own unique interpretation, that Page and others are as within their rights to claim authorship of their own interpretations of this material as Muddy Waters, Davy Graham, Willie Dixon, Bert Jansch, Blind Willie Johnson, Robert Johnson, and all the other artists Led Zeppelin would knowingly "borrow" from over the years. In the early part of the twentieth century, the legendary "patriarch" of American country music, A.P. Carter, copyrighted dozens of songs written decades before his arrival in the Appalachians, many of which had their origins in ancient Celtic tunes from the British Isles. As a result, to this day a venerable old masterpiece like "Will the Circle be Unbroken" is still spuriously credited to Carter.

Similarly, Bob Dylan—widely considered the most groundbreaking and original songwriter of the late twentieth century—described his own debut album as "some stuff I've written, some stuff I've discovered, some stuff I stole." He was talking mainly about arrangements, such as his "Man of Constant Sorrow," lifted wholesale from Judy Collins' "Maid of Constant Sorrow." Or, most brazenly, the steal of Dave Van Ronk's innovative arrangement of "House of the Rising Sun," which Van Ronk resented hugely. Later on, "Masters of War" would be sung to the tune of "Nottamun Town"; "Girl from the North County" from "Scarborough Fair"; "Blowin' in the Wind" from an old anti-slavery song, "No More Auction Block"; "Don't Think Twice, It's All Right" from a traditional Appalachian tune, "Who's Gonna Buy Your Chickens When I'm Gone." None of which ever received any due credit on Dylan's album sleeves. John Lennon believed Dylan's "4th Time Around" to be a deliberate parody of his "Norwegian Wood." But then what was "All You Need Is Love" if not Lennon's "re-reading" of "Three Blind Mice"?

Jeff Beck was at it too, now admitting that Truth included more than one outright steal, including the track "Let Me Love You"—credited on the sleeve to one Jeffrey Rod (i.e. Beck and his then vocalist Rod Stewart)—based on an earlier Buddy Guy track of almost the same name. "We just slowed it down and funked it up a little with a Motown-style tambourine," Beck reveals in the sleeve notes for the 2005 remastered CD version of Truth. "There was a lot of conniving going on back then: change the rhythm, change the angle, and it's yours. We got paid peanuts for what we were doing and I couldn't give a s*** about anybody else." Other Jeffrey Rod compositions included "Rock My Plimsoul" (B.B. King's "Rock Me Baby"); "Blues De Luxe" (B.B. King's "Gambler's Blues"); and "I've Been Drinking" (from the Dinah Washington original "Drinking Again").

Page has also subsequently acknowledged the origins of some of the material he repurposed for Zeppelin. "The thing is they were traditional lyrics and they went back far before a lot of people that one related them to. The riffs we did were totally different, also, from the ones that had come before, apart from something like 'You Shook Me' and 'I Can't Quit You,' which were attributed to Willie Dixon." More to the point, he says: "I'm only the product of my influences. The fact that I listened to so many styles of music has a lot to do with the way I play. Which I think set me apart from so many other guitarists of that time."

Nevertheless, the accusations of plagiarism would have a debilitating effect on

Zeppelin's long-term credibility. It's one thing to "assimilate" old songs, quite another to claim credit for having built them from the bottom up. Even today when sampling is the norm in the hip-hop world, woe betide any artist that omits to credit original sources. On a purely musical level then, while Page has often told me how, for him, the first Zeppelin album "had so many firsts on it, as far as the content goes," in fact the first Zeppelin album was less a new beginning for Page than a culmination of everything that had gone before. All it really proved was that Zeppelin were great "synthesizers" of existing ideas. That this was accomplished in an era when such notions were still considered outside acceptable bounds says something about fortune and the talent to influence it. With Jimmy Page at the helm, Led Zeppelin would have both.

In fact, the real innovations of that first album were in the advanced production techniques Page was able to bring to bear and the sheer weight of musicianship he had assembled to execute them. Being able to produce such power and cohesiveness from a lineup that was barely a month old at the time the album was recorded was extremely impressive; to capture that energy on record, however, little short of astonishing; his previously unknown talent as a producer overshadowing even his dexterity as a guitar player. Not least in his innovative use of backwards echo—an effect that engineer Glyn Johns told him couldn't be done until Page showed him how—and what Jimmy calls "the science of close-mic'ing amps." That is, not just hanging microphones in front of the band in the studio, as was the norm at the time, but draping them at the back as well, or floating them several feet above the drums, allowing the sound to "breathe." Or taking the drummer out of the little booth they were routinely shoved into in those days and allowing him to play along with the rest of the band in the main room. This would lead to a lot of "bleeding"—the sound of one track seeping into another, particularly when it came to the vocals—but Page was happy to leave that in, treating it as "one more effect" that gave the recording "great atmosphere, which is what I was after more than a sterile sort of sound."

Or as Robert Plant later put it, listening to what Page had done on the first Zeppelin album "was the first time that headphones meant anything to me. What I heard coming back to me over the cans while I was singing was better than the finest chick in all the land. It had so much weight, so much power."

The core material may have been derivative, the "light and shade" aspect not nearly so interesting or new as Page still insists—certainly not compared to the multifaceted aspects of the music then being made by the Beatles and the

Accusations of plagiarism would have a debilitating effect on Led Zeppelin's long-term credibility.

Stones, or even Dylan and The Who, all of whom had alternated between electric and acoustic instrumentation for years, playing not just with light and shade but helping shape the parameters of rock music as a creative genre—but it had never been done with such finesse and know-how, or quite so much determination to succeed at any cost. Indeed, the first Zeppelin album was an almost cynical attempt to outdo its immediate competitors—Hendrix, Clapton, Townshend, and of course the unwitting Beck—while at the same time demonstrating that the man at the back, lurking in the shadows—Page himself—had more up his sleeve than mere conjuring tricks. This was a rock visionary with incredible mastery over his tools, a musical sorcerer who had stood off to one side watching for long enough.

Now it was time to do, to be, to overcome. And if anyone was going to get credit for that tremendous achievement, it was Jimmy Page. When Glyn Johns—who'd also worked with the Beatles, the Stones, and The Who, and who Page had known since his days as a teenager playing in a local hall in Epsom—asked for a producer's co-credit on Led Zeppelin, Page gave him short shrift. "I said, 'No way. I put this band together, I brought them in and directed the whole recording process, I got my own guitar sound—I'll tell you, you haven't got a hope in hell.'" Nor anyone else that would come along. ❷

When Giants Walked the Earth: A Biography of Led Zeppelin by Mick Wall is published by Orion.

The Maestro: Jimmy Page, no longer the sideman.

Bringing it on home: Led Zeppelin—(l to r)
John Paul Jones, John Bonham, Robert
Plant, and Jimmy Page—about to go onstage
at one of the most important shows of their
careers, at the Bath festival in 1970.

TWO BY FOUR

By: Dave Lewis

Led Zeppelin II was a record that would dislodge The Beatles' *Abbey Road* from the top of the US chart, and go on to shape the craggy face of modern rock music. Not that Jimmy Page realized it at the time— by the time the album was finished he'd lost confidence in it!

Whole lotta motor:
Led Zeppelin strikes a pose in front of an *Inspector Morse*-style Mk II Jaguar.

When Jimmy Page formed Led Zeppelin out of the ashes of The Yardbirds in late 1968, the guitarist could never have envisaged the success his new band would enjoy in their first year together. Zep's debut album was released in the US in January 1969 and quickly climbed the *Billboard* chart off the back of their debut tour there. Its UK release (in March of the same year) gave them a belated boost in their homeland, aided by a series of club gigs and some well-received BBC radio sessions. But it was Zep's second album that truly defined the band—and molded the entire genre of rock music itself.

ed Zeppelin II was a twisted, swaggering beast of a record, born out of the experiences the four-piece (Page, along with singer Robert Plant, drummer John Bonham, and bassist John Paul Jones) were gaining from being part of, to coin a *Spinal Tap*-ism, a living, breathing rock band on the road.

It was in the US that Zeppelin first really made its mark, and their label (Atlantic Records) was anxious to reap full benefit from what was fast becoming their biggest dollar earner since Cream. Zeppelin's astute manager Peter Grant also saw the vast potential in his band and the momentum they were building, and was happy to go along with Atlantic's call for a second album to be released by late summer '69. All this hurled Zeppelin into a hectic period of touring and recording commitments that, by the year's end, would establish them as the most important and fastest-emerging band on the scene, rivaling The Beatles and The Rolling Stones in record sales and box office receipts.

Fueled by the grueling stint on the road and the chemistry so apparent in their live shows, Page and his bandmates began

"The first time I saw [Led Zeppelin] was at the Fillmore East. They were sensational."

– *Led Zeppelin II* Engineer
Eddie Kramer

formulating ideas for their second album. The first batch of recording sessions took place at Olympic Studios in Barnes, west London, in April '69. It was the same place where they had recorded their debut album in a little over a staggeringly quick 30 hours. But the sessions for what would become *Led Zeppelin II* would not prove to be quite so fast.

The initial recording sessions saw the band working on "What Is and What Should Never Be," a drifting, melodic song that would highlight Robert Plant's growing maturity as a lyricist, and "Whole Lotta Love"—the song that would soon become their onstage anthem—led by Page's distinctive, stuttering guitar riff that would later change the face of rock forever.

But their time in Olympic Studios was limited, and by the end of the month Zeppelin was back on the road in America. Atlantic Records were so eager for a second album, though, that they informed Peter Grant that the band should continue recording during their second US tour. Unbeknownst to the group, label executives were aiming ambitiously for a July release date. While Grant was happy for the sessions to recommence, thankfully he did not buckle to Atlantic's scheduling demands—and this would prove to be the first of many occasions when the formidable figure of Peter Grant, rather than the record company, dictated how Zep would conduct their business.

During the US tour, the band began road-testing some of their new material; "Whole Lotta Love" made its full stage debut at a date at the Winterland Ballroom in San Francisco on April 26, 1969. Live, Zep were also regularly featuring a version of Howlin' Wolf's "Killing Floor" that would be retitled and reworked as "The Lemon Song" when they took it to the studio. Plant threw in lines from Robert Johnson's ▷

Led Zeppelin circa 1970.

Plane sailing: Led Zeppelin attempts to smuggle some copies of *Led Zeppelin II* into Hawaii.

"Travellin' Riverside Blues," and this live arrangement of the song was similar in structure to the version recorded by US rock band The Electric Flag.

John Bonham had been showcasing an extended drum solo dubbed "Pat's Delight" (a reference to his wife) that he would later take into the studio and rename "Moby Dick."

By the time the tour rolled into Los Angeles, Jimmy Page had called up engineer Chris Huston to book in some sessions at Huston's Mystic Sound studio. This was a low-ceilinged, 16-square-foot room with four-track recording facilities. (Page was no stranger to the place, as he had previously worked in the studio on a session with Screaming Lord Sutch.)

"The sessions came out great," Huston recalls. "Jimmy was very easy to get on with. We did the tracks live, with Plant standing in the middle of the room with a handheld microphone. You can hear that at the end of 'The Lemon Song,' where Plant sings 'floor floor floor'—that echo was recorded in real time."

Both "The Lemon Song" and Bonham's drum solo piece were initially laid down at Mystic Sound.

It's worth noting that for the *Led Zeppelin II* sessions, Page had now switched to using a Gibson Les Paul guitar as opposed to a Telecaster that had dominated his late Yardbirds and early Zeppelin work. He was already in possession of a vintage 1958 Les Paul, but added another model during the early American tours. "I had been mainly using the Telecaster, both onstage and in the studio," Page remembered. "We were at the Fillmore at the time, and Joe Walsh, who was then playing guitar with his outfit The James Gang, said he had a Gibson Les Paul for sale—a 1959 model. He wanted to sell it for five hundred dollars—a right price at the time. Once I started playing it, that was it."

UNDER THE COVERS

THE ALBUM ARTWORK EXPLAINED: The distinctive *Led Zeppelin II* artwork was designed by David Juniper, and has the four faces of the group members superimposed on an old photo of the *Jasta* division of German pilots, featuring the notorious Red Baron. Juniper edited the picture and added the face of English actress Glynis Johns (who played the mother in the film version of *Mary Poppins*) and, rumor has it, members of Zep's road crew plus blues guitarist Blind Willie Johnson.

It has been surmised that the inclusion of Johns was an inside joke reference to producer Glyn Johns, who had worked with Page on Zeppelin's debut album. Glyn Johns often claimed he had produced the record, and it may have been a retort by Page and friends to include the Glynis Johns photo.

The design was wrapped in an elaborate gatefold sleeve that opened up to show the shadow of a Zeppelin airship. The sleeve's distinctive outer coloring earned the album the nickname "The Brown Bomber" in America.

Back in the UK in June, Zeppelin did more recording at Morgan Studios in Willesden, North London. Here they laid down another batch of tracks, notably "Thank You," "Livin' Lovin' Maid (She's Just A Woman)," and "We're Gonna Groove." The latter was a cover of a B.B. King/J. Bethea stomper that did not make the final running order of *Led Zeppelin II*, despite becoming their live set opener for brief period in early 1970. (It would, however, eventually see the light of day on the posthumous *Coda* outtakes collection, released in 1982.)

Another track recorded at the Morgan sessions that was also destined never to make the cut. The band had been working on an up-tempo, riff-led song titled "Sugar Mama," but it was later discarded.

Aborted songs notwithstanding, the growing confidence for the new, in-progress *Led Zeppelin II* material led the band to preview two of the tracks during sessions recorded for BBC Radio One in June '69. A version of "What Is and What Should Never Be" was recorded on June 16 at Aeolian Studios for broadcast on the June 22 edition of Chris Grant's show, the endearingly titled *Tasty Pop Sundae*. A little over a week later, at the BBC's Maida Vale studios, Zeppelin recorded another version of the same track alongside a superb version of "Whole Lotta Love." This became part of a session broadcast on John Peel's legendary *Top Gear* show on June 29.

During the Maida Vale recording, Jimmy Page also taped an interview with DJ Brian Matthew for broadcast on the BBC's World Service, in which Page told Matthews that Zep's second album was three-quarters completed.

"We're finishing off mixing in New York and it should be out in the first week of August," Page said. He also revealed that it would be called *Led Zeppelin II*. Asked by Matthew to select a track representative of the album, Page cited "What Is and What Should Never Be": "It's got a bit of everything,"

Whole lotta Zep: early Zeppelin in full flow could be mesmerizing.

> *"Led Zeppelin II* would establish them as the most important and fastest-emerging band on the scene, rivaling The Beatles and Stones in record sales and box office attraction."

Page added as a link to the airing of the June 24 BBC session of the track. And he was right.

But before they could draw breath, the band was dispatched back to America for their third US tour, that kicked off in July '69. Peter Grant had arranged the tour to include a variety of high-profile outdoor festivals, including the Atlanta Pop Festival, the Newport Jazz Festival, and the Dallas International Festival. Surprisingly, their ambitious manager had declined an invitation for Zeppelin to play Woodstock, opting instead for dates in Phoenix, New Jersey, and Connecticut. But this proved to be a canny move. "I said no to Woodstock because I knew we'd just be another band on the bill," Grant reflected years later.

New York was the next stop for Led Zep's crazy train, notably at A&R Studios in New York in August '69. During the tour, Page hooked up with engineer Eddie Kramer, noted for his work with Jimi Hendrix on *Electric Ladyland*. Kramer had also worked at Olympic Studios when Page and Jones were session musicians in the mid-sixties. Kramer later recalled: "John Paul Jones was the first to make me aware of Zeppelin when he told me he was joining a group with Jimmy Page. This was before I left England to work in the US. The first time I saw them was at the Fillmore East. They were sensational. I'd known both Jimmy and John Paul from working with them at Olympic, and had followed their careers over the years. I periodically bumped into them, and then I was asked to work on their second album."

Further tracks were developed at this point: "Heartbreaker" was recorded in two parts—initially at A&R Studios, with the famous Jimmy Page virtuoso guitar solo added across town at Atlantic Studios. The finishing touches to "Bring It on Home" were also perfected there.

LED ZEPPELIN'S ONLY SINGLE

In the USA, singles taken from albums gained valuable radio airplay that, in turn, led to all-important album sales. Consequently, Zeppelin manager Peter Grant had no problem with Atlantic Records issuing an edited version of "Whole Lotta Love" as a single there. Its ascent to the Top Five of the *Billboard* chart by January 1970 confirmed Zep as the hottest act of the new decade.

Grant had no plans to allow such a release in the UK, but Atlantic Records presumed differently and went ahead and pressed an initial quantity of the 3:12 edit of the song backed with "Livin' Lovin' Maid (She's Just A Woman)." Allegedly, around 500 copies were distributed to press and radio stations and another 500 ended up in a warehouse in Manchester ready for release.

Grant immediately requested they be recalled, citing a clause in Zep's contract which stated that he (and he alone) would have control of any single releases. At the time, of course, Zeppelin was an integral part of the underground rock scene, and had no desire to make the obligatory appearance on *Top of the Pops*.

As *Led Zeppelin II* was selling more than most singles, Grant promptly pulled the plug on the planned UK release of the single, and issued a curt statement saying that Zeppelin intended to issue a special track as a single in the future. That single never appeared.

The catalogue number allocated to the UK edit of "Whole Lotta Love" (584 309) was subsequently given to Clarence Carter's UK single "Take It off Him and Put It on Me." Copies of the withdrawn UK "Whole Lotta Love" single now command a price tag of six hundred dollars (five hundred pounds), making it one of the rarest UK singles of all time.

It seemed that Zep would record whenever they had a moment to spare. Other studios used during this period included New York's small independent setup Juggy Sound, which was used to lay down the Tolkien-inspired "Ramble On." The band also attempted to record in a run-down studio in Vancouver which had no proper working headphones. They also spent more time at A&M Studios in Los Angeles and the Mayfair, again in New York.

Their second album might have been nearing completion, but it was yet to be mixed. Towards the end of the tour, Page met up with Kramer to complete the final mixing. This was done over a marathon session at New York's A&R Studios, gaining Kramer a credit on the album as Director Of Engineering. ▷

Led Zeppelin II was released in the UK on October 22, 1969.

> "It took a long time. It was insane. We'd put down a rhythm track in London, add vocals in New York, put in a harmonica . . . in Vancouver, and then go back to New York to do the mixing." – JIMMY PAGE

"Jimmy was an excellent producer, and I think we complemented each other," Kramer recalls. "When he and I mixed 'Whole Lotta Love' we just flayed around the console, twiddling every knob we could. We somehow managed to stretch our limitations and create an effective sound. Working with Jimmy Page was a lot different to working with Jimi Hendrix . . . apart from the fact they were both influenced by the blues, and they were both able to alternate between playing delicately and intensely. Page usually didn't go for the blasting, huge wall of sound, he went for a more refined approach."

Page asked Kramer to bring a cohesion to the sound of the various tracks, as they had been recorded in many separate locations. "I wound up cutting a few new tracks, overdubbing some of the tracks they already had, and then I mixed the whole album with Jimmy," Kramer reveals.

The fragmented nature of the sessions did give rise to a rare lack of confidence from Jimmy Page at the time: "It [the second album] took a long time on and off, having to write numbers in hotel rooms," Page said in late '69. "It was insane, really. We'd put down a rhythm track in London, add the vocals in New York, put in a harmonica, say, in Vancouver, and then go back to New York to do the mixing. By the time the album came out I'd lost confidence with it."

But he need not have worried.

Led Zeppelin were back on the road before they knew it, reconvening for a series of European dates. They returned to the UK to play a prestigious show at London's Lyceum Theatre (where Bob Marley's *Live!* album was later recorded), on October 12. On these

regular Sunday night Lyceum specials, staged by promoter Tony Stratton Smith, each band that played was expected to showcase a full album. And there was talk of utilizing this gig as a platform to launch *Led Zeppelin II* and perform the record in full.

However, with only a handful of songs from the album rehearsed for live action, this idea was quickly vetoed, and in London Zep premiered only two tracks: "What Is and What Should Never Be" and "Heartbreaker." Even on the subsequent US tour in November, the band added only Bonzo's "Moby Dick" as support to their second album.

It must have baffled the Atlantic Records executives to no end to have the edited version of "Whole Lotta Love" climbing the US *Billboard* singles chart, but to be conspicuously absent from the band's current set—another prime example of Jimmy Page and company pleasing themselves rather than pandering to corporate rock ethics.

Live performances of songs from the new album may have been thin on the ground initially, but it didn't really matter. When *Led Zeppelin II* was released in the US in late October '69 it already had advance orders for half a million copies. It was an instant success, and by the end of the year it had dislodged The Beatles' *Abbey Road* from the top spot, where it remained for seven weeks. It was clear indication that Zeppelin were set to rule the US chart in the seventies as much as The Beatles had done in the sixties.

In the UK it was a similar story. *Led Zeppelin II* was unleashed on an unsuspecting UK public on October 22, 1969, and the record swiftly established

ZEPPELIN GOES POP!

"WHOLE LOTTA LOVE" ON TV

It's ironic when you consider that although Led Zeppelin was never a singles band, they still manage to be present every week on *Top Of The Pops*—the UK TV show that celebrates the singles chart itself.

In November 1970 "Whole Lotta Love" dented the UK Top 20, but Zep wasn't the band behind the single. Rather, it was CCS—or Collective Consciousness Society—and their version of the song. It was CCS' big-band arrangement of "Whole Lotta Love" that was subsequently adopted by *TOTP* as its theme tune in the mid-seventies. After a period of absence, the program revived the song as its theme in 2000, taking elements of the Zeppelin original and adding a drum 'n' bass makeover. In 1996, dance act Goldbug took "Whole Lotta Love" into the UK Top Five with a remix that merged the Pearl & Dean cinema ad theme with the song.

A year later, Zep's surviving band members sanctioned a belated UK release for a new edit of "Whole Lotta Love." It was released as a CD single to promote the reissuing of the Zeppelin catalogue at mid-price, and it reached number 21 on the chart.

Zeppelin playing to 200,000 people at the 1970 Bath festival—a "crucial" show, according to Robert Plant.

LED ZEPPELIN II
BACKTRACKING

"WHOLE LOTTA LOVE"
Zeppelin's penchant for borrowing blues influences and reshaping them got them into legal trouble on three of the tracks on *Led Zeppelin II*. Most famously, they were issued with a lawsuit over "Whole Lotta Love." It took some 15 years for Chicago bluesman Willie Dixon to claim that his composition "You Need Love"—as recorded by Muddy Waters in 1962—was used without credit as the basis for the lyrics of the opening track on *Led Zeppelin II*. He successfully won a court case in 1985 for royalties.

"WHAT IS AND WHAT SHOULD NEVER BE"
This song was previewed in June 1969 at the BBC sessions, and then premiered at Zeppelin's Lyceum show on October 12, 1969. It was revived by Page and Plant for their *Unledded* MTV recording in August 1994, and was also performed by Page with The Black Crowes on their 1999 US tour dates.

"THE LEMON SONG"
ARC Music, the copyright holders of "Killing Floor," written and recorded by Howlin' Wolf, were quick to identify that the composition (written under his real name Chester Burnett) appeared on *Led Zeppelin II* with the title "The Lemon Song," and was credited as a group composition. An out-of-court settlement was agreed, and for a while UK copies of the album listed the track as being titled "Killing Floor" on the insistence of publishers Jewel Music. Jimmy Page revived the *Led Zeppelin II* arrangement when he played with The Black Crowes.

"THANK YOU"
It has also been noted that the chord structure of "Thank You," Plant's emotional love song to his then wife Maureen, bears a resemblance to Traffic's 1968 song "Dear Mr. Fantasy." It is known that Page did some demo recordings with Steve Winwood immediately before he joined Zeppelin. This song was chosen as the opening number for Page and Plant's MTV *Unledded*. In the nineties, it was also covered by Tori Amos and Duran Duran.

"HEARTBREAKER"
For the live performances of this song, Jimmy Page often extended the solo to include snippets of Bach's "Bouree in C Minor" and Simon & Garfunkel's "59th Street Bridge Song (Feelin' Groovy)."

"LIVIN' LOVING MAID (SHE'S JUST A WOMAN)"
This track was viewed as something of a throwaway number by both Page and Plant, and therefore no full live performances of it have been logged. However, Robert Plant did revive the song on his 1990 *Manic Nirvana* tour, turning it into a rousing Beach Boys-style singalong encore.

"RAMBLE ON"
Surprisingly, this was another song Zeppelin never played live in full. On their spring 1969 US tour, Plant did throw in lines from it during extended versions of "Communication Breakdown" and "Whole Lotta Love." Post-Zeppelin, it was performed many times by Page and Plant on their 1995/6 and 1998 world tours.

"MOBY DICK"
The riff of this John Bonham epic can be traced back to the band's arrangement of the John Estes song "The Girl I Love She Got Long Black Wavy Hair," as recorded for the BBC in 1969 and available on the *BBC Sessions* album.

"BRING IT ON HOME"
Another Willie Dixon tune, "Bring It on Home" was borrowed for the closing song of *Led Zeppelin II*. Though credited to Page/Plant, this was actually a cover of Sonny Boy Williamson's 1963 arrangement issued on the Chess album *Real Folk Blues*. "Bring It on Home" was named in the same legal action as "Killing Floor," but did not include the changing of songwriting credits. The song developed into a lengthy live performance number played from 1969 up until 1972. One of Zep's last performances of it, as an encore at the June 1972 LA Forum show, can be heard on the *How the West was Won* live album, released in 2003..

a top-five placing. By the time the group were completing an eight-date UK tour early in 1970 (including the memorable show at London's Royal Albert Hall), the album had climbed to the number-one position. *Led Zeppelin II* went on to enjoy a remarkable 138-week unbroken run on the UK chart, and was still riding high when Zeppelin's next album was released a year later.

During 1970, Zeppelin added three more tracks from their second album to their live shows: "Thank You," "Bring It on Home," and "Whole Lotta Love." It was the band's dynamic interpretations of those staple tracks from the *Led Zeppelin II* album that elevated Zeppelin to the position of the world's top live attraction—a position and status they would retain for the rest of their existence.

Recording in a variety of studios had allowed Jimmy Page the luxury of experimenting with sound. A key element was the art of "distance-miking"—a trick he had picked up from his days as a session man. This technique enhanced the sound of John Bonham's straight-from-the-wrist drumming considerably, and also had a huge effect on Plant's wailing vocals. "I discovered that if you moved the microphone away from the drums, the sound would have room to breathe," Page recalled. "I kept exploring and expanding that approach."

Led Zeppelin II also signaled the emergence of Robert Plant as the group's lyricist, and he brought in arrangements, lyrical concepts, and hints that pointed to the breadth of styles the band were prepared to investigate. "On that album we were definitely deviating from the original Zeppelin intensity, but without losing quality," Plant remarked after the record's release. "In fact we gained a quality, because my voice was being used in differing ways instead of confining it to a safe formula."

Despite the millions of units that *Led Zeppelin II* has shifted since it was released, perhaps the album's greatest achievement is the influence it has had on so many of the bands that have come along afterwards. *Led Zeppelin II* has spawned an endless stream of imitators, all ready to popularize this distinctive style of aggressive rock that would later be called heavy metal. From Aerosmith to Def Leppard, to today's guitar bands like The Music, The Darkness, and Black Rebel Motorcycle Club, Zep's second album has been a hard-rock yardstick. The ferocious riffs, the gentle melodies, the thunderous rhythm section . . . the record has it all.

While *Led Zeppelin IV* may be the band's biggest-selling record, and the *Physical Graffiti* double set may be their most diverse work, there is no question that *Led Zeppelin II* is the record that really established them.

But back in 1970, as the gold and platinum sales awards flooded in, Jimmy Page, Robert Plant, John Bonham, and John Paul Jones had already moved on. They may have inadvertently invented heavy metal, but there was so much more musical territory to explore. With *Led Zeppelin II* they had already laid down the definitive hard-rock statement. The call of the east, mandolins, Mellotrons, and an important date with "a lady who's sure all that glitters is gold" were beckoning now. ❷

A Bustle In Your Hedgerow

★ ★ ★ ★ ★ ★ ★ ★ ★ ★ ★ ★ ★ ★

When the reigning kings of rock holed up in the Welsh countryside to write a new album, no one expected the folky pastoral results. Critics hated it, fans didn't get it, but *Led Zeppelin III* is arguably the band's most important record.

By: Mick Wall ★ ★ ★ ★ ★ ★ ★ ★ ★ ★ ★ ★

By the time Led Zeppelin returned from their latest US tour in April 1970—25 "heartland" dates, no New York, no LA, just deep inside the belly of the beast—what Robert Plant called "the craziness count" had definitely gone up. John Bonham, whose bouts of homesickness seemed to be growing in direct proportion to how successful the band became, began drinking more heavily and taking out his frustrations on hotel rooms. The show at the hockey arena in Pittsburgh at the end of March had to be stopped when a bloody brawl erupted in the audience. Elsewhere, cops hassled the band members at their own shows, blaming them for the uncontrolled antics of the audience.

"I don't think we can take America again for a while," John Paul Jones said at the end of the tour. "America definitely unhinges you. The knack is to hinge yourself up again when you get back."

Plant suffered, too. "More than anyone, Robert seemed on the brink of collapse," tour manager Richard Cole later noted.

As usual at the tour's end, they took refuge in West Hollywood, though no longer staying at the Chateau Marmont—the Manson murders the year before had thrown all of LA into a fog of paranoia, and manager Peter Grant decreed the Marmont's spread of isolated bungalows too easy a target for any potential "nutters," of which there were more than a few now following the band around on tour. Instead, they had relocated to the Hyatt House (or the "riot house," as Bonzo and Plant now dubbed it) a few blocks up on Sunset. There, a never-ending parade of girls found their way up to the ninth floor where the band and their entourage were sequestered for a week. Richard Cole remembers the limo for the shows being so weighed down by girls that "the trunk [had] become stuck on the riot house driveway, requiring a push off the curb . . . absolute madness."

Yet just as Zeppelin were reaching the height of their on-the-road notoriety, they were also on the cusp of making their most enduring music. The monumentally successful *Led Zeppelin II* album was only the beginning. In fact, they only really began to make the giant leaps forward musically that would cement their reputation as one of the all-time rock greats with what came next, starting with what was arguably their first proper album together: *Led Zeppelin III*.

Written and conceived, in large part, in reaction to both criticism of their first two albums and their own frustrations at being forced to write and record so quickly and under so much pressure, the beginnings of the songs—and indeed the album that followed—were undertaken in much less stressful circumstances. The end result would take everyone by surprise. The whole tenor of the album—acoustic-based songs, rooted in folk and country, as well as their already well-established blues influences—were the last thing anyone, including Jones and Bonham, who were largely excluded from the songwriting process, would have predicted at that point.

Until then the question had been: how would they top the ecstatic thrill of that titanic second album? Would they be able to come up with another "Whole Lotta Love"?

The answer was: they didn't even try to. "People

that thought like that missed the point," Jimmy Page told me years later. "The whole point was not to try and follow up something like "Whole Lotta Love." We recognized that it had been a milestone for us, but we had absolutely no intention of trying to repeat it. The idea was to try and do something different; to sum up where the band was now, not where it had been a year ago."

And where the band was now—or where Page and Plant were, anyway—was halfway up a mountainside in sunny Wales.

With the final show of the US tour canceled when an exhausted Plant's voice gave out, they flew home from Las Vegas on April 20. Between their first show in December '68 and their latest in April 1970, Zeppelin had performed in the US no less than 153 times. They were now playing for guarantees of up to $100,000 per show (more than $625,000 in today's money). It was also now, in the spring of 1970, that they received their first substantial royalty payments. That year, the band began to live large. Twenty-four-year-old John Paul Jones bought himself a big new place in Chorleywood, Hertfordshire, where he and

Land rover: Robert Plant driving near his farm in Kidderminster.

his wife Mo and their two daughters moved into as soon as the band returned from America. Twenty-two-year-old John Bonham finally moved out of the council flat in Dudley he'd been living in since he'd joined the band two years before, and relocated the family to a 15-acre farm in West Hagley, on the borders of Worcestershire and the West Midlands. Plant, not 22 until August, had already paid $100,000 the year before for a similar dwelling, Jennings Farm, near Kidderminster. He now set about spending several more thousands of dollars refurbishing it. Page kept the boathouse in Pangbourne that he'd owned since his Yardbirds days, and bought Boleskine House—home of occultist Aleister Crowley 50 years before—on the banks of Loch Ness.

But while Bonham and Jones immersed themselves in nest building, Plant was restless, and began talking to Page on the phone about a remote eighteenth-century cottage in Wales that he recalled from a childhood vacation. He told Jimmy how his father would pack the family into his 1953 Vauxhall Wyvern and take them for a drive up the A5 through Shrewsbury and Llangollen into Snowdonia; places with strange names, full of tales of swords and sorcery.

The cottage, named Bron-Yr-Aur (Welsh for, variously, "golden hill," "breast of gold," or even "hill of gold," pronounced Bron-raaar) had been owned by a friend of his father's, and stood at the end of a narrow road just outside the small market town of

Led Zeppelin at their Albert Hall show in 1970.

Machynlleth in Gwynedd. Plant further intrigued Page by telling him of the giant Idris Gawr, who had a seat on the nearby mountain of Cader Idris, and how legend had it that anyone who sat on it would either die, go mad, or become a poet; how King Arthur was said to have fought his final battle in the Ochr-yr-Bwlch pass just east of Dolgellau.

Page, who had only just begun to restore the interior of his own new mythological abode, Boleskine, to its former glories, was equally taken by the idea of some time away from it all. Before committing full time to The Yardbirds, he had been an occasional solo traveler, moving through India, America, Spain, and elsewhere. Now, with his new French model girlfriend Charlotte Martin by his side, and Plant talking of bringing his wife Maureen and infant daughter Carmen (and his dog Strider, named after Aragorn's alter ego in *The Lord of the Rings*), plans were laid for a sojourn into the Welsh mountains.

Both men had also been very taken by the debut album the year before by Bob Dylan's former backing group The Band, *Music From Big Pink*, famously named after the country house it was recorded in in Upstate New York.

Page and Plant weren't the only musicians newly influenced by The Band's ramshackle musical blend of rock, country, folk, and blues. Eric Clapton had been so bowled over he had actually flown to Woodstock and asked to join the band, an overture they merely laughed at as they sat there rolling another joint. George Harrison had also since flown out to hang with The Band in LA, where they'd fetched up to record their second album.

Suddenly everyone, including all of Led Zeppelin, had beards, along with a new pastoral chic in sharp contrast to the blend of mod sharpness and pre-Raphaelite foppery that had dominated their look early on. There were other influences too, such as Van Morrison's *Astral Weeks*, whose deeply spiritual, if somewhat bleak mix of folk and soul Plant was particularly taken with. And Joni Mitchell, whom Page now became besotted with, partly through her inspiring use of different acoustic guitar tunings, which were almost a match for his own in their range and obscurity, and partly through her remarkably honest and clearly autobiographical songs—and of course her long blonde hair and aquiline features.

The huge impact of Crosby, Stills & Nash, whom Plant had seen at the Albert Hall in London just before Zeppelin played there in January, had also been noted with intense interest by both men.

Above all, there was simply the desire to prove something that neither the critics nor even the fans had picked up on yet, which was the fact that Led Zeppelin was not a one-trick pony. That there was more to Jimmy Page, certainly, than a growing collection of great rock riffs, not least his deep ▷

> "The whole point was not to try and follow up something like 'Whole Lotta Love' … The idea was to try and do something different."
>
> **Jimmy Page**

29

"We were living in this falling-down mansion in the country. The mood was incredible."

Robert Plant on Headley Grange

and abiding interest in the acoustic guitar.

As soon as Plant suggested the cottage, Page saw the potential. As he would later explain: "It was the tranquillity of the place that set the tone of the album. After all the heavy, intense vibe of touring, which is reflected in the raw energy of the second album, it was just a totally different feeling."

*W*hen in May Page and Plant arrived at Bron-Yr-Aur, situated along a steep track that leads through a ravine, they found a stone dwelling so derelict it had no electricity, running water, or sanitation. Fortunately, as well as their respective partners, they had also brought Zeppelin roadies Clive Coulson and Sandy Macgregor with them, both of whom were now saddled with domestic chores.

"It was freezing when we arrived," Coulson remembered. He and Macgregor would be sent to carry water from a nearby stream and gather wood for the open-hearth fire, "which heated a range with an oven on either side." There were Calor Gas heaters but only candles to light the place. "A bath was once a week in Machynlleth at the Owain Glyndwr pub. I'm not sure who got the job of cleaning out the chemical toilet."

Evenings off would also be spent at the pub, where they mingled with local farmers, the local biker gang, and some volunteers restoring another old house nearby. When invited to join in on *Kumbayah* one night, Page apologized and explained he didn't play guitar.

Meanwhile, back at the cottage, where Page did play the guitar and Plant warbled on his harmonica, the songs began to come, sometimes just scraps, sometimes fully formed. Songs that would "prove there was more to us than being a heavy metal band," as Page put it. Chief among them, "Friends," built on some esoteric scales Page had brought back with him

from a trip to India in his Yardbirds days, laid over a conga drum; Plant's dreamy "That's the Way"; the rousting (misspelled on the record) "Bron-Y-Aur Stomp."

There were also several begun there that would find a home not just on the next Zeppelin album but also on their next four albums, including the bare bones of "Stairway to Heaven," "Over the Hills and Far Away," "Down by the Seaside," "The Rover," "Poor Tom," and (similarly misspelled) "Bron-Yr-Aur."

Of the tracks that did make the third album, there was also "Tangerine," with its nicely low-key, deliberate-mistake intro, a song originally begun at a disastrous final June '68 Yardbirds session in New York as a song called "My Baby," now reborn in Wales as a country-tinged, Neil Young-inspired dirge.

"Bron-Y-Aur Stomp" had also begun life as another, electric number, "Jennings Farm Blues," laid down at Olympic Studios in London the previous autumn. Here it was transformed into a jugband hoedown dedicated to Plant's dog Strider. "Walk down the country lanes, I'll be singin' a song," Plant warbled cheerily. "Hear the wind whisper in the trees that Mother Nature's proud of you and me."

The song that really summed up the spirit of adventure at Bron-Yr-Aur was one that arrived almost unbidden late one afternoon as Page and Plant traipsed through the surrounding flower-decked hills, then in full spring bloom. Stopping to smoke a joint and admire the view, Page took the guitar he'd been carrying on his back and began

No quarter: Zeppelin rocks it to America in 1970.

strumming some random chords, half-remembered from Bert Jansch and John Renbourn's arrangement of the traditional "The Wagoner's Lad."

To his delight, Plant began singing along in a much more restrained voice than usual, ad-libbing the opening to what was originally called "The Boy Next Door," but later became "That's the Way." Afraid to lose the moment, they pulled a cassette recorder out of a knapsack and recorded the rest of it then and there. Afterwards they celebrated by sharing some squares of Kendal Mint Cake, then made their way back to the cottage where they sat in front of the fire, eating a full English breakfast and drinking cups of cider mulled by red-hot pokers, listening to endless repeats of the tape.

"We wrote those songs and walked and talked and thought and went off to the Abbey where they hid the Grail," Plant later told writer Barney Hoskyns. "No matter how cute and comical it might be now to look back at that, it gave us so much energy, because we were really close to something. We believed. It was absolutely wonderful, and my heart was so light and happy. At that time, at that age, 1970 was like the biggest blue sky I ever saw."

Jones and Bonham were equally taken with the rough tapes of the songs Page and Plant had returned from Wales with. But back at Olympic at the start of June, the band struggled to recreate the atmosphere in the stale environs of a professional recording facility. So they decided to decamp once again, this time for a dilapidated mansion in Hampshire named Headley Grange, where, with the aid of the Rolling Stones' mobile studio, they hoped to have the album finished before returning to the road in America in August.

Headley Grange had been found by Grant's secretary, Carole Browne, through an ad in *The Lady*. Once again, Page was attracted to the setting more by its history than by its practical application. Headley Workhouse, as it was originally known, was a three-story stone manor built in 1795 in order to "shelter the infirm, aged paupers, orphans, or illegitimate children of Headley" and nearby Bramshott and Kingsley. In 1875 it was bought by a builder who converted it into a residence and renamed it Headley Grange.

With the advent of mobile ⟶

"It was like, 'Jesus, what's happening here then?' In the end you knew you'd seen something you were never going to forget."

Roy Harper on Zep's 1970 Bath Festival show

Led Zeppelin III allowed Page to indulge his love of acoustic guitar.

studios and the sixties fashion for "getting it together in the country," the Grange began to be rented out to rock groups by its widowed owner. Both Genesis and Fleetwood Mac had recorded there previously.

With both Page and Plant still enchanted by their newly consummated creative union, they were especially susceptible to their surroundings, and the austere, often bleak mansion appealed to the same sense of adventure as their trip to Wales.

"It really looked to me as if it had been . . . not derelict, but it looked as if it had hardly been lived in," Page revealed. "It was quite interesting considering the tests we were going to put it to."

As Plant put it, "We were living in this falling-down mansion in the country. The mood was incredible."

It wasn't all work, though, with the band breaking for two weekends to play some gigs. The first two shows were in Iceland, on June 20 and 21, at a converted gymnasium in Reykjavik, from where they returned to Headley with a new, distinctly non-acoustic battle cry of a number called "Immigrant Song," Plant solemnly intoning, "We are your overlords" to chilling effect. The staff at the

venue was on strike at the time, so the local student body ganged together to help put on a show. "The students took over," Plant says now, "and got the whole thing going and it was just amazing. When we played there it really did feel like we were inhabiting a parallel universe, quite apart from everything else, including the rock world of the times."

The following Sunday evening, they were back for their second Bath Festival appearance, this time held in Shepton Mallet at a much larger site than the first, where more than 150,000 people eventually showed up over the duration of the two-day festival. The official

Already well along the road to greatness: Bonham, Plant, Page, and Jones in 1970.

line peddled by Zeppelin manager Peter Grant to the press was that the band was playing at Bath despite an offer of $200,000 to play in America that weekend—almost certainly Grant's shrewd attempt to drum up a bit of useful PR for the event. Nevertheless, it became another key moment in the winning over of the British music press.

BP Fallon, then working as PR for T. Rex but soon to become Zeppelin's publicist, was at Bath and remembers it well: "I was there as a punter, me and my girlfriend, on acid in the VIP enclosure at the very front. The sunset was tickling the skies, and this Led Zeppelin monster exploding into action yards away was like a f***** rocket going off and carrying us to Mars and beyond. Whoosh! Sonic sex! Beyond brilliant, you know?

"But there was no strategic follow-up, not really. People in Britain knew that Led Zeppelin were doing very well in America, but mostly they were lumped in with Ten Years After or Savoy Brown or Keef Hartley or whoever, this blues-based Second British Invasion Of America."

It was after Bath, though, that Zeppelin began their rapid ascent in Britain to what Fallon describes now as "full-on and on fire. After that, Led Zeppelin were treble-mega in Britain. Tick that box! Next!"

Zeppelin's near-three-hour set began with a halo of sunlight descending into the horizon behind their heads, the band dressed, as per their new pastoral mode, as tweedy troubadours, heavily bearded, Page even sporting what looked like a scarecrow's hat.

"I remember Jefferson Airplane and Janis Joplin were also on the bill," said Plant, "and I remember standing there thinking: 'I've gone from West Bromwich to this! I've really got to eat this up.' The whole thing seemed extraordinary to me. I was as astonished as the audiences some nights."

It was also at the Bath Festival that Page first met Roy Harper, destined to become the titular subject of another of the songs on *Led Zeppelin III*, "Hats off to (Roy) Harper." Rustic jester and folk troubadour Harper exerted an unusual influence on everyone he came into contact with, including Led Zeppelin.

Harper was a stereotypical English eccentric whose formative years had seen him feign madness to get out of the RAF, the result of which was five years in and out of mental hospital and prison. He spent the early part of the sixties reading poetry and busking around Europe.

Having washed up in London in 1964, he became a fixture on the folk circuit, where Page had first noticed him, before eventually recording his own albums, all quite distinct, all utterly uncommercial.

Seeing Harper wandering around backstage at Bath, Page approached him and asked to be shown how he played an instrumental from his first album, *Blackpool*.

"So I played it for him," Harper remembers, "and he said: 'Thanks very much.' The only thing I thought as I watched him leave was: 'That guy's pants are too short for him.'"

It wasn't until he saw Zeppelin play that evening that he realized who Page was. "During the

Plant with Zeppelin at the International Center Arena in Honolulu, September 1970.

second song ["Heartbreaker"], all the young women in the crowd started to stand up involuntarily, with tears running down their faces. It was like, 'Jesus, what's happening here then?' In the end you knew you'd seen something you were never going to forget."

Although neither of them knew it then, it was also the start of a long relationship between the two guitarists, with various Zep members appearing at Harper shows and Harper opening occasionally for Zeppelin. Nevertheless, he was taken aback some weeks later when he discovered his name on the next Zeppelin album.

"I went to their office one day and Jimmy said, 'Here's the new record.' 'Oh . . . thanks,' I said, and tucked it under my arm. 'Well look at it then!'" I discovered 'Hats off to (Roy) Harper.' I was very touched."

As he should have been. Over the next few years, that one track would introduce the perennially unsuccessful Harper to millions of album buyers around the world. "As far as I'm concerned," Page explained, "hats off to anybody who does what they think is right and refuses to sell out."

Or as Plant would later jokingly recall: "Somebody had to have a wry sense of humor and a perspective which stripped ego instantly—[and] we couldn't get Zappa."

B ack at Headley Grange, Led Zeppelin continued honing their new material. Eventually there would be 17 near-complete tracks. To the acoustic-based material from Bron-Yr-Aur they now added "Hats off to (Roy) Harper," a piece of spontaneous combustion initiated by Page one night, inspired by some frenzied slide-guitar channeling of Bukka White's "Shake 'Em on Down" (credited on the sleeve to "Charles Obscure").

There was also "Gallows Pole," a rollicking reinvention of a centuries-old English folk song

called "The Maid Freed from the Gallows," a striking contemporary version of which Page remembered fondly from the B-side of a 1965 single by Dorris Henderson that she'd dubbed "Hangman," and which he had stuck in his mind.

There were also a handful of electric, more obviously Zep-sounding tub-thumpers like "Immigrant Song," "Celebration Day," and "The Bathroom Song" (so called because everyone said the drums sounded like they had been recorded in the bathroom), later changed to "Out on the Tiles." Plus, the foundation of what would become one of their finest ballads, the exquisite blues "Since I've Been Loving You," begun at Olympic during the same truncated sessions that produced the original electric "Jenning's Farm." The band had played a shorter, tighter version live at Bath, but it wasn't until now that they'd tried to finish it.

That said, the genesis of what was destined to become one of Zeppelin's most famous tracks can again be fairly clearly pinned down to an earlier, typically unaccredited blues jam by Moby Grape titled "Never." As the Grape remain one of Plant's favorite San Francisco groups of the period, it's inconceivable that he wasn't already acquainted with "Never." Indeed, the opening lines of "Since I've Been Loving You"—"Working from seven to eleven every night, it really makes life a drag, I don't think that's right"—are almost identical to those on "Never," which go: "Working from eleven to seven every night, ought to make life a drag, yeah, and I know that ain't right."

With Plant also displaying his new Van Morrison and Janis Joplin influences on the scatted vocal amid the sound of John Bonham's squeaking bass-drum pedal and John Paul Jones' jazzy bed of keyboards, while playing the bass pedals of the Hammond organ with his feet, all it needed to round it off was a spine-tingling guitar solo from Page.

The tape op at the session was a young guy named Richard Digby Smith. "I can see Robert at the mic now," he later recalled. "He was so passionate. Lived every line. What you got on the record is what happened. His only preparation was an herbal cigarette and a couple of shots of Jack Daniel's . . . I remember Pagey pushing him: 'Let's try the outro

chorus again, improvise a bit more.' There was a hugeness about everything Zeppelin did. I mean, look behind you and there was Peter Grant sitting on the sofa—the whole sofa."

I n an effort to try to complete the album, by now they had abandoned Headley in favor of the more polished surrounds of Island's No. 2 studio at Basing Street in Notting Hill Gate. It was during these sessions that the first rough recording of another new song, "No Quarter," written by Jones, was etched out.

All other considerations went out the window, though, as Page battled to come up with a suitable solo to finish off "Since I've Been Loving You." But by the time their US tour began in Cincinnati on August 5, 1970, the album still wasn't finished and Page was left with no option but to repeat the grueling process that had characterized the previous summer's US tour, jetting off to the studio between shows.

Fortunately, he was able to call on his old friend Terry Manning at Ardent Studios in Memphis for help. "I'd pick Jimmy up at the airport and drive him straight to the studio to begin work," Manning recalls. "Peter always accompanied Jimmy too. No one else, though. I think Robert came in for one day, Bonham came in for one. That was it."

Manning remembers editing "a lot" out of "Gallows Pole" and Page trying—and repeatedly failing—to find the right solo for "Loving You." "In the end Jimmy accepted that the demo solo done in England wasn't going to be bettered, and so that was the one they eventually used. Listening back now, it's my all-time number-one favorite rock guitar solo. We took three or four other takes, and tried to put takes together and come up with something, and they were all great. But there's something magic about that one take [he did], that stream of consciousness."

Page worked alone with Manning on the mix of the album. Manning says the much looser approach—the tape echo at the start of "Immigrant Song," the wayward segue of "Friends" and "Celebration Day," the occasional voices you can hear in the background, what a quarter of a century later would be called lo-fi—was "all thought out, not accidental at all."

It was this aspect, he says now, that demonstrated to him what "a really brilliant producer" Page was.

"Not to demean or cast any aspersions," he adds, choosing his words carefully, "but I think he harmed himself perhaps in a few ways later on. But at that particular time, the very early days, Jimmy was an incredibly insightful, true musical genius, in my opinion—and I've seen a lot of musical people. I would say that very little happened by accident. When it says "produced by Jimmy Page," it seriously was.

"He asked me, 'What do you think about leaving the beginning of the 'Celebration Day' ▷

"At that particular time, [Jimmy] was an incredibly insightful, true musical genius, in my opinion—and I've seen a lot of musical people."

Terry Manning, mixing/mastering engineer on *III*

33

thing on [referring to the moment when Bonham can be heard shouting 'F***!']?" No one ever seemed to pick up on it. But he said, 'That's not why I wanna leave it, not 'cos that's cool. I like the sonic texture of everything. I like the feel that you're really there.' We really talked all that through."

It was also Manning that Page would ask to help master the album. With albums produced, mixed, and largely made on computer these days, mastering a vinyl record is almost a lost art. Back in 1970, though, it was still one of the most crucial parts of the recording process.

Using a lathe to transfer the sound from acetate on to vinyl, great care and an even greater set of ears were essential. Page and Manning were well aware that over the years, many potentially marvelous albums had been ruined because of poor technique at the mastering stage, and they approached the job with great seriousness. That is, until the final moments, when adding the usual catalogue numbers that would be stamped onto the run-out groove of the finished record.

"Working with Big Star, we had added some messages of our own on there," Manning says. "I mentioned this to Jimmy and said, 'Anything you wanna write?' And he said: 'Ooh, yeah . . . '"

Due to the enormous quantities of copies the pressing plant knew they would need to fill the advance orders alone for *Led Zeppelin III*, they had requested two sets of masters—not unusual for the biggest-selling American acts in those days. As a result, Page would come up with four separate "messages," one per side of each master.

"We'd been talking about the Aleister Crowley thing," Manning says. "He said, 'Give me a few minutes.' And he sat down and he thought and he scribbled some things out, and he finally came up with 'Do What Thou Wilt Shall Be The Whole Of The Law' and 'So Mote It Be' and one other one which I've forgotten."

I suggest perhaps either "Love Is the Law" or "Love under Will," Crowley's other two most famous maxims. "I suspect the latter," Manning replies. "Sounds the most familiar."

Released on October 23, 1970, two weeks after its release in America, *Led Zeppelin III* was already at number one in the US by the time it went on sale at home in Britain, where it would also top the chart. Nevertheless, it was destined to become one of Zeppelin's most overlooked albums, misunderstood and largely reviled by the critics.

Even the fans seemed confounded. And although the album would eventually sell in millions, it remains one of the comparatively weakest sellers in the Zeppelin canon. Indeed, by the start of 1971 it had all but disappeared from the charts, while its more popular predecessor maintained a steady presence in both the US and UK Top 40s.

But if many were left nonplussed by the unexpected change in musical direction, the same critics who had previously attacked them for being shallow peddlers of roisterous clichés now accused them of daring to undermine such perceptions by singularly failing to repeat the trick.

At best they assumed the band had been unduly influenced by the recent success of Crosby, Stills & Nash, whose remarkable debut album had seen a seismic shift in critical opinion on where rock was—and should be— heading at the dawn of the new decade. It was a charge Page, in particular, whose background in acoustic roots music was well-established long before it became the fashionable sound of southern California, was furious over.

"I'm obsessed—not just interested, obsessed—with folk music," he said, pointing out that he'd spent many years studying "the parallels between a country's street music and its so-called classical and intellectual music, the way certain scales have traveled right across the globe. All this ethnological and musical interaction fascinates me."

But no one was listening. Instead, the critics screamed betrayal. Under the headline "Zepp Weaken!", *Disc & Music Echo* typically enquired: "Don't Zeppelin care any more?" There were occasional flashes of insight from the press. Lester Bangs—who had previously chastised Zeppelin for their "insensitive grossness"—wrote in *Rolling Stone*: "'That's the Way' is the first song they've ever done that's truly moved me. Son of a gun, it's beautiful."

According to Terry Manning, however, Page had anticipated such reactions. "He was quite apprehensive but quite determined. We spoke of these matters as we were in the studio completing it. He would say, 'This is so different, this is going to shock people.' And it did."

"I felt a lot better once we started performing it," Page told Dave Schulps in 1977, "because it was proving to be working for the people who came around to see us. There was always a big smile there in front of us. That was always more important than any poxy review."

With an irate Page refusing to explain or make excuses to the press in 1970, it was left to Robert Plant to defend the album. "Now we've done *Zeppelin III*, the sky's the limit," he told *Record Mirror*. "It shows we can change. It means there are endless possibilities and directions for us to go in."

Ready to knock 'em dead. Backstage at the Bath Festival, June 28, 1970.

It was an entirely prophetic statement, as the next Zeppelin album would demonstrate in no uncertain terms. But that was still a year away, and for now the band was forced to live through the first dip in what until then had been a steady upward surge of their commercial fortunes. By the start of 1971 "Zep to Split" stories were even beginning to pepper the British music papers.

But if *Led Zeppelin III* polarized opinion, long-term it went a considerable way to cementing their reputation, confounding expectations and proving there was more to them than simply being the "new Cream" they had started life as.

Instead of more wall-shaking, heavy rock classics, the third Zeppelin album should be looked at now as the first convincing marriage of Page's fiery occult blues and Plant's swirling Welsh mists. It was the first serious proof of the band's ability to move beyond the commercial straitjacket that would eventually leave contemporaries like Black Sabbath and Deep Purple marooned in a creative cul-de-sac, churning out copycat hits until they finally ran out of steam, key members came and went, and their reputations would be sealed forever as second-rung niche acts, truly loved only by heavy metal fanatics.

Besides, with bands like

> "Jimmy knew they could not be more than the greatest heavy rock band if they didn't expand into new avenues."
>
> **Terry Manning**

all-out rock assault. With "Immigrant Song" becoming another Top 20 single, reaching number 16 during a 13-week run on the *Billboard* chart, their 1970 summer tour of the US was their biggest yet, topped off with two sold-out three-hour shows at Madison Square Garden on September 19 and 20, their first time at New York's most famous venue.

The same month, they were voted Best Group in the annual Readers' Poll in *Melody Maker*—the same music paper that had slated *Zeppelin III* for "ripping off" Crosby, Stills & Nash. The first act for eight years to oust The Beatles from the top spot in what was then the UK's most prestigious music magazine, Zeppelin returned to London for a special reception where they were also presented with more gold discs.

Yet for all the band's public defiance, and *Led Zeppelin III*'s not inconsiderable sales, behind the scenes there was a palpable sense of disappointment when the album slipped unobtrusively from both the UK and US charts within weeks of topping them, at a time when *Led Zeppelin II* was still riding high around the world.

Used to fighting fires, Peter Grant moved swiftly to reassure Jimmy Page that no one at Atlantic, certainly, was perturbed by this disappointing downturn in events. The album had still sold more than a million copies in the US and had gone gold (for advance orders of more than 100,000) in the UK—the sort of figures they'd have been throwing lavish parties to celebrate a year before. The fact that the second album had sold more than five times that amount in the preceding 12 months was, if anything, a freak result, he argued, not the kind of thing one should expect every time Zeppelin released a new album.

Nevertheless, there were tensions over at Atlantic's Broadway offices. Relatively speaking, *Led Zeppelin III* had been a commercial failure. The feeling—though politely disguised in earshot of Page, if not Grant—was that the band had shot themselves in the foot by releasing something so radically different from the winning formula established by their first two albums.

In order to appease both sides, Grant suggested the band take the rest of 1970 off. That is, abort their plan to tour Britain over Christmas and instead return to the studio. Although he was reluctant to spell it out to Page, Grant knew it was essential that the band get another, hopefully more representative album out as soon as possible. By going into the studio now, he argued, they would be in no rush this time, either.

So concerned was Grant, in fact, that he turned down an offer of a million dollars for a New Year's Eve concert to be performed in Germany and linked by satellite to a large chain of cinemas in America. The reason he said no, he later explained, was because "I found out that satellite sound can be affected by snowstorms."

In reality, he was more concerned for Led Zeppelin's career as recording artists. He felt sure their next album would be make or break.

For Peter Grant and Led Zeppelin, there were more than a mere million bucks at stake in whatever they did next. There was their entire all-that-glitters-is-gold future. ◗

Sabbath now doing the job for them—"We used to lie on the floor of the rehearsal room, stoned, listening to the first two Zep albums," recalls Sabbath's Geezer Butler, who admits that his band's most famous song, "Paranoid," "was just a rip off of "Communication Breakdown"—the determinedly non-metallic direction of the new Zeppelin material was, in retrospect, not only a brave move but also an exceptionally shrewd one.

As Terry Manning says, "None of it was accidental. Jimmy knew they could not be more than the greatest heavy rock band if they didn't expand into new avenues, into more than just beating you on the head with a riff. You take a band like The Beatles, or Pink Floyd, the kind of bands that kids of fifteen love today as much as the kids of thirty or forty years ago, and they sound totally different from their first album to the middle of their career to the end of their career.

"And Jimmy knew that. He wanted to be more. The first two Zeppelin albums are quite different from The Yardbirds. He wanted to keep going, keep expanding. He would talk about rhythms, and people like Bartok, Karl Heinz Stockhausen, or John Cage. He was totally into Indian classical music, Irish folk music, all sorts of things."

That would become ever more clear on subsequent Zeppelin albums, where Page's fondness for such seemingly disparate musical bedfellows as funk, reggae, doo-wop, jazz, synth-pop, and rockabilly could be felt amid the symphonic slabs of rock.

For now, the third album showcased what Page describes as "my CIA." That is to say, "my Celtic, Indian, and Asian influences. I always had much broader influences than I think people realized, all the way right through, even when I was doing

[session] work. When I was hanging around with Jeff [Beck] before he was in The Yardbirds, I was still listening to all different things."

As if to add insult to injury, the gatefold sleeve of the third album was often more positively reviewed than the music inside. Designed by an old college pal of Jimmy's who liked to go by the name of Zacron, then a tutor at Wimbledon College of Art, the end result was a self-consciously "surreal" collection of seemingly random images—butterflies, stars, zeppelins, colorful little smudges—on a white background.

The most striking element was a rotatable inner disc card, or volvelle, based on crop rotation charts, which when turned revealed more indecipherable sigils and occasional photos of the band, peeping through holes in the outer cover. Critics cooed, but it veered away drastically from what Page had actually asked for, and was more to do with Zacron's own taste, rotating graphics being a signature of his work since 1965.

Zacron later recalled Page telling him, "I think it is fantastic." But Jimmy told *Guitar World* in 1998, "I wasn't happy with the final result."

Zacron had got far too "personal" and "disappeared off with it . . . I thought it looked very teeny-bopperish. But we were on top of a deadline, so of course there was no way to make any radical changes to it. There were some silly bits—little chunks of corn and nonsense like that."

ut on the road, the band were still going from strength to strength, with whatever acoustic subtleties employed on their new album sacrificed in concert for

WHEN ALL IS ONE AND ONE IS ALL

The making of
Led Zeppelin IV

By: Barney Hoskyns

It had no title, no band name on the sleeve, no singles released to radio. But the album that the record company said would bomb made Zeppelin the biggest band on the planet. Forty years after its release, this is the inside story of a rock classic.

HE SCENE IS the Atlantic Records HQ in New York City, the date is early September 1971. The event is a tense standoff between, on the one hand, Atlantic co-founder Ahmet Ertegun and, on the other, the ectomorphic guitarist along with the behemoth manager of a band who have just hit town to play a show at Madison Square Garden. Sitting in are legal representatives for both sides.

The issue at hand is the cover and sleeve design of Atlantic 7208, Led Zeppelin's fourth album for the label. The manager, Peter Grant, is laying down the whole of the law—or at least the wishes of the guitarist, his master—and informing Ertegun that the record will be released without a title and without even the band's name on the cover. Ertegun is having kittens, throwing his hands in the air in disbelief. How can you put an album out without your name on the cover? It's suicidal!

"It went down like a lead balloon," recalled Phil Carson, then head of Atlantic in England. "[Atlantic] were like, 'That's crazy. It'll never sell.' But Peter said, 'Listen, this record would shift units if we put it in a f***** brown paper bag.'"

Peter Grant, the behemoth who is already terrorizing the industry, won't give an inch and says he won't hand over the master tapes until Ertegun agrees to Jimmy Page's demands. When "G" finally leaves after a long afternoon's wrangling, Page stays on to press his point. "[The lawyer] was saying, 'You've got to have this,'" he remembered of the showdown. "So I said, 'Alright, run it on the inside bag. Print your 'Rockefeller Plaza' or whatever it is down there.'

"In the end I went back to the label and said, 'Trust me, people will find it,'" Phil

GETTY

Carson said in 2003. "You have to remember that by the time the album came around, the band was responsible for about 20 to 25 percent of Atlantic's total sales. My job as chief liaison officer was to keep Led Zeppelin happy and keep those successful records coming."

Two months later, the fourth Zeppelin album appears with nothing on the front cover bar a framed photo of a bearded codger hunched under a bundle of sticks—a picture hanging on a wall whose flowery paper is badly peeling. On the back cover, behind what turns out to be a partially demolished home, a modern council tower block looms behind a row of derelict terrace houses.

"The picture of the old man was Robert's," Richard Cole, Zeppelin's legendary tour manager, tells me brusquely. "None of us could work out why . . . he wanted that old bit of rubbish on the cover."

To Jimmy Page, a mite preciously, the cover represents "the change in the balance which was going on. There was the old countryman, and the blocks of flats being knocked down. It was just a way of saying that we should look after the earth, not . . . pillage it." To the more prosaic John Bonham, who had once lived in a tower block a stone's throw from the one on the back cover, "it means I'd rather live in an old house than a block of flats." (Led Zeppelin's drummer had already been granted that particular wish.)

Even on the album's inner sleeve, the band's name is conspicuous by its absence. Instead, it features four runic symbols, plus the titles of the eight tracks and some cursory credits. Along with Barrington Colby's sinister inner-gatefold illustration, "The Hermit," the symbols prove irresistible to the growing fan base of besotted

adolescents in thrall to the enigma Led Zeppelin projects.

Releasing an album without "Led Zeppelin" on the cover (or even on the spine) sends a message to anyone who ever accused them of being a "Superhype," the name Grant and Page had chosen for their production company. Smarting from the negative press they'd suffered since the band formed, Page wants to prove that their music can stand on its own merits.

"[The press] didn't really start bothering me until after the third album," he told *Guitar World*'s Steven Rosen more than 20 years later. "After all we had accomplished, the press was still calling us a hype. So that is why the fourth album was untitled. It was a meaningless protest, really, but we wanted to prove that people were not buying us for the name."

"The genius of Jimmy Page that people are always missing is the idea of the anti-establishment 'punk' things he was doing," Zep fan Jack White told me in 2006. "Things like releasing records with no information and no writing on the cover. I mean, that's pretty bold. It's a lot more punk than the Sex Pistols signing a contract in front of Buckingham Palace."

Punk or not, the courage of Zeppelin's convictions was soon vindicated when the untitled album—referred to as *IV*, *Led Zeppelin IV*, *ZoSo*, *Runes*, *Four Symbols*, or (silently) as ○⚗⊛ℓ — became their best-selling album to date. (It currently ranks as the twelfth best-selling album of all time.) If their first three albums made them stars, their fourth turned them into superstars. Within two years they were unquestionably the biggest band on the planet. ●▸

FOUR SYMBOLISM
The origins of the album's four symbols explained.

By: Dave Lewis

Ever on the lookout for new ideas to present the band in a different light, the art-schooled Jimmy Page came up with the idea of an unpronounceable title made up of four distinct symbols, or runes, for their fourth album. "After all the crap that we'd had with the critics, I put it to everybody else that it'd be a good idea to put out something totally anonymous," Page remembers. "At first I wanted just one symbol on it, but then it was decided that since it was our fourth album and there were four of us, we could each choose our own symbol. I designed mine, and everyone else had their own reasons for using the symbols that they used."

The use of four symbols as the title for *IV* only added to their overall mystique, and the saga of what they represent (if anything) still rages today on Zep internet forums and message boards.

The four symbols were first introduced to the rock media via a series of teaser ads placed in the music papers in the weeks leading up to the album's release—each ad depicting a particular symbol alongside a sleeve of a previous Led Zep album.

The symbols for John Paul Jones and John Bonham were selected from Rudolph Koch's *The Book of Signs*. Jones' is a single intersecting circle, said to symbolize a person who possesses both confidence and competence (as it's difficult to draw accurately).

John Bonham's three interlocking rings is said to represent the triad of mother, father, and child. It was also—somewhat appropriately, given the late drummer's penchant for alcoholic

beverages—the logo for Ballantine beer.

Robert Plant's symbol was apparently his own design, though it can also be traced to a book titled *The Sacred Symbols of Mu* by Colonel James Churchward. The feather in the circle represents the feather of Ma'at, the Egyptian goddess of justice and fairness, and is the emblem of a writer. "The feather is a symbol on which all sorts of philosophies have been based," noted Plant. "For instance, it represents Red Indian tribes."

Jimmy's symbol is often referred to as "ZoSo," and there have been various theories put forward surrounding its origin. Some point to it being used as early as 1557 in representing Saturn. It has also been noted that it is made up of astrological symbols for Saturn, Jupiter, and perhaps Mars or Mercury. The symbol also appeared in almost identical form in a rare nineteenth-century dictionary of symbols titled *Le Triple Vocabulaire Infernal Manuel du Demonomane*, by Frinellan (a pseudonym for Simon Blocquel), published by Lille, Blocquel-Castiaux in 1844. "My symbol was about invoking and being invocative," Page told *Classic Rock*'s Mick Wall in 2001, adding, "That's all I'm going to say about it."

Whatever their meaning, these symbols have, become synonymous with each member of Led Zeppelin, and over the years have been adapted by Plant, Jones, and Page in presenting their respective solo projects. Most recently they have been used by Plant, whose feather design was adapted for the back cover design of last year's *Band of Joy* album, and by Page, who used his enduring "ZoSo" image as the embossed cover on his deluxe pictorial autobiography *Jimmy Page by Jimmy Page*.

ROSS HALFIN

Combining the bruising power of *Led Zeppelin II* with the unplugged side of *Led Zeppelin III*, the album swung wildly from blues-rock strut ("Black Dog") to canyon reverie ("Going to California"), retro blast ("Rock and Roll") to medieval mandolins ("The Battle of Evermore"). It also featured an epic, eight-minute track called "Stairway to Heaven"—not, as it turned out, a cover of Neil Sedaka's bouncy Brill Building hit from 1960.

"Music is very like a kaleidoscope," Robert Plant told *NME* the following year. "And I feel that particular album was just a case of us stretching out. It was a very natural development."

"My personal view is that it's the best thing we've ever done," John Bonham maintained in *Melody Maker*. "It's the next stage we were at, at the time of recording. The playing is some of the best we've done and Jimmy is . . . mint!"

More terse were the reflections, years later, of the classically trained multi-instrumentalist whose composing and arranging skills were so vital to Zeppelin's music: "After this record," John Paul Jones stated for the record, "no one ever compared us to Black Sabbath."

Led Zeppelin's fourth album started life a year before the Ertegun standoff, on the band's previous visit to the Big Apple. With *Led Zeppelin III* about to be released, the final date of their sixth US tour also found them at Madison Square Garden, in a state of near-exhaustion from the relentless criss-crossing of a country they had now conquered.

"We were fed up with going to America," Jimmy Page said in 1973. "We'd been going twice a year, and at that time America was really a trial, an effort."

Playing two shows at the Garden on Saturday, September 19, 1970, Zeppelin was on the verge of collapse and could hardly wait to fly home. Moreover, the news had just winged its way across the Atlantic that Jimi Hendrix had been found dead in London, casting a dark pall over both shows. After the fourth song, "Bring It on Home," Robert Plant paid tribute to the guitar magus who had once raved that John Bonham had "a right foot like a pair of castanets."

Bonham himself was not just exhausted, he was also pining for his wife Pat and four-year-old son Jason. "We did three tours last year and finished off feeling: 'We've just about had enough,'" Bonzo told *Melody Maker*'s Chris Welch. "We had done so much in such a short space of time, we were drained. We had offers to go everywhere—France, America. And we could have done them, but what would be the point? We were tired. We had worked hard, and Peter had probably worked harder than any of us. We enjoyed working but we needed the break before we got stale." The break they did get led to groundless rumors that Zeppelin were on the point of splitting up.

Grant wasn't in the best of shape, either, and saw an opportunity to do something about his ballooning weight by checking into a health farm. Meanwhile, Page and Plant remembered the tonic that "a small, derelict cottage in South Snowdonia" had provided the previous spring, and decided to return there, to Bron-yr-Aur, to see if it might inspire a similar spurt of creativity. Their only company this time came in the form of roadies Sandy MacGregor and Henry "The Horse" Smith.

"After this record, no one ever compared us to Black Sabbath."
John Paul Jones

"We drove to Bron-yr-Aur in a white-paneled truck," remembers Smith, the American who had worked alongside Richard Cole on US tours by Zeppelin and the Jeff Beck Group. "It was like a camping trip. Jimmy was wearing the high wellies and cardigan sweaters, and that famous hat he wore at the Bath festival. It was the folksy look. In some ways it was grounding for them. Jimmy was a city kid, where Robert was more of a country boy. And Robert had been to Bron-yr-Aur as a child, so he remembered it as a safe, secure place. It was interesting to see them work that part of life out to where serenity was."

A humble stone structure standing in the midst of a sloping sheep pasture, Bron-yr-Aur "just felt like a good thing" to Smith. "Like, if you want to write you need to get away. And this was a great place to go to get away because there was *nobody* around. The sheep would almost come into the house while Jimmy and Robert were working on songs. There were a couple of times when Robert and I went out back and sat in the grass by the stream. And he was talking about songs and looking for a little inspiration for some lyrics. I remember talking about little animals in the grass, parting the grass and seeing what was underneath."

I n 2003, prior to interviewing him in nearby Machynlleth, I persuaded Plant to drive me up to Bron-yr-Aur, in a muddy, burgundy 4x4. That afternoon he waxed nostalgic about what the place had meant to him and Page: "In among it all when we set off for the Welsh mountains was the question: 'What sort of ambition do we have? And where is it all going? Do we want world domination and all that stuff?' We didn't really have anything to do with the Stones or The Beatles or anybody, but we lived on the side of a hill and wrote those songs and walked and talked and thought and went off to the abbey where they hid the grail. No matter how cute and comical and sad it might be now to look back at that, it gave us so much energy because we were really close to something. At that time and that age, 1970 was the biggest blue sky I ever saw."

On their second visit to the cottage, Page and Plant worked on a number of songs both old and new, some scarcely more than sketches that would remain on the back burner: things like "Down by the Seaside," "Over the Hills and Far Away," "Poor Tom," and "The Rover." Also coming along nicely was the music for "Stairway to Heaven," on which Page had been working in his home studio for some months.

By December, Page and Plant were reunited with John Bonham and John Paul Jones at Island Studios in London, where some of *Zeppelin III* had been recorded (and the majority of it mixed). Here, early versions of "Stairway to Heaven" (sans lyrics), "When the Levee Breaks," and other tracks were attempted. After Bron-yr-Aur, however, the studio vibe left much to be desired.

"You really do need the sort of facilities where you can take a break for a cup of tea and a wander 'round the garden and then go back in and do whatever you have to do," Page reflected. "Instead of that feeling of walking into a studio, down a flight of steps and into fluorescent lights . . . and opening up the big soundproof door and being surrounded by acoustic tiles."

As they had done with *III*, Zeppelin chose to decamp to a damp mansion in Hampshire. "For the third album, I'd suggested going to Mick Jagger's house with the Stones' mobile," says engineer Andy Johns, who had already used the unit to record the Stones' *Sticky Fingers*. "Now, Pagey is a wise fellow and doesn't like to expend money when he doesn't have to. 'How much would that cost?' he says. 'Well,' I reply, 'the truck's about £1,000 a week and Stargroves is about £1,000 a week.' He says: 'I'm not paying Mick Jagger £1,000 a week! I'll find somewhere better than that.' So they found this old mansion, and we went down there and it was somewhat seedy. There was stuffing coming out of the couch, springs coming out of the bed. But it wasn't a bad place."

"We've done a good deal," John Paul Jones informed *Disc*'s Caroline Boucher shortly before Zeppelin set off for Headley Grange. "We've broken the back of it, and recording starts this month. But rather than . . . thinking of the riffs and lyrics in the studio, we decided this place in Hampshire was definitely the best place to get the numbers down before we were there."

"Maybe the spark of being at Bron-yr-Aur came to fruition by saying, 'Let's go to Headley,'" Page told me in 2003. "It was: 'Let's go to Headley with a mobile truck and see what comes out of it.' And what came out of staying in the house was the fourth album. Although some things were recorded outside of that location—like 'Stairway to Heaven'—the germ of it was Headley."

Things didn't commence well. January 1971 found the house significantly colder and damper than it had been the previous spring. "It was horrible," John Paul Jones recalled. "There was virtually no furniture, no pool table, no pub nearby . . . We all ran in when we arrived, in a mad scramble to get the driest rooms." The house boasted central heating but the boiler was so ancient it had given up the ghost. "It seems more dilapidated than it was the last time we were here," Bonham remarked mopily to Richard Cole as he wandered through its rooms.

Page, however, "loved the atmosphere" of Headley Grange, convinced there were ghosts in the house. "Jimmy had a room right at the top that was haunted, I'm sure of it," says Richard Cole. "None of us would go up there. It had an old electric fire. The rest of us didn't particularly like the place. By now they all had lovely houses and had been living in five-star hotels. They recorded in the worst f****** places imaginable. I don't know whether it was because in the back of Jimmy's mind he thought, 'If I can make the outside surroundings as unpleasant as possible, they'll get on with it!'"

"You didn't have . . . [any] recreational pursuits at all," Page noted of the distraction-free environment. "It was really good for discipline and getting on with the job. I suppose that's why a lot of these came at Headley Grange. For instance, 'Going to California' and 'Battle of Evermore' came out of there."

It wasn't all hard work. Richard Cole recalls that the band ate like "million-dollar Boy Scouts" at Headley, lubricated by cider purchased in the local village. "There weren't any serious drugs around the band at that point," the road manager remembered. "Just dope and a bit of coke. They were playing at being country squires. They found an old shotgun and used to shoot at squirrels in the woods—not that they ever hit any." Attired in a gamekeeper's cap and tweed jacket, farmer Bonzo regularly repaired to the nearest pub after the band had finished for the day.

Since nobody was taking notes—and since the memories of the surviving members are understandably hazy—it is difficult to be sure exactly what Zeppelin did after settling in at Headley. Up to 14 songs—enough for a double album—may have been tried out before Andy Johns showed up with The Rolling Stones Mobile Studio after a week. Among them were a slightly zippier version of "No Quarter" (later recorded for *Houses of the Holy*) which began life as one of Jonesy's keyboard instrumentals; "Down by the Seaside," a Plant-steered homage to Neil Young dating back to the first stay at Bron-yr-Aur; The Faces-esque "Night Flight"; a version of Leroy Carr's "Sloppy Drunk" that morphed into "Boogie with Stu"; and possibly other Bron-yr-Aur songs ("Poor Tom," "The Rover," "I Wanna Be Her Man") that had failed to make it on to *Led Zeppelin III*. Rehearsal bootlegs from the period do not establish definitively what was rehearsed at Headley and what wasn't.

One that definitely was is "Black Dog," a track conceived by John Paul Jones. "We were always trying to encourage Jonesy to come up with bits and pieces," Page recalled in 1983. In Joe Smith's book *Off the Record* (1988), Robert Plant recalled that "sometimes John Paul would contribute the main leading part of a song, and then it would be a pretty quick arrangement of bits and pieces so that the thing fitted together rather quickly."

Inspired by a twirling, circular blues riff on "Tom Cat" (a track on Muddy Waters' critically reviled psychedelic album Electric Mud, from 1968), "Black Dog" had been developed by Jones on the train home from a pre-Headley Grange rehearsal at Page's boathouse in Pangbourne, Berkshire. "My dad had taught me this very easy notation system using note values and numbers," he told Mojo's Mat Snow in 2007. "So I wrote it on a bit of paper on the train . . . probably the ticket."

Easy the system might have been; fiendishly complex the unfolding time signatures of "Black Dog"—named for an elderly Labrador that wandered in and out of Headley Grange—turned out to be. So much so that when it was first attempted in rehearsal the song imploded amid a collective fit of hysterical

Jimmy Page "loved the atmosphere" of Headley Grange, and was convinced there were ghosts in the house.

laughter. Subsequent run-throughs—and arguments—can be heard in riveting detail on the *Stairway Sessions* bootleg.

"It was originally all in 3/16 time," Jones remembered, "but no one could keep up with that." Least of all Bonham, who understandably struggled with the jarring juxtaposition of the song's basic 4/4 rhythm with the 5/8 riffing of Jones and Page in its B-verse section. "I told Bonzo he had to keep playing four-to-the bar all the way through 'Black Dog,'" Jones recalled years later. "If you go through enough 5/8s it arrives back on the beat." Bonzo was unconvinced, and to most ears the B-verse rhythm still sounds wrong.

Equally complex groove-wise was "Four Sticks." Intended as a trance-like raga with Indian overtones, the song had the band flummoxed from the outset, fluctuating as it did between five- and six-beat meters. "I had real problems working out where the beat should go," said Jones. "Rhythmically it was quite unusual. But I was the only one in the band who could do that, because of my background as an arranger."

MUCH SIMPLER IN construction were "Going to California" and "The Battle of Evermore," acoustic songs that picked up where *Led Zeppelin III* had left off. One night at Headley, after the others had hit the sack, Page spotted a mandolin Jones had bought on tour in America in 1969. "I just picked it up and started playing a sequence," Jimmy told Stuart Grundy and John Tobler. "It probably consisted of the most basic chords on a mandolin, but from that I worked out the sequence to 'The Battle of Evermore.'"

Starting out, in Page's words, as "an old English instrumental," the chords quickly meshed with a lyric Robert had begun at Bron-yr-Aur, inspired by his immersion in J.R.R. Tolkien's fantasy novel, *The Lord of the Rings* and in the military history of the Middle Ages. "The Battle of Evermore" references the Battle of Pelennor Fields from *The Return of the King*, while the Queen of Light represents Eowyn, the Prince of Peace, Aragorn, and the Dark Lord most likely Sauron. The name check for the Ringwraiths was an even more explicit nod to Tolkien. Plant also alludes to English and Celtic history in a line about "the angels of Avalon."

"You don't have to have too much of an imagination or a library full of books if you live near the Welsh border," Plant told Robert Palmer of the *New York Times* years later. "It's still there. On a murky October evening, with the watery sun looking down on those hills over some old castle and unto the river, you have be a real bimbo not to flash occasionally. Remember, I wasn't living in London. There you can be a fashion victim, but you can't feel like your average working man's Celt."

A companion piece to "The Battle of Evermore," "Going to California" had no Tolkien references, but similarly stemmed from what Page described as "a late-night guitar twiddle" at Headley. The next afternoon, with Jones pitching in on mandolin, Plant completed what was essentially an ode to LA's Laurel Canyon as personified by Joni Mitchell, the Canadian songstress who'd made the city her home early in 1968. "Someone told me there's a girl out there with love in her eyes and flowers in her hair," Plant sang.

"Songs as sort of fey as 'Going to California' were basically just joining in with Neil Young's vibe," Plant told Mick Wall in 1988. "Like, you know, [Young's album] *Everybody Knows This is Nowhere*. For me, I was back there in that sort of environment where harmony was the answer to everything, to create harmony and to promote . . . the brotherhood of man."

"Robert was more of an American type of peacenik than maybe the others were," says Henry Smith. "He was more of a caring soul. I remember times that we would sit down in the seventies and go, 'Whatever happened to this peace-love generation? What made it stop in America and what made it stop in Europe?'"

It was to Plant's great chagrin that, as he told me in 2003, "the people who lived in Laurel Canyon avoided us . . . because we were in the tackiest part of the Sunset Strip with tacky people like Kim Fowley and the GTOs." Years later, nonetheless, Joni Mitchell expressed sincere appreciation for Led Zeppelin's unlikely championing of her music.

The funky, mid-tempo stomp of "Misty Mountain Hop" coupled Plant's hippie inclinations with his Tolkien obsessions, the mountains in question featuring in both *The Hobbit* and *The Lord of the Rings*. Plant's lyrics drew allegorical parallels between long-hairs and *The Hobbit* (he was hardly the only flower child of his time to regard Tolkien's books as sacred texts of fantasy). The song concerned a drug bust, either in London or in San Francisco, and a consequent desire to flee to a place "where the spirits go now/Over the hills where the spirits fly . . ."

As with "The Battle of Evermore," "Misty Mountain Hop" came together quickly at Headley Grange. The song's core riff came from Page—"I just came up with that on the spot," he remembered—before being developed one morning by Jones, who'd woken earlier than the others and plonked himself down at a Hohner electric piano. "Jonesy put the chords in for the chorus bit, and that would shape up," Page recalled. "We used to work pretty fast. A lot of that would have been made up during the point of being at Headley."

Page had already spent many hours working out the different sections of what would become "Stairway to Heaven," layering six- and 12-string guitars at his new eight-track studio in Pangbourne. "When we were recording it," he said, "there were little bits, little sections that I'd done, getting reference pieces down on cassette, and sometimes I referred back to them if I felt there was something that seemed right that could be included."

"I wanted to try this whole idea musically," Page continued, "this build towards a climax, with John Bonham coming in at a later point . . . to give it that extra kick." He was also determined to break a rule drummed into him and John Paul as young gunslingers on the London session scene of the sixties, which was that a track should never under any circumstances speed up. (Possibly Page was unaware that Boz Scaggs had beaten him to the punch with the extended Les Paul heroics of Duane Allman on 1969's 13-minute "Loan Me a Dime." Less likely would have been his unawareness of Spirit's 1968 instrumental "Taurus," which partially influenced the opening guitar melody of "Stairway to Heaven"—Spirit was, after all, one of Robert Plant's favorite bands.)

One evening at Headley, Page and Jones worked on the song on acoustic guitar and electric piano after Plant and Bonham adjourned to the pub. The *Stairway Sessions* bootleg features the pair experimenting with the transition from the song's bridge to its final solo section. "Both Jimmy and I were quite aware of the way a track should unfold and the various levels it would go through," Jones later remarked. "We were quite strong on form. I suppose we were both quite influenced by classical music, and there's a lot of drama in the classical forms."

The next evening, with Jones and Bonzo popping up to London for a party at rock 'n' roll hangout the Speakeasy, a frustrated Plant sat by the fire with a strumming Page and grappled with the lyrics to "Stairway to Heaven." "I was holding a pencil and paper, and for some reason I was in a very bad mood," Plant recalled. Suddenly the pencil seemed to move of its own will and the song's opening couplet appeared as if by magic on the page.

The next day, Plant all but finished the lyrics in the presence of his bandmates. "By the time we'd gone through it a few times, Robert was obviously penciling down words," Page told Dave Schulps of *Trouser Press*. "About 75 to 80 percent of the words he wrote on the spot. Amazing, really. In other words he didn't go away and think about it, or have to sort of ponder and ponder and ponder."

"I'm pretty sure the first time I heard 'Stairway to Heaven,' John Paul was playing it on a recorder," says Richard Cole. "Whenever they got together to write or record, Jonesy would come down with a carload of instruments, usually acoustic. This particular time he came down with the mandolins, and I remember Robert sitting on a radiator working out the words."

"It was done very quickly," Plant himself said of a song he famously came to disown. "It was a very fluid, unnaturally easy track. There was something pushing it, saying: 'You guys are okay, but if you want to do something timeless, here's a wedding song for you.'"

The tune had come to them at last.

Andy Johns arrived at Headley Grange with the Stones mobile in late January. Thrown in at no extra expense were Stones co-founder/pianist Ian "Stu" Stewart and a battered upright piano. Parking the truck round the

"I wrote it on a bit of paper on the train . . . probably the ticket."
John Paul Jones on "Black Dog"

Led Zeppelin performing at peace and in action, 1971/72.

GETTY

"We'd recorded a couple of tracks and the sound pressure was building up as it always did with those buggers," Johns says. "I'd been experimenting with Blind Faith and Blodwyn Pig, and I was always thinking about how to record things with just two microphones, because my mother loved classical music. Listen to the Blind Faith song "Can't Find My Way Home." It's just two mics, and that includes the vocals and the drums. So we carted Bonzo's kit out to this huge lobby where the ceiling was at least 25 feet high. It sounded really good. How could he not like *this*? 'Bonzo!' I said. 'Come and listen!' He came out to the truck . . . he said, 'It's got *thrutch!*'"

"Thrutch"—one of Bonzo's favorite onomatopoeias—was an understatement for the drum sound on "When the Levee Breaks." The primordial thwack of the groove, with its fat, booming echo (courtesy of a new Binson unit), was like industrial funk. What made it even more remarkable was that Johns had dispensed with a separate mic for the bass drum.

"We could have used one but we didn't need to," Page told *Guitar World*. "[Bonzo's] kick sound was that powerful. And his playing was not in his arms, it was all in his wrist action. Frightening! I still do not know how he managed to get so much level out of a kit."

No wonder the group delayed the entrance of Plant's vocal for almost a minute-and-a-half.

Bonham was less enamored with "Four Sticks." So frustrating did he find the song's awkward rhythm that, in a moment of rage, he downed a can of Double Diamond and instead launched into the drum intro to Little Richard's "Keep A-Knockin." It was one of those impetuous impulses that takes a band off on a tangent and winds up creating something completely new—in Jimmy Page's words, "a spontaneous combustion number."

Page instantly piled in with Bonzo, cranking out a gnarly, neo-rockabilly riff that combined the influences of guitarists like Scotty Moore and Cliff Gallup. Jonesy got stuck in on bass, and Plant ad-libbed a vocal line over the top. Even Ian Stewart joined in, hammering out a piano part that was pure Jerry Lee Lewis. Fifteen minutes later, "Rock and Roll"—originally called "It's Been A Long Time"—was all but written and recorded.

For all their love of early R&B and rockabilly—live, they often inserted medleys of classics like Elvis' "That's Alright, Mama" and Eddie Cochran's

"It was a very animal thing, a hellishly powerful thing, what we were doing."

Robert Plant on recording *Led Zeppelin IV* at Headley

back of the house, Johns ran wires through the windows of the drawing room, the walls of which were covered with empty egg cartons for acoustic baffling. Though he had misgivings about mobile studios—"you end up talking to the band through a closed-circuit camera and a mic instead of through the studio glass, [which] can get a bit impersonal"—Johns acknowledged that the band felt more at home at Headley.

"It's that old cliché about a place in the country," Plant reminisced to interviewer Rick McGrath at the end of the year. "The microphones coming in through the windows, and a fire going in the hearth, and people coming in with cups of tea and cakes, and people tripping over leads, and the whole thing is utter chaos. It was a good feeling, and we did it as easy as pie."

"As musicians and performance-wise they were so fast," Johns recalls. "You could get three or four tracks done in a night. Jimmy and John Paul were session musicians—and the best session musicians. Bonzo would play the same thing on everything, so it wasn't like he had to figure out something new."

It was Bonzo who prompted Johns to come up with the album's most famous experiment. Tired of hearing the drummer moan about never capturing the sound he heard in his head, one evening Johns asked him to stay behind. The band had already made one stab at covering Memphis Minnie's 1929 blues "When the Levee Breaks" at Island, but the results—in Page's words—"sounded flat." Johns suggested to Bonham that they drag his Ludwig drum kit out of the drawing room into Headley's hallway and dangle two Beyerdynamic M160 mics from the top of the stairwell.

"Somethin' Else" into the breakdown section of "Whole Lotta Love"— "Rock and Roll" marked a new departure for Zeppelin. It also made the point that they were as passionate about fifties rock 'n' roll as any of the other seventies acts—from Don McLean on *American Pie* to John Lennon on *Rock 'N' Roll*—who were busy paying homage to the stars of that era. Page's collection of early Sun and rockabilly singles was rumored to rival even his collection of Aleister Crowley artifacts.

Plant, too, was a connoisseur of American oldies: the lyrics he wrote, virtually on the spot, amounted to a high-speed hymn of nostalgia, referencing The Diamonds, The Monotones, and The Drifters as he sought to rekindle the innocent magic of rock's early days.

"We just thought rock 'n' roll needed to be taken on again," Robert told Chuck Eddy in 1988. "So we had all these little rock 'n' roll nuances, like in "Boogie with Stu" and "Rock and Roll." I was finally in a really successful band and we felt it was time for actually kicking ass. It wasn't an intellectual thing, 'cos we didn't have time for that, we just wanted to let it all come flooding out. It was a very animal thing, a hellishly powerful thing, what we were doing."

Following the week of rehearsals at Headley, the band spent a mere six days in the house with the mobile studio. "Looking back, I suppose what we really needed was at least two weeks solid with the truck," Page admitted. "But as it turned out we actually only had about six days. Usually we need a full week to get everything out of our system and to get used to the facilities."

In no time they were back at Island studios in London, primarily ➤➤

to record "Four Sticks" and "Stairway to Heaven," but also to take care of the overdubs for the album. "A lot of times we'd leave Jimmy alone to do his layering and overdubs," says Richard Cole. "You'd leave on a Friday afternoon, and then when you turned up on a Monday morning you'd hear something completely different."

Zeppelin had already used Island's Studio One for two of the third album's highlights—the dreamy Bron-yr-Aur strum along "That's the Way" and the harrowing blues ballad "Since I've Been Loving You"—and so were used to the room's cavernous resonance.

"It wasn't a little den," says Digby Smith, one of Andy Johns' assistants at Island. "You could get a 70-piece orchestra in there. The problem was controlling the liveness of it. So the sound was heavily compressed by Andy. It seemed like whenever he was at the desk, everything got bigger and louder—the excitement levels rose. The quality of the sound he could create, and the speed with which he worked, really impressed me. The confidence he exuded fed through to the band. He had great style. Every take was a performance. If George Martin was the fifth Beatle, then Andy at that point was the fifth member of Zeppelin."

One evening, Smith had barely arrived home—"looking forward to a well-deserved night off"—when the phone rang. It was studio manager Penny Hanson, asking if he could come straight back to the studio and deputize for Bob Potter. The session was for "Stairway to Heaven."

"Zeppelin had been in for a couple of nights and were due in for one more," Smith says. "When I walked in, Jonesy was sitting at a keyboard and Jimmy was playing acoustic guitar, surrounded by four tall, beige baffles that almost obscured him. Seventy percent of Bonham's drum sound came from a Beyer M500 ribbon microphone hanging four or five feet over his head. I don't think Robert had even done a guide vocal for the song."

Although it was a complex song—in Smith's words, "a medley of two or three tunes tied together"—the first take almost nailed it. Johns called everyone in to listen, increasing the volume to what Smith recalls as "hooligan level."

"There's a two-inch tape somewhere of Take 1 that's awesome, no mistakes from beginning to end," says Smith. "Bonham and Jones and Plant all agree that that's the one. The only person not saying anything is Jimmy. So Bonham turns to him and says, 'What's wrong?' Page says nothing's wrong. Bonham goes, 'No, something's wrong. What is it?' 'There's nothing wrong.' 'Well, is that the take or *isn't* it?' 'It's alright.' 'It's alright. So you

want us to do it again.' 'I think we've got a better take inside us.'"

Fuming, Bonham picked up his sticks, stomped down the steps from the control room, and planted himself behind his kit. "I can still see him sitting there, waiting to come in, seething," says Smith. "And when he finally comes in, he's beating the crap out of his drums and all the meters are going into the red. And they come back up into the control room, play it through, and it's just that little bit more urgent. And Bonham gives Pagey a metaphorical hug and says, 'You were right.'"

It was now time for Jones to overdub the three recorders he played on "Stairway to Heaven," enhancing the already Elizabethan feel of Page's picking. Which left the vocal, and the small matter of the guitar solo, which Page opted to play not on one of his then-preferred Les Pauls but on the old Telecaster that Jeff Beck had given him in 1966.

"Instead of headphones we set up some big playback monitors—as big as Page was—and Jimmy leant on one of them with a cigarette in his mouth," says Digby Smith. "We did three takes of lead guitar and comped the solo from those three takes. I was audacious enough, even as a fresh-faced 19 year old, to point out that one of Andy's switches didn't quite work and that there was an alternative solution that might. And Jimmy was like, 'This kid's good.' After the solo, Robert went out and did the vocal— one take, maybe two."

"Robert was sitting at the back with me and I said, 'Come on, it's your turn now,'" says Johns. "He said, 'I'm not finished. Play it again.' And he's got this legal pad in front of him. So I played it through again and he said, 'Okay, I'm ready now.' It was two takes, one punch-in."

"Four Sticks," which they'd so singularly failed to nail at Headley, was finally sussed out at Island. Re-energized by seeing Ginger Baker's Air Force at London's Lyceum on February 1, Bonham came to the studio determined to do the track justice. But it took four drumsticks to make it work, hence the song's eventual title.

"It was two takes, but that was because it was physically impossible for him to do another," Jimmy Page said of Bonzo's playing on the track.

To Page, the guitars on "Four Sticks" were almost as important as those on "Black Dog." "I can see certain milestones along the way like 'Four Sticks,' in the middle section of that," he told Steven Rosen. "The sound of those guitars—that's where I'm going." After the guitars had been recorded, Jones overdubbed the synthesizer solo on the song's second middle-eight section. By the time it was complete, "Four Sticks" just about worked as an exotic oddity, its crabbed oriental feel making it a missing link between *Led Zeppelin III*'s "Friends" and *Physical Graffiti*'s "Kashmir." When ◆◆

Top: Led Zeppelin with Sandy Denny, who sang on "The Battle of Evermore."
Above: Page with his signature Gibson EDS 1275 6/12 double-neck.

"It was a very fluid, unnaturally easy track. There was something pushing it, saying, 'You guys are okay, but if you want to do something timeless, here's a wedding song for you.'"

Robert Plant on the writing of "Stairway to Heaven"

Left to right: Richard Cole and Robert Plant
in a hotel room in New York

Page and Plant stopped off in India the following year, they recorded versions of both "Friends" and "Four Sticks" with some inebriated members of the Bombay Symphony Orchestra.

Even after all that, "Four Sticks" was, says Andy Johns, "a bastard to mix." "When I originally recorded the basic tracks I compressed the drums," he said. "Then when I went to mix I couldn't make it work. I did it five or six times." Zeppelin only ever played "Four Sticks" once live, though Page and Plant returned to it when putting together their *UnLedded* project in 1994. Plant also included it in his *Strange Sensation* repertoire in 2005.

In addition to Page's many overdubs at Island—among them the directly injected guitars on "Black Dog"—was a guest vocal from Alexandra "Sandy" Denny, who duetted with Plant on "The Battle of Evermore." "It was really more of a playlet than a song," Robert said in April 1972. "After I wrote the lyrics, I realized I needed another, completely different voice, as well as my own, to give that song its full impact."

Denny had been the lead singer with folk rockers Fairport Convention, who had strongly influenced the acoustic side of Zep, and jammed with them on a wild night at LA's Troubadour club the previous September. "There was a great mutual appreciation society between Fairport and Zeppelin," Plant told me in 2003. "I mean, can you say that the White Stripes might hang out with The Hives? No, and yet it was far more of a divide between Zeppelin and Fairport."

Elvis and the Gibson double-neck that had discontinued. The BBC sessions, April 1971, caught the band at their peak.

The association with Denny went still further back. "Sandy was big mates with Jimmy from their school days," says Fairport's bassist Dave Pegg. "She knew Jimmy from way back from when she was at art school in Kingston." (Pegg himself went way back with Zeppelin, having played with Bonham in Midlands band A Way of Life.)

Andy Johns recalls, "Robert said, 'We're going to have Sandy come down.' I thought it was a brilliant idea. Of course she fitted right in—she sang like a nightingale with Robert singing at the same time. Literally, she was the inspiration for the whole thing. I went: 'Wow!'"

Denny, who was about to part ways with her subsequent group Fotheringay, was a magnificent addition to the track. "I don't think it took more than 45 minutes," Robert Plant recalled. "I showed her how to do the long 'Oooooh, dance in the dark' bit so there'd be a vocal tail-in. It was perfect against my bluesy thing."

As great as she sounds on the song, Denny left the studio feeling like she'd been thoroughly overshadowed by Plant. As she admitted to journalist Barbara Charone from *Sounds* in 1973, "Having someone outsing you is a horrible feeling, wanting to be strongest yourself."

By the time Zeppelin finished up at Island they had 14 tracks, enough to make the album a double—or, more eccentrically, a series of four separate EPs, a suggestion that was floated by Page. In the end, both ideas were discarded. "We have enough here for two albums," Page said, "but we won't put out a double album. I think people can appreciate a single album better."

"No Quarter" would appear in more brooding form on the next album, *Houses of the Holy*. "Boogie with Stu," like "Night

"We have enough here for two albums, but . . . I think people can appreciate a single album better."

Jimmy Page on *Led Zeppelin IV*

Flight" and "Down by the Seaside," would show up on *Physical Graffiti*, the one after that. "The Rover," also included on *Physical Graffiti*, existed only in rudimentary acoustic form at this time. Talking to Bob Harris on *The Old Grey Whistle Test* in 1975, Robert Plant referred to this and other material on *Physical Graffiti* as "old, crazy stuff . . . really good stuff that we thought, we can't keep it in the can any longer."

On February 9, with PR man Bill Harry busy dispelling rumors that Zeppelin would split after a 12-date tour of the UK and Ireland, Page and Andy Johns packed up the tapes and flew to LA with Peter Grant to mix the album at the famed Sunset Sound studios. Just after they landed at LAX, they felt the tremors of the Sylmar earthquake that shook the city just after six that morning—an eerie coincidence, given that "Going to California" had a Plant line about the mountains and canyons starting to "tremble and shake."

Johns had used Sunset Sound before, having mixed an album there by Doug Feiger's pre-Knack outfit Sky. But his ulterior motive for mixing in LA wasn't entirely to do with recording.

"I was seeing this bird, Jeanie, not to mention her friend Jackie," he says. "I was so excited to get there that I left my two tapes on the plane. These are 15-IPS tapes, and I think I had two of them and Jimmy had two. So we're standing out front, and there's two limos, and I suddenly realize the tapes are on the plane. And going back the wrong way to get your stuff is far more difficult than getting on with it. I'd left 'Stairway to Heaven' and 'Going to California' under my seat." Luckily the reels were retrieved, and Page and Johns set off to Hollywood.

Unfortunately, the acoustics at Sunset Sound proved to be deceptive. "We wasted a week wanking around," Page moaned after returning to England. "It had sounded all right to me but the speakers were lying. It wasn't the balance, it was the actual sound that was on the tape. All I can put it down to was the fact that the speakers in LA and the monitoring system in that room were just very bright. It wasn't the true sound."

"We should have just gone home," Johns later conceded. "But I didn't want to and I don't think Jimmy did either. We were having a good time, you know?"

The one mix salvaged from the Sunset Sound fiasco was the storming "When the Levee Breaks." Radically slowed down by Page and Johns, it stands with "Black Dog" as a vital counterweight to the album's airier moments. "It is probably the most subtle thing on there as far as production goes," Page told Dave Schulps, "because each 12 bars has something new about it, though at first it might not be apparent. It's got different effects on it, which now people have heard a number of times but which at the time hadn't been used before: phased vocals and harmonica solos backwards… a lot of backwards echo."

Page was particularly proud of the panning and "extreme positioning" he and Johns achieved during the final two minutes of "When the Levee Breaks." "At the end of it, where we've got the whole works going on this fade, it doesn't actually fade," Jimmy said. "As we finished it, the whole effects start to spiral—all the instruments are now spiraling. This was very difficult to do in those days, I can assure you, with the mixing, and the voice remaining constant in the middle. You hear everything turning right around."

"When the Levee Breaks" aside, the mixes met a distinctly frosty reception when played to the other members of Zeppelin. "Jimmy brought the tapes back and they sounded terrible," Robert Plant told *Disc*.

"I thought my number was up," Andy Johns confessed later. "But the others seemed to look to Jimmy, even though it was just as much my fault."

Johns had in any case by now fallen foul of the band's increasing control-freakery. "They were very much unto themselves—a clique," he says today. "There was a tremendous amount of paranoia, because all they knew was each other: 'It's us against them, because they're going to get us.'"

Like many who worked with Zeppelin over the years, Johns gripes that Jimmy Page, in particular, likes to take credit for everything and anything the group ever did. "Jimmy thinks he invented the f****** electric guitar," he told me last year. One of the reasons Page constantly switched engineers was so that none of them could take credit for Zeppelin's sound.

"Jimmy told me years ago, 'I'm not having anyone saying they're the sound of Led Zeppelin—I am the sound of Led Zeppelin,'" says photographer Ross Halfin, one of Page's closest confidantes. "And you know something? He is. You can play any Zeppelin album apart from *In through the Out Door* and it sounds like they recorded it this morning. And ❧

THE *BACK TO THE CLUBS* TOUR

By: Dave Lewis

They had been accustomed to filling the stadiums of the US, but when Led Zeppelin undertook their first tour of 1971—a 14-date trek across the UK—they played to venues with a capacity of less than 1,000 in what was dubbed the *Back to the Clubs* tour.

"The audiences are becoming bigger and bigger," explained Jimmy Page at the time. "By going back to places like the Marquee, we aim to reestablish our contact with the people who got us off the ground in the beginning."

In a rare act of charity, Peter Grant charged the promoters the same fee as they had done when they originally appeared an the venues concerned in the band's early days. Inevitably there were complaints from fans unable to get tickets, especially as this would be the last opportunity to see Zeppelin in such intimate surroundings.

The tour kicked off with a visit to trouble-torn Ireland. On the evening of March 5, 1971, fans inside the Ulster Hall Belfast witnessed Led Zeppelin perform "Stairway to Heaven" for the first time. They also premiered "Black Dog," "Going to California," and "Rock and Roll" from their as-yet unreleased fourth album, which eventually surfaced some six months later.

Paul Sheppard saw the band at Bath Pavilion for the princely sum of 70 pence (the equivalent of about one dollar today). "The volume was incredibly loud for such a small venue,"

he remembers. "For the acoustic set, they sat on old, canvas-backed metal chairs. Robert made a reference to The Mixtures, who had a hit at the time with 'The Pushbike Song.' 'Tobacco Road' [a Nashville Teens hit from '64] made an appearance in the 'Whole Lotta Love' medley."

Up in Newcastle, then-17-year-old schoolboy Phil Tait queued for hours to get tickets for their show at the Mayfair club and managed to take a few photos. "Cameras were banned at the venue, so I was very lucky to get my equipment through. I used a Kodak with a large flash-gun attachment—something that you see in old films of the 1950s. Getting it past the doorman was not easy. Luckily my greatcoat had big pockets."

Other choice venues included Nottingham Boat Club, the Belfry Golf Club in Sutton Coldfield, and the famous Marquee club in London. They also appeared at the BBC's Paris Cinema in London for John Peel's *In Concert* Radio One show. An hour-long edited broadcast of that show (including "Stairway to Heaven"), was aired on April 4, 1971. Listeners of the show on that spring Sunday evening could have no inkling at the time that they were privy to the very first radio play of a song that would subsequently rack up some six million plays on radio stations around the world over the next 40 years.

The *Back to the Clubs* tour.

that is 100 percent Jimmy."

Remixing the album was in any case put on the back burner while Zeppelin set off on the scaled-down *Back to the Clubs* tour of the UK.

"The boys came to me after Christmas and talked about their next tour," Peter Grant told *Melody Maker*'s Chris Welch. "We decided to do the clubs and forget about the bread and big concert halls. We're going to restrict prices to about 12 bob [about one dollar in today's money] a ticket."

Given the troubles in Northern Ireland, it was brave to start the tour at Belfast's Ulster Hall on March 5. There was additional trepidation in giving live debuts to four songs from the forthcoming album—especially to the ambitious "Stairway to Heaven," which prompted Page to invest in a custom-made Gibson EDS 1275 6/12 double-neck so he could switch from a six to a 12-string guitar.

Page had seen the double-neck on the cover of bluesman Earl Hooker's 1969 Arhoolie Records album *Two Bugs & A Roach*, and Elvis Presley had played one in his 1966 movie *Spinout*, but Gibson had discontinued production of them. So it was a minor coup to get his hands on one at all.

"When you just play the six-string neck," he later told Zep specialist Howard Mylett, "all the other strings start ringing in sympathy like the strings in a sitar . . . it can sound like a harp."

As the Belfast bootleg makes clear, the response to "Stairway to Heaven" was polite but equivocal: no Zeppelin fan had ever heard anything quite like this from them before. "There was always a slight resistance to new material," John Paul Jones later remarked. "The first time we played 'Stairway to Heaven,' it was like, 'Why aren't they playing 'Whole Lotta Love'? Because people like what they know. And then 'Stairway to Heaven' became what they knew."

Phil Carson, then head of Atlantic Records in England, remembers it differently: "The audience was stunned," he told *Q*'s James McNair in 2003. "Here were Zeppelin, who were very much riff-oriented, with this almost orchestrated song. After the first few times they'd played it live, Peter said, 'You know what? You've really got to shut up after this song. Bonzo, don't hit the snare drum.' The idea was that if the band seemed reverent towards the song, then that would impact on the audience."

Though it was rooted in uncharacteristically altruistic motives, the *Back to the Clubs* tour was only a qualified success for Zeppelin. Asunder a dollar. Page remarked to *Record Mirror*, "We couldn't win either way . . . first we were this big hype, now we were at fault for not playing places big enough for everybody to see us."

The day after the tour's final show, at the Marquee on March 23, Page's French partner, Charlotte Martin, gave birth to their daughter Scarlet Lilith Eleida. The day after *that*, Zeppelin were forced at the last minute to postpone their second live session for BBC's Radio 1 because Plant had strained his vocal cords. The session then took place on April Fool's Day, with John Peel introducing the band. Stellar versions of "Black Dog," "Going to California," and "Stairway to Heaven" proved just how comfortable Zep had become with the new material on the UK tour.

By mid-April, Page and Andy Johns were booked into Olympic—where Zeppelin had recorded their game-changing debut album with Johns' elder brother Glyn—to start the new mixes. (All were credited as being "with Andy Johns" except "The Battle of Evermore," which employed assistant engineer George Chkiantz). Due to further live bookings, the mixing process continued into June. "It's that long, dragging-out thing of mixing a lot of the tracks," Robert Plant said at the time. "It's a drag having to do it twice, but we're coming to the tail end of it now."

Plant was nonetheless starting to feel energized about the finished album. "Out of the lot, I should think there are about three or four mellow things," he said in June. "But there's also some nice strong stuff . . . and exciting, and the flame is really burning higher and higher."

Shortly before a police-provoked riot brought Zeppelin's July 5 show at the Vigorelli Stadium in Milan to a violent halt, the finished mixes were finally delivered for mastering to Trident Studios in Soho.

Equally excited about the album was Bonham, who took an acetate back to his West Hagley home and blasted it at top volume to local friends. Among the privileged few was Glenn Hughes—later of Deep Purple, then of power trio Trapeze—who was treated to a private listening party in early August.

Bonham told Hughes he wanted to play him the new album. "We must have played it 10 times from tip to toe, "Black Dog" to "When the Levee Breaks," Hughes says. "John was grinning and crying and smoking and back-slapping and

dancing. And what I heard—on an amazing stereo, turned up to 11—was life-changing. "When the Levee Breaks" just did me in, it became embedded in my soul. I didn't think, 'This is going to become one of the biggest-selling albums of all time,' I thought, 'Here I am with a great guy, we're young, we're f***** rocking, he's becoming my mentor, he's giving me advice, he's dropping the needle back to this moment and telling me how Jonesy did this or Pagey did that.' In fact, he was giving me a historical lesson on the making of *Led Zeppelin IV*. It was one of the biggest moments of my life."

Having agreed between them that Led Zeppelin's fourth album would be untitled—and wouldn't even feature their name—the four members instead chose to represent themselves with runic symbols from Rudolph Koch's *Book of Signs*. "Jimmy said we should all choose a symbol from the book to represent each one of us," Jonesy recalled. He later discovered that Page had had the infamous "ZoSo" symbol designed personally for him—"typical, really."

The symbols helped cement Led Zeppelin's occult standing within their exponentially expanding fan base. "ZoSo" in particular turned a generation of teenage American boys into disciples of Page's guitar sorcery and with an obsession with Aleister Crowley. "My symbol was about invoking and being invocative," Page has said. "And that's all I'm going to say about it."

"To this day I don't know what Jimmy's sign meant," says Richard Cole. "For all I know he could have been having a f***** laugh with everyone . . . No one really delved into what he did, to be honest with you. It was as much of a mystery to us as it was to everyone else."

It was Page, too, who commissioned the rather bad drawing that graced the inside of the gatefold cover. Barrington Colby's *View in Half or Varying Light* showed a cloaked elder—the Hermit of the tarot pack, as it turned out—standing atop a mountain with a lantern, while below him a tiny, long-haired figure clambers up the rocks towards him. For Page, this represented "the ascension to the beacon and the light of truth."

When the album finally appeared—released on November 8, 1971 in America and November 19, 1971 in the UK—it was almost a year since Zeppelin had begun work on it. The frustrating delays had taken their toll on the band as they toured Europe, America, and Japan without a record to promote. "I'm pleased with the new album, but I'm disgusted at the amount of time it's taken to get it off," Plant told *Disc* on returning from Japan at the end of September. "The whole story of the fourth album reads like a nightmare."

Oddly, given its eventual phenomenal sales, the album never topped the US chart, being kept off the number-one spot by Carole King's *Tapestry*. By May 1975, however, it had been in the Top 60 continuously for three-and-a-half years. "Stairway to Heaven," meanwhile, had become a kind of ritual invocation.

"The song was going nuts on the radio, but it was an eight-minute cut," says Jerry Greenberg, then president of Atlantic Records and currently manager of Zeppelin tribute band Led Zepagain. "I called Peter and said, 'Listen, we've got the same thing going on as we had with 'Whole Lotta Love.' Will Jimmy go in and edit the track?' Peter said no. So I did the exact same thing as I did with 'Whole Lotta Love'; we did our own edit. It had to go to at least five minutes; there was no way you were going to make a three-minute version of 'Stairway to Heaven.' But the same thing happened; Peter would not allow it to come out as a single. The only way anybody was going to get 'Stairway to Heaven' was to buy *Led Zeppelin IV*. And it was their biggest-selling album ever."

Looking back on the evolution of Zeppelin's music, the fourth album seems to consolidate everything they'd achieved with the first three. But whereas the acoustic tracks are what most people recall of *Led Zeppelin III*, it's the power numbers that really define the fourth album.

"I'm not sure they didn't change direction and do the acoustic thing on *Led Zeppelin III* knowing they were going to go back to the other side on the fourth album," says Richard Cole. "The third album was almost like a break in the pattern. They didn't want to make it look like that was all they could do. Then when the fourth one came out, there was just absolutely no dispute as to what they were about."

Asked in 1990 if there was anything he would change about Zeppelin's fourth album, Jimmy Page replied with a laugh that he would "do it with click-tracks, synthesizers, and sampling" and then retire. "I've really got fond memories of those times, and the album was done with such great spirit," he said. "Everyone had a smile on their face." ◗

> ## "I'm not having anyone saying they're the sound of Led Zeppelin—I am the sound of Led Zeppelin."
> ### Jimmy Page

BOMBAY NIGHTS

In October 1972, Robert Plant and Jimmy Page made an impromptu visit to Bombay, where they jammed with local musicians.

By: Rob Hughes

Lack of information has only served to amplify the mythical aspect of Led Zeppelin's three low-key visits to India in the space of 12 months in the early seventies. Jimmy Page and Robert Plant first visited the sprawling city of Bombay on the back of their Japanese tour of September 1971. A few months later, on their way to play Australia in February 1972, they surreptitiously slipped into the country with tour manager Richard Cole after being denied entry to Singapore because of their long hair and beards. The trio swung around Bombay in a taxi cab, armed with 8-mm film cameras. The footage can now be seen on *YouTube*.

But the most intriguing of these clandestine trips was the one in October 1972. Following Zeppelin's six-date tour of Japan, Page, Plant, and Cole set up camp in Bombay's five-star Taj Mahal hotel—and duly played a gig. Their arrival in the country came at a time when Indian rock music was still in its infancy. There were several such bands in Bombay—chief among them being Atomic Forest, Human Bondage, and Velvette Fogg—but they were almost wholly in thrall to Western imports.

"In the early seventies there wasn't much original music sung in English here, only Hindi," explains Nandu Bhende, the singer of Velvette Fogg. "There was definitely a scene among the college kids in the metros . . . but, frankly, we just copied Led Zeppelin. It was much later that we took all those influences and started making our own music."

Bhende first encountered Page and Plant at the Taj Mahal hotel, where the Led Zeppelin pair were staying on their third trip.

"There was a nightclub downstairs at the Taj hotel where we used to perform as a rock band, and Plant and Page walked into our rehearsal," he recalls. "I remember Plant sat on the drum set and nearly broke it, because he was hitting it so hard. He was all over the place. He wanted to connect. But Page was very quiet, just sitting around and not communicating too much. I thought they looked quite effeminate, which was really odd to me, because they were so strong in their music and sound. It felt like a macho act, but in real life they weren't like that at all."

A few days later, on a Monday night (most likely October 16), Plant and Page gave an impromptu concert at Bombay nightclub Slip Disc, accompanied by two local musicians and primitive stage gear. Bhende was in the audience that night.

"The Slip Disc was really a hole, not a very huge

place at all," he says. "But it was packed. Plant and Page didn't have any equipment and hadn't rehearsed. They just walked out onstage with the two musicians here [Xerxes Gobhai, bassist from Human Bondage, and Jameel Shaikh, drummer with Bhande's own band, Velvette Fogg]. I remember Page going for a Stratocaster and it being in very bad shape, so he picked up my bandmate's guitar, an old German thing, and played that instead. They started with 'Rock and Roll' and played for 20 or 25 minutes. There was a long jam at the end, when Plant started talking about Bombay, then they did 'Black Dog.' Plant and Page looked like they were having fun. The crowd went absolutely wild."

The show was supposedly recorded onto cassette by the club's resident DJ, Arul Harris, after which it fell into the possession of Atomic Forest's Keith Kanga. Unfortunately, the tape is now lost, as are definitive memories of the time, although Gobhai recalled also playing "Whole Lotta Love." College student and journalist Khalid Mohammed subsequently claimed that Plant and Page sang a previously unheard tune, "Kashmir," but Zeppelin experts insist that "Kashmir" wasn't written until 1973.

Due to the spontaneous nature of the event, it received scant notice in the press. Some photos of the gig did, however, appear in the November issue of Bombay youth magazine *Junior Statesman*, accompanied by a brief interview.

"You know why we came?" Plant told the writer. "To see if we could set up a recording studio. But the customs regulations are tough, man. Like, it will take us six months to get our equipment out of Bombay airport."

That trip also marked the occasion when Plant and Page, the latter armed with a state-of-the-art Stellavox qaudraphonic tape machine, recorded in the studio with Indian classical musicians, arranged for them by Ravi Shankar disciple Vijay Raghav Rao. The result, the much-bootlegged *The Bombay Sessions*, yielded radically different versions of "Friends" and "Four Sticks," featuring sarangi, sitars, and tablas. The ensemble was credited as the Bombay Symphony Orchestra, though Page was less than happy with the quality of the sessions themselves. Once back in England, according to Richard Cole, the Bombay tapes went into storage.

Yet nothing can deflect from the monumental cultural impact of Page and Plant's visit.

"They were idols of ours before they came here," marvels Bhende, "so we just could not believe that a front-ranking band of that stature could perform in India. None of us could have ever dreamt it was going to happen." ❼

"PLANT AND PAGE LOOKED LIKE THEY WERE HAVING FUN. THE CROWD WENT ABSOLUTELY WILD."
—Nandu Bhende, observer

Richard Cole, Jimmy Page, and Robert Plant rub shoulders with Indian musician Xerxes Gobhai at Bombay's Slip Disc club.

(Continued on page 50)

THE·HOUSE THAT ZEPPELIN BUILT

More than five decades ago, Led Zeppelin released their fifth album, *Houses of the Holy*. Let's celebrate Zeppelin's unsung masterpiece.

By: Mark Blake

> **"WE WOULDN'T MAKE THE SAME RE- CORD TWICE. IT WAS A CASE OF, 'LET'S KEEP MOVING.'"**
> —Jimmy Page

In March 1973, advertisements started appearing in the press for Led Zeppelin's new album, *Houses of the Holy*. One featured a black-and-white drawing of a man with his hands bound behind his back and his head jammed between the buffers of two railway carriages. Another featured a uniformed figure with their head exploding in a cloud of smoke and flames, above the words "Led Zeppelin. *Houses of the Holy*. The Effect is Shattering . . ."

Even ads for Pink Floyd's enigmatic-looking new album *The Dark Side of the Moon*, released that month, couldn't equal the confidence of Zeppelin's campaign. Since 1971's fourth album, they had dispensed with images of themselves on album sleeves. Now, they no longer needed a band picture or even an album cover in their ads; the crushed skull and exploding head did the job just fine.

Released on March 28 1973, *Houses of the Holy* rapidly topped the UK and US charts.

In truth, *Houses of the Holy* is a more subtle record than that schlock-horror ad campaign suggests. Yes, it's a bit messy and almost perversely eclectic, but it also contains at least four classic songs (five if you're in the mood for a good pub argument). Taken as a whole, it bottles Zeppelin's gleeful energy and anything-goes experimentalism just at that point before they became the biggest rock group on the planet.

Zeppelin's fifth album always gets passed over for their fourth, with its ubiquitous "Stairway to Heaven," or 1975's magisterial *Physical Graffiti*. But *Houses of the Holy* is the sound of a band entering their most imperial phase, just before fatigue, cynicism, and hard drugs impinged on their well-being. In a strange way, it's Zeppelin's last "innocent" album—if anything about Led Zeppelin could ever be described as innocent.

Although they'd emerged in 1968, Zeppelin was always a band for the seventies. Jimmy Page had toured America with his old group The Yardbirds. There, he'd spotted a gap in the market for a band that could build on the power and dynamism of Hendrix and Cream.

By the end of 1969, rock music had become big business. Critics mourned the end of the hippie dream and the rise of the "breadheads." But there was now a new audience to be catered for: teenagers who had been too young for the Summer of Love and wanted their own heroes. There were arenas to be filled and dollars to be made. Led Zeppelin saw their chance, and took it.

Rolling Stone critic John Mendelssohn described their self-titled 1969 debut album as "weak, unimaginative, limited, monotonous", sparking a tense relationship between the band and the press that was never resolved. But *Led Zeppelin* and its follow-up *Led Zeppelin II* both cracked the Top 10 in Britain and America. Those who dismissed the group as stone-age grunters were further ◆▶

Jimmy Page in May, 1972.

disarmed by 1970's *Led Zeppelin III*, which included a clutch of almost tender folk songs. It proved, said Page, "that there is another side to us."

This message was driven home on 1971's fourth LP (the one most people call *Led Zeppelin IV*). Its centerpiece, "Stairway to Heaven," conveyed more of the band's light and shade, and became a hit on US FM radio. Zeppelin's refusal to release singles, together with their reluctance to woo the press, all added to the mystique. *IV* went gold on the day of its release. But by the time they started *Houses of the Holy*, the stakes were higher than ever.

"We wouldn't make the same record twice," said Page. "It was a case of, 'Let's keep moving.'"

Work began on the album in April 1972 at Mick Jagger's Berkshire manor house, Stargroves. The Rolling Stones had moved to France a year before to avoid Britain's punitive new tax laws and make *Exile on Main St.* The four members of Zeppelin shipped over to Stargroves to rehearse and record their new material.

"It was a nice mansion, if you like mansions," engineer Eddie Kramer told Zeppelin biographer Barney Hoskyns. Kramer showed up at Stargroves with an American girlfriend in tow, but "Robert Plant bagged her straight away." Meanwhile, Page bagged Jagger's bedroom, one of the few furnished rooms in the house, and Bonham's kit was set up in a large, conservatory style space downstairs. When the group wandered outside, Kramer recorded Plant singing and Page strumming an acoustic guitar in the sunshine. "You can hear the fun we were having," the guitarist said. "And you can also hear the dedication and commitment."

Dedication and commitment were never a problem for Page. "I don't think Zeppelin was ever complacent," said Robert Plant. "By the time we got to *Houses of the Holy*, there was a conscientious air about Jimmy's work."

Page had come to the sessions loaded with song ideas worked up beforehand at his home studio. One of the songs he brought to Stargroves would become the album opener. "The Song Remains the Same" started as an instrumental fanfare for the album's second track, "The Rain Song." Then Plant heard it. "Robert had different ideas," said Page. "He said, 'This is pretty good. Better get some lyrics—quick!'"

Plant's lyrics referenced Zeppelin's globetrotting adventures, with "sweet Calcutta rain," a nod to a trip to India he and Page had made before starting the album. Page's jangling 12-string guitar created an exotic noise like a mini orchestra. Plant's voice was slightly sped up.

The press ads for *Houses of the Holy* that began to appear in March 1973.

Listen to it now and it almost sounds like Yes.

While progressive and glam rock were thriving in the outside world, Zeppelin created music in a bubble. Nothing ever seemed to make its way in, apart from the blues, soul, and fifties jukebox records they'd grown up with.

"The Song Remains the Same" also had a cinematic, larger-than-life feel that Zeppelin would go back to on "Achilles Last Stand," the dominant track on 1976's *Presence*. But while the latter track sounded like the end of the world, "The Song Remains the Same" sounded like a band having the time of their lives.

Even the ballad "The Rain Song," all about a broken romance, didn't sound *that* heartbroken. John Paul Jones created the song's mournful violins and cellos with a Mellotron, that unwieldy, primitive synthesizer featured on the Moody Blues' 1967 hit "Nights in White Satin." But, as Jones dolefully recalled, "They had the guy who invented it working for them, and I didn't."

Jones did a sterling job. Never one for self-aggrandizement, it's difficult to overstate his role on the whole album. He's there throughout, sometimes in the foreground but more often than not multi-tasking at the back. Jones also brought song ideas to Stargroves. One of these, "No Quarter," the album's only downbeat track, had been attempted during sessions for the fourth LP. Now, though, they found an arrangement that gelled.

Between them, Jones' grand piano, bass, and synthesizer, Page's eerie-sounding guitar, Plant's treated vocals, and a restrained John Bonham, a mysterious song about an unspecified snowbound rendezvous was conjured up. You

never knew exactly what was going on, but whatever it was sounded dramatic and life-changing. "No Quarter" swept *Houses of the Holy* out of the daylight and into the Arctic gloom. It was a brilliant counterpoint to everything else on the album.

"I knew instantly ["No Quarter"] was a very durable piece and something we could take on the road and expand," Jones told Zeppelin historian Dave Lewis. You can only imagine how much it must have peeved him, then, when Page and Plant lifted its title for their Jones-less '94 collaboration album, *No Quarter: UnLedded*.

After further sessions at London's Island and Olympic studios, with engineers Keith Harwood, Andy Johns, and George Chkiantz, Zeppelin went back on the road in America in June. In between dates, they checked into New York's Electric Lady studios with Kramer to mix the Stargroves tracks.

The band had worked hard to cultivate an aloof image, believing that it helped sales. But it also had a downside. By now, Zeppelin had notched up four UK and US Top 10 albums. But it was the Rolling Stones, not Led Zeppelin, who were bagging magazine front covers and having society author and social butterfly Truman Capote trailing them around America on tour. "All we read was, the Stones this or the Stones that," John Bonham complained in *NME*. "And it pissed us off." Perhaps that's why Stargroves was never mentioned in the credits on the original *Houses of the Holy* LP.

The Stones may have stolen their thunder, but Zeppelin sounded invincible at their own shows. "Right through, the majority of the music was built on an extreme energy," explained Plant. That was never more apparent than at the LA Forum and Long Beach Arena on June 25 and 27 (two shows preserved on the 2003-released live album *How the West Was Won*). That "extreme energy" was further distilled on the three *Houses of the Holy* tracks played during the gigs, despite the new album not being out for another nine months.

On "Over the Hills and Far Away," Plant revisited the role he'd played on *Led Zeppelin II*'s "Ramble On"—the hippie romantic with a well-thumbed copy of *The Lord of the Rings* under his arm. After a deceptively folky intro, Page's scything guitar blew the song out of Middle Earth. Meanwhile, on "The Ocean," a sort of heavy metal sea shanty, Bonham's drum fills challenged the jabbing rhythms on *Led Zeppelin IV*'s "Black Dog" for sheer unadulterated power. The Beastie Boys would later sample Page's opening riff on "The Ocean" for their own "She's Crafty" in 1986 (the lawsuit-tempting rappers also sampled Bonham's monster drum pattern from "When the Levee Breaks" on *IV* for "Rhythm & Stealin'"). However, despite the song's burly swagger, the

Led Zeppelin onstage in New York, 1973.

lyrics on "The Ocean" had a twist. They weren't about sex or hobbits, but partly inspired by Plant's three-year-old daughter, Carmen.

If one single song summarizes the (almost) innocence of *Houses of the Holy*, then it's "Dancing Days," also premiered at those 1972 shows, and one of the best Led Zeppelin tracks you'll never find on any official "best of" compilation. "Dancing Days" was the goofy pop-rocker with the wonky guitar and organ riff (that man Jones again) that opened Side Two of the LP. Until that first round of Zeppelin CDs appeared, listeners kept the album's inner sleeve/lyric sheet close at hand, to check that Plant really did sing: "I saw a lion he was standing alone with a tadpole in a jar." He did. Perhaps the clue as to why could be found elsewhere in "Dancing Days'" talk of "suppin' booze." Either way, it was the brightest-sounding song on a very bright-sounding album.

Which just leaves the two tracks that have been polarizing opinion ever since. Side One of *Houses of the Holy* ended with a circular funk rock jam called "The Crunge." Bonham and Page played as if they were reading each other's minds, and Plant ad-libbed the vocal to which he added a James Brown pastiche ("Has anybody seen the bridge?"). The song baffled listeners not used to their long-haired, White rock bands playing dance music, even if Zeppelin's definition of dance music (see also *Physical Graffiti*'s "Trampled Underfoot") usually suggested a man dancing with one foot in plaster. "The Crunge" is no exception. Nowadays, though, it just sounds like "the giggle" that Page told the press it was. And besides, the riff is fantastic.

Unfortunately, the lilting lovers rock of "D'Yer Mak'er," forever damned as "Led Zeppelin's reggae song," hasn't weathered as well. The problem is that it wasn't reggae enough, which was partly due to the rhythm section's lack of conviction. "John [Bonham] wouldn't play anything but the same shuffle beat all the way through," said Jones. "He hated it, and so did I."

Page insisted pedantically that "D'Yer Mak'er" was "more a fifties thing" than reggae. Which is why the lyrics on the inner sleeve ended with the question: "Whatever happened to Rosie and the Originals?", a reference to a fifties doo-wop ensemble; the kind of obscure group Plant has been dropping into conversation for years as a way of putting doltish rock journalists off their stride. If you hear "D'Yer Mak'er" unexpectedly, it sounds better than you remember it. But even after all these years it's difficult to love to some.

Houses of the Holy was completed in August 1972. The sessions had proved fruitful, and there were several songs left over. The discarded title track (a bouncy pop-rock song and distant relative to "Dancing Days"), together with "The Rover" (another of Plant's questing lyrics roped to a wonderful grinding guitar riff) and "Black Country Woman" (acoustic fun and games recorded on the lawn at Stargroves) were all carried over to *Physical Graffiti*. The other leftover, "Walter's Walk," only surfaced on the 1982 compilation *Coda*.

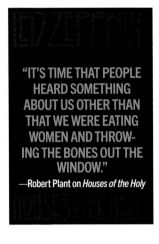

"IT'S TIME THAT PEOPLE HEARD SOMETHING ABOUT US OTHER THAN THAT WE WERE EATING WOMEN AND THROW-ING THE BONES OUT THE WINDOW."
—Robert Plant on *Houses of the Holy*

By the time *Houses of the Holy* appeared in March 1973, Zeppelin was getting the begrudging respect that had been denied them for so long. After all, it was hard for the press to ignore them when all 24 dates on their November 1972 UK tour sold out in four hours. *HOTH* itself went to number one on both sides of the Atlantic. Though not everyone was convinced. It was an "an inconsistent work," said the *Disc and Music Echo*, who were more impressed with that mystical sleeve featuring naked kids crawling over the Giant's Causeway. "So there's some buggers who don't like [the album]," shrugged Page. "Good luck to 'em. I like it, and a few thousand other buggers too."

On May 5, Zeppelin broke US box office records playing to 56,800 at Florida's Tampa Stadium. It was proof that they owned the post-Woodstock crowd. They toured with a private jet, groupies at their beck and call, and enough booze and drugs to make them think their heads had exploded—or, at least, been jammed between the buffers of two railway carriages.

Their story would get very dark very soon. But for now the sun was shining. *Houses of the Holy*, the best Led Zeppelin album no one talks about, had helped make them the biggest rock 'n' roll band in the world. Who needed Truman Capote and the Rolling Stones anyway? ◗

BRING IT ON HOME

Recorded at Mick Jagger's country pile, *Houses of the Holy* was the sound of a band at the top of their game. Producer Eddie Kramer was there with them, and these are his memories of the eight songs that make up their great unsung album.

By: Mick Wall

In late April 1972, Led Zeppelin decamped to Stargroves, Mick Jagger's Berkshire mansion, to start work on their fifth album. According to Robert Plant, it was a chance for Zeppelin to show another side to their personality. "It's time that people heard something about us other than that we were eating women and throwing the bones out of the window," the singer said at the time.

The man they initially brought in to help them get their goal on tape was renowned South African-born producer/engineer Eddie Kramer. Kramer had worked with Zeppelin on *III*, on which he was credited as "Director of Engineering," although his most recent encounter with the band had ended badly following an argument during sessions the previous year at Electric Lady studios in New York. "Everything was going fine until they ordered in some Indian food," says Kramer today. "A whole bunch ended up on the floor. I was pretty possessive about the place and I asked them to clear it up. And they all walked out!"

All that had been forgotten by the time Kramer got the call to fly to England to work with Zeppelin again. When he arrived at Stargroves, the band was in buoyant mood. "The weather was good, the atmosphere among the band was very jolly," he says. "Jimmy had Jagger's bedroom. Everyone was happy."

The Rolling Stones Mobile truck would be used to capture Zeppelin at play. Kramer saw his role as "helping them achieve whatever sounds Jimmy wanted. He was the boss, very clearly."

Kramer assisted Zeppelin to record eight tracks at Stargroves, four of which would end up on the album. (Three of the others—"Black Country Woman," "The

Rover," and "Houses of the Holy" itself—would appear on the next album, *Physical Graffiti*, while the final track, "Walter's Walk," surfaced on the posthumous collection *Coda*, released in 1982). He also mixed many of the tracks that made up *Houses of the Holy*.

"These days, bands want it so perfect that they miss the magic that a band like Led Zeppelin had," says Kramer. "You've got to leave all the hair in. It's rock 'n' roll."

1. THE SONG REMAINS THE SAME

The latest in a string of classic Zeppelin album openers. Prior to album sessions, this song was rehearsed with the working title "Worcester and Plumpton Races"—a reference to Page and Plant's respective homes. When they worked on it in the studio, that title was changed to first "The Overture" and then "The Campaign." It was only when Plant started scribbling verses for it that it ceased to be an instrumental and became his paean to the music of the world, whatever form it takes.

"The whole album had a very upbeat quality to it," says Kramer. "You can hear that straight away from this opening track. A much brighter sound than on earlier Zeppelin albums. There was a unity of spirit and a unity of direction of sound. A lot of that had to do with Pagey and the fact he had a very clear idea of what he wanted. I believe Jimmy later had Robert's vocals sped up a bit so that they become another layer to all those gorgeous guitars.

2. THE RAIN SONG

If there's one Zeppelin song that unites people in its greatness, then it's this smoldering, otherworldly epic. Page wrote it in response to a

conversation he had with George Harrison, in which the former Beatle asked why Zep never did any ballads.

Working on demos for the album at his Plumpton studio, Page came up with this epic-in-waiting with the tongue-in-cheek working title "Slush"—incorporating a subtle use of the opening notes of Harrison's "Something" into the arrangement. At one point it was intended to have been a further extension of "The Overture," but that changed when Plant added lyrics and it was retitled "The Rain Song."

"I love this track because of the typically esoteric Pagey guitar tuning, but also because of the role John Paul Jones plays on it," says Eddie Kramer. "This was definitely the album where Jonesy finally stepped out of the shadows. I knew him from before Led Zeppelin, when he was a session musician. He was a superb arranger who could conduct an orchestra while playing bass with one hand. I once saw him do that. That Mellotron he plays on this is what lifts the track to another emotional level. And the piano, which he also plays, is like raindrops, or maybe teardrops. I don't think they'd ever done a track so subtle before. That's the test of a great arranger: to do something so subtle yet which has such power. Quite beautiful."

3. OVER THE HILLS AND FAR AWAY

Another feature of the album that Kramer identifies is how most of the tracks have their own boutique ending: the orgasmic "Oh!" at the end of "The Song Remains the Same"; the echoing guitar at the climax of "The Rain Song." "Over the Hills and Far Away" (originally titled "Many Many Times") finishes with a similar coda, created by Page using a reverb guitar effect with Jones' keyboard part.

"I can't remember exactly, but I think it was something I suggested at the mixing stage," says Kramer. "I used to do something similar with Hendrix sometimes—fade the track out, then bring it back, like an extra breath." What really makes this track, though, he says, "is that it really shows off the Zeppelin preoccupation with light and shade, acoustic and electric."

4. THE CRUNGE

One of two tracks on the album that splits the vote with fans, this knockabout tribute to James Brown was something that Jimmy Page had been tinkering with since 1970.

"This is one of those tracks that sounds like it just started completely off the bat as an impromptu jam in the studio," says Kramer. "But what you quickly learn about working with musicians of the caliber of Led Zeppelin is that nothing is ever brought to the recording that hasn't been worked over, in Jimmy Page's mind at least, to the Nth degree."

It's preceded by some studio chat between Page and engineer George Chikianz, who you can hear talking just as Bonham comes in on the intro. The track also has John Paul Jones on a pioneering EMS VCS3 synthesizer.

"Of course, it is a fantastic jam, with Bonham and Jonesy especially really going to town. But the tension is very tightly held. I'd set Bonzo's drums up in the conservatory, and the sound he got in there was phenomenal. But they all knew what they were doing. And I love all that James Brown stuff Robert does about taking it to the bridge, because of course there is no bridge in this track. Hence the in-joke ending:

> "THESE DAYS, BANDS WANT IT SO PERFECT THAT THEY MISS THE MAGIC THAT ... LED ZEPPELIN HAD."
> —Eddie Kramer

Zeppelin playing at the Capital Centre in Landover, Maryland May 25, 1977.

GETTY

6. D'YER MAK'ER

The title might have been filched from an old music-hall joke ("My wife's gone to the West Indies . . ." etc.), but the song was originally Plant's attempt at a fifties doo-wop pastiche. He wanted to release the reggae-tinged track as a single—Atlantic even distributed promo copies to DJs—but not everyone liked it. John Paul Jones was vocal in his derision of the track.

"A real love it or hate it track, which I still love," says Kramer. "Those huge drums that kick in at the start are like bombs going off. What's amazing, though, is how John Bonham keeps the bombs going off while playing this extraordinarily subtle and brilliant rhythm. Robert's voice is also superb, kind of a meeting of doo-wop and reggae.

"All credit must also go to Jonesy, whose bass takes the reggae rhythm to a whole different place. I could go on about this one for hours. Suffice to say nothing like it had ever really been attempted by a rock band before, and it caused a lot of controversy when people first heard it."

7. NO QUARTER

The only studiedly "down" track on the album was first tried out at Headley Grange during sessions for Zeppelin's fourth album, at which time it was much faster than the final versions. On *Houses of the Holy* it was John Paul Jones' personal showcase.

"This was the album where Jonesy really came into his own, and this is the track that proves it," says Kramer. "I wasn't there when they finally recorded it, but they had demo versions of it going back a few years. It really demonstrates that Led Zeppelin could do anything they turned their minds to now—and do it better than anybody else. They were able to really stretch out now and experiment, which allowed the space for Jonesy to come in and do his thing on the arrangements. It wasn't just his brilliance as a keyboard player or even a writer, it was also the subtlety of his arrangements, and the economy of notes that made this track such a powerful statement. Genius."

8. THE OCEAN

Already part of the band's encores long before it was released, the album's closing track was Plant's ode to Zeppelin's legions of fans. John Bonham counted in the song with the line, "We've done four already but now we're steady and then they went one . . . two . . . three . . . four . . ."—something which became a ritual when it was played live. Listen carefully and you can hear the studio telephone ringing in the background at around 1:37.

"This was another one where Bonzo's drums just sound amazing," says Kramer. "Some of the stuff Jimmy asked him to do in Led Zeppelin . . . it was complicated s*** and Jimmy would have to run through it with him a few times. But once he locked in, once he knew precisely what he had to play, then he would f*** with it and blow your mind, put a fill where you would not expect it. We'd all be laughing because it was just so insane. But we were going for ambient sound, so we utilized every aspect of the house and its grounds we could. I remember putting a Fender amp in the fireplace and putting a mic up in there. Jonesy's bass was in another room. Everybody's gear was in a different room. There was no CCTV, but I put talkback mics all around so people could yack to each other." ●

'Where's that confounded bridge?'"

There was even an idea to include some dance steps on the sleeve as a guide for happyfooted Zeppelin fans. Wisely, the idea was scrapped.

5. DANCING DAYS

One of the great overlooked Zeppelin rockers. The seeds of this track went back to a visit Page and Plant had made to India the year before, for a date Jimmy had arranged with a collection of musicians in Bombay, recording rough-and-ready versions of "Friends" and "Four Sticks." The snake-hipped riff and slouching melody were inspired by a raga they overheard at a wedding during their stay.

"By the time they started playing the track with me, it just had the most amazing vibe," Kramer recalls. "Just a glorious groove. They all enjoyed playing it so much. The way Bonzo played it was what really made it, though. He just found a way to make the rhythm bounce and snap. I'll never forget playing it back to them from the mobile truck and how excited they all were. It was a lovely sunny day, and there was Jimmy and Robert and a couple of others all sort of linking arms and dancing on the lawn. I don't think even they could believe how good they sounded."

HOW THE WEST WAS WON

In May 1973, Zeppelin kicked off their US tour. Label boss Phil Carson saw three months that changed everything.

By: Phil Carson

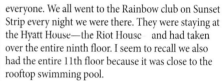
Phil Carson in 1973.

As president of Atlantic Records in those days, I had been Led Zeppelin and Peter Grant's go-to guy since the beginning. As a musician myself, I had built up a great relationship with the band, even playing bass onstage during an encore at a show in Germany, doing "Whole Lotta Love."

Zeppelin's 1973 tour of America was their ninth over there, but it was clear right away that this one was different. For a start, the band looked different. Glam rock had seen bands like the Stones and the Faces taking on a much more glamorous look onstage, and Zeppelin was the same. This tour was the first time Jimmy wore his "moon and stars" suit; Robert still went on bare chested, but he'd be wearing a puff-sleeved blouse; even Bonzo had a glittery star on his T-shirt. The show was more colorful too; their first to have a professional light show, with lasers and dry ice.

They also had the Starship—a 40-seater Boeing 720 with the words "Led Zeppelin" emblazoned down the side. Inside, the whole layout was totally over the top. It had lounge seats and dinner tables, a fully stocked bar and a TV lounge. There was also an electric Thomas organ which Jonesy would entertain

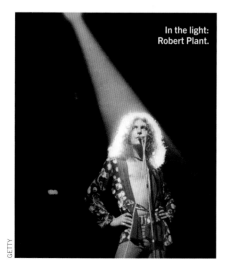
In the light: Robert Plant.

the various guests with, and a cabin at the back with a double bed in it and a fireplace—a glowing electric pseudo-coal fire. The bed even had seat belts on it so you could take off and land in a horizontal position.

Having a plane like that at their disposal, they could base themselves pretty much anywhere and just fly out to gigs. That said, the places they chose to base themselves were not necessarily geographically suitable. One base was in New Orleans. Because they wanted to get back to the Quarter by one o'clock in the morning, they would run out of venues with the last notes of the last song still ringing in your ears, then jump in the limos and race for the airport. I remember one show, in St. Louis, they were supposed to be onstage at eight o'clock, but I remember still being in the bar at the Maison de Puis in New Orleans at about 10 to eight. Needless to say, we were somewhat late for that show.

In those days, there was no real airport security. The plane would taxi up to a predesignated point, nowhere near the terminal building, then this line of limousines would come. Everybody had a limo—I had a limo. Even the tour doctor had a limousine. He was there in case anybody needed a vitamin B shot—and that's all I'm gonna say about him.

The rules hadn't been written yet. And even where they had, we broke them. The band played an outdoor stadium in Tampa, Florida, and there were nearly 60,000 people there, breaking the record set by The Beatles at Shea Stadium. Don't forget this was for one band, not even a headline act with support bands. This was just Led Zeppelin on their own. I'll never forget the reaction when they came onstage. Mind-blowing!

Of course, whenever Zeppelin hit LA, it was party time for

everyone. We all went to the Rainbow club on Sunset Strip every night we were there. They were staying at the Hyatt House—the Riot House—and had taken over the entire ninth floor. I seem to recall we also had the entire 11th floor because it was close to the rooftop swimming pool.

John Bonham celebrated his 25th birthday on that tour in LA. They had played the Forum that night, and afterwards a big party was thrown for him at this big place in Laurel Canyon. George Harrison was there. I remember lots of champagne, and no doubt other things. Then George stuck John Bonham's birthday cake on his head, so John chased him and threw him in the pool. I remember George later saying that it was the most fun he'd had since The Beatles.

For Bonzo's birthday party, the band gave him a motorbike, and I recall him riding it down the hotel corridor. That was when it started to get a little scary, so I ducked back into my room very quickly.

The tour ended in July in New York, with three nights at Madison Square Garden. I was at the first show, but I wasn't feeling well and I didn't go to the other two shows. But there is something I distinctly remember about that first show. I got there late, and as I was coming in they were playing "How Many More Times," and it was the most eerie feeling. The floor of the Garden was shaking. I'm talking about a

> "BY 1973 THEY HAD BUILT THEIR EMPIRE AND NOW THEY WERE SURF-ING THE WAVE."
> —Phil Carson

The band performs during the filming of *The Song Remains the Same.*

John Paul Jones entertains Atlantic Records boss Ahmet Ertegun (second from left) aboard the Starship.

In full flight, Germany 1973.

concrete walkway, and the floor was actually shaking. Because the riff is such a powerful f***** riff, and the Zeppelin timing being what it was, right on it all the time, making the crowd stamp its feet, it set up this vibration. I was actually having trouble walking, it was moving so much.

I do recall that I shared a two-bedroom hotel suite with John Bonham for those shows. It was quite a lot of fun, but it did spell for me the last time I would ever share a hotel suite with John. He had this propensity for ordering lots of stuff from room service. At one point, there were about seven room service carts lined up outside the door—and when the bill came it was split down the middle.

By 1973, drugs had started to come into the picture. I never did any drugs, so I wasn't really part of that side of things. But things hadn't changed radically. Away from the tour, I didn't live that far from where Jimmy lived in those days, in Sussex, and a lot of time we would go to each other's houses for lunch on a Sunday, that sort of thing.

But it was a different Jimmy Page once you got on tour. That's true of any artist, but magnified in Jimmy's case because of the vastness of what Led Zeppelin had become by then. All of them were normal types when they were at home. John Paul Jones is still with the same wife now he had then. It was probably more difficult for Jimmy, though,

to build a solid foundation of real friends, because he is by nature a little reclusive. Then becoming as big as they got, that sealed his fate, in a way.

By 1973 they had built their empire, and now they were surfing the wave. It was a culmination of all the touring they'd done before and the quality of the records. There would be more huge tours, but I don't think those peaks were ever achieved again after that particular tour. After 1973 the mold had been set. And what came after that was only to be expected, as it were. Certainly from a touring standpoint, I'm not convinced that it ever achieved those heights again. That was it. Led Zeppelin was a unique force of nature. And that is exactly what you got. ●

THIRTY-FIVE YEARS GONE

The band is getting death threats. John Paul Jones wants to leave. A backlash against the rock aristocracy is rumbling. So how did Zep manage to pull *Physical Graffiti* out of the bag?

By: Barney Hoskyns

Something is rotten in the state of rock. The heady euphoria of the late sixties has degenerated into decadence and self-satisfaction. Working-class guitar heroes have become remote, nouveau aristocrats in limousines, attended by inner courts of dealers and debauched nymphets.

The music itself is becoming ever more pompous and self-satisfied. Double and even triple albums proliferate as artists lose all traces of humility. No one had ever imagined that rock 'n' roll could get so pretentious: how did we get from Elvis' Sun sessions to *Yessongs*? Nor did anyone predict the sheer scale of the post-Woodstock rock industry, with stadiums now the venues of necessity for the likes of Elton John and the Eagles.

A sense of enervation grips even these gods as, exhausted, they return for inspiration to their fifties and sixties roots on covers albums such as *Pin-Ups* (Bowie), *Rock 'N' Roll* (Lennon), *These Foolish Things* (Ferry), *Moondog Matinee* (The Band).

True, there are faint rumblings of discontent from the emerging generation of CBGB rebels ready to kick over the old statues. And true, reggae has delivered its first global icon in the shape of Bob Marley.

And what of the biggest rock band of all? The mighty Led Zeppelin, a cult phenomenon beloved of every suburban stoner in America, coming off the back of an insanely successful 1973 US tour that packed 56,800 worshippers into Tampa Stadium in Florida, breaking the single-concert attendance record The Beatles had set eight years before. The news that the English quartet's next release will be a double album does not fill the hipper rock critics with unbridled enthusiasm. Granted, Zeppelin isn't Emerson Lake & Palmer, but in many ways they remain exemplars of "progressive" rock, not shy about turning "Dazed and Confused" and "No Quarter" (or John Bonham's infamous drum marathon "Moby Dick") into half-hour live epics of Mellotrons and meandering self-indulgence. Whatever else "Stairway to Heaven" is—the most-played record on radio ever—it is the slow-building prog-rock anthem to end them all.

Let's not forget that Led Zeppelin is the band who, more than any other, declared war on the single by refusing to release a 45-rpm edit of "Whole Lotta Love."

The new album in question is, of course, late. When Zeppelin commence their 1975 US tour ➤➤

"IF YOU WANT TO LEAVE, YOU'VE GOT TO DO WHAT YOU'VE GOT TO DO—BUT THINK ABOUT IT . . ."

PETER GRANT TO JOHN PAUL JONES

St. Mark's Place, New York,
July 2010.

in January, the record still isn't the stores, despite attaining platinum status on advance orders alone.

So is it any good? Will it be Zeppelin's *Exile On Main St.* or their *Tales From Topographic Oceans*? It could so easily be a low-water mark of arrogance and aloofness—maybe even a Swan Song, the name of the new custom-made label on which it is being released. And how will it go down with the critics who've dismissed Zeppelin ever since their explosive arrival in America in late 1968?

After the relatively unloved *Houses of the Holy*— the proggiest but also the most underrated of all Zeppelin's albums—will *Physical Graffiti* be a new beginning? Or could it be the end?

Led Zeppelin almost did come to an end—or at least almost lost one of their members—before the *Physical Graffiti* sessions even started. Not long after the band gathered to rehearse new songs in October 1973, bassist and all-round multi-instrumental wizard John Paul Jones drove to see their larger-than-life manager Peter Grant at his moated home Horselunges in East Sussex. There he bared his soul, telling Grant that Zeppelin had all become too much for him. The group's very own Quiet Man had now endured nine tours of the US alone and wasn't sure he could stand hanging around, sleep-starved, in one more airport lounge or hotel lobby. He told "G"—or dryly joked to him—that he had been offered the post of choirmaster at Winchester Cathedral, a job too tempting to be dismissed out of hand.

The welcome experience of some proper down time after four relentless years of touring and recording had prompted Jonesy to reevaluate his priorities. Not one of nature's born rock stars— indeed, a self-effacing and scholarly prodigy from the suburbs of southeast London—the super-sessionman known formerly as John Baldwin decided he didn't want to miss any more of the experience of his daughters Tammy and Cindy growing up in leafy, green-belt Sussex.

That very summer, Jones had allegorized his double life in the filming of his fantasy sequence for the endlessly protracted Zeppelin "home movie" that became *The Song Remains the Same*. Pursued by sinister nightriders, he galloped home to his wife Mo and their girls and was seen in the bosom of their flickering hearthside, a gentle and doting paterfamilias. A more pointed contrast to the sixth floor of the Continental Hyatt House in LA it would be hard to imagine.

"By that time the security thing in the US was getting ridiculous," Peter Grant told keeper-of-the-Zep-flame Dave Lewis in 1993, two years before his death. "We started getting death threats—in fact, straight after the '73 tour . . . there was a very serious one. It got very worrying."

Grant told Jones, "If you want to leave, you've got to do what you've got to do—but think about it." Though G informed guitarist Jimmy Page about Jones' unrest, Robert Plant and John Bonham were initially kept in the dark and given the story that Jones was ill.

"I remember Jonesy had some personal issues," remembers Ron Nevison, the engineer on the sessions, "but I didn't ask and I wasn't told. So we spent a week or so just running down songs. I don't think we even recorded much."

Philadelphia-born Nevison had come to London at the behest of Island's Chris Blackwell and started out as a tape op at the label's Basing Street studio off Ladbroke Grove in West London. Commissioned to build a mobile studio in an Airstream trailer Ronnie Lane had shipped back from America during a Faces tour, Nevison—and the mobile studio—had come to Led Zeppelin's attention after both were used by The Who for the recording of *Quadrophenia*.

"It was state-of-the-art with a Helios console," says Nevison. "It was the same one the Stones had in their truck: 16 tracks like most of the big studios had." In

"I HAD TO ASK TO LEAVE THE PROJECT . . . THEY ALL SHOUTED AND SCREAMED AT ME . . . ESPECIALLY BONHAM, WHO CALLED ME ALL SORTS OF NAMES."

—Ron Nevison, Engineer

Top: *Physical Graffiti* engineer Ron Nevison. Bottom: The LMS (Ronnie Lane Mobile Studio), as it appeared at *Classic Rock*'s High Voltage Festival.

mid-October he drove the Airstream from Lane's place in Richmond down to Headley Grange, the damp eighteenth-century house where Zeppelin had recorded much of *Led Zeppelin III* and their untitled fourth album. The sonic petri dish for such storming masterpieces as "Immigrant Song" and "When the Levee Breaks"—tracks recorded using the Stones' mobile—Headley Grange was a place where the group had long felt at home.

"Headley was found by our secretary, Carole Browne," Zeppelin's legendary tour manager Richard Cole told me in 2006. "She used to read *The Lady* and she'd seen an advert saying the place was for rent. I think she sent a dispatch rider down there to see if it was suitable and had enough rooms and if they could put a mobile studio in there.

"It wasn't very comfortable. I mean, the band was used to five-star hotels and had lovely homes by then. I sometimes think they recorded in the worst places imaginable because, in the back of Jimmy's mind, it meant they had to get on with it so they could get out of there." (And yes, that is a reference to the alleged frugality of a man frequently referred to as Led Wallet.)

Plant and Bonham had too many dismal memories from previous visits to sleep at the Grange. Instead they checked into the nearby Frencham Pond hotel. "Page stayed behind at Headley," Cole said with a laugh. "He was quite happy in that f***** horrible cold house."

With Jones absent, Page, Plant, and Bonham ran through new ideas and jammed on old blues and rock 'n' roll classics. "We were just hanging around and messing around," Ron Nevison says. "They were doing Elvis covers and stuff like that."

A tape dated October 17 documents the trio playing versions of Elvis' "Baby I Don't Care," "Jailhouse Rock," "One Night," "Don't Be Cruel," and "The Girl of My Best Friend," along with the Drifters' "Money Honey" and Eddie Cochran's "Summertime Blues"—most of them classics that Zeppelin regularly dropped into the live medley sections of "Whole Lotta Love" and other epics. It was even fleetingly suggested that these and other tracks might comprise a covers album of their own.

Eventually the three grew weary of waiting for Jones and dispersed to the four winds. Ron Nevison was about to do the same when he ran up against the intimidating intransigence of Zeppelin at the height of their fame.

"I'd made a commitment to Pete Townshend to start the *Tommy* film in late January," Nevison recalls, "and because of Jonesy not appearing for a week, I had to ask to leave the project. But when I called up and told them I couldn't continue, they were really nasty to me on the phone. They all shouted and screamed at me, and it was very upsetting. Especially Bonham, who called me all sorts of names. I don't think anybody in the history of Led Zeppelin had ever quit a project before."

Peter Grant demanded that Nevison remain at Headley to engineer the debut album by a new supergroup formed from the ashes of Free and Mott the Hoople. Ten days later, "Bad Company" was in the can. It became an instant multi-platinum success for Swan Song when it was released the following year.

An audible sigh of relief was heard throughout the Zeppelin hierarchy when news subsequently came in that Jonesy had had a change of heart during Christmas. "Eventually I think he realized he was

Left: "In My Time of Dying" was based on an old Blind Willie Johnson song. Right: Rolling Stone Ian Stewart played on "Boogie with Stu."

doing something he really loved," Peter Grant said. "It was never discussed again." By the New Year, Zeppelin was back in harness at the Grange, their bass player's crisis behind him.

When they reconvened, Jimmy Page ran the band through an assortment of riffs he'd been working on at Plumpton Place, his landscaped pile in Sussex. These included the building blocks for "In the Light," "Ten Years Gone," and "The Wanton Song"—the latter a song that borne out of soundchecks on the 1973 US tour—along with an instrumental epic bearing the not-entirely-coincidental working title "Swan Song." Meanwhile, Robert Plant brought with him a small cache of lyrics inspired by a vacation he and his wife Maureen had taken in Morocco after the tour had wrapped.

Otherwise, however, the band was winging it as only they knew how. "At this point," Page told Jaan Uhelszki in 1997, "we had this beautiful freedom that we could try anything, do anything, which was what the beauty of how the band was, and how the music was made, as opposed to how things are today."

"Some artists like to sit down and plan an album," Robert Plant declared. "We just can't do that. Our music is more an impromptu thing. You know, it drops out of your mind, it falls out of your head, and onto the floor, and you pick it up as it bounces. That's how it works. But what else can you expect? We hire this recording truck and trudge off to some crude old house in the country. The last thing you expect is the music to fall right into place. But eventually it does."

If there were any clear ideas about how Zeppelin wanted the next album to sound, most involved doing something very different from *Houses of the Holy*. "The last album was difficult to get into because it was so complex," Page stated in the pages of *Circus*. "We used intricate rhythm patterns and hid a lot of ideas in the lyrics. The next one will still have complex songs, and will have an acoustic guitar piece based on a solo I used to do [during "White Summer"], but most of the album will get back to something people think we've been drifting away from: straightforward rock 'n' roll."

If that phrase implied songs in the vein of, well, "Rock and Roll," it was misleading. The eight tracks Zeppelin wrote, rehearsed, and substantially recorded at Headley Grange between January and March of 1974 were hardly straightforward—not even "In My Time of Dying," the one that most obviously returned them to the blues roots that set them on their way in the first place.

True, this near-12-minute Delta mutation, which had begun life in the hands of the gruff-voiced Blind Willie Johnson, was in Page's words "a good example of something more immediate" that "sounded like a working group." But it was also much more than that: a launching-pad for one of the most devastating items in the Zeppelin songbook, featuring multiple tempo changes and abrupt funk turns à la "Black Dog."

Still, the point is made: the new album would boast a raw force that the more smoothly produced *Houses of the Holy* had forsaken, its production more live and true to the ambience of Headley's old walls. "I look at it as a document of a band in a working environment," Page told *Guitar World* in 1993. "People might say it is sloppy, but I think this album is really honest. [It] is a more personal album,

and I think it allowed the listener to enter our world." One of the things fans came to love most about the album was the retention of, for example, the spoken asides on "In My Time of Dying" and "Black Country Woman."

As with the fourth album, John Bonham's drum kit was—for the most part—set up in what Ron Nevison refers to as the "bombastic entryway" to Headley Grange—the entrance hall, at the foot of the stairwell, where Bonzo and engineer Andy Johns had captured the bone-crunching stomp of *IV*'s "When the Levee Breaks."

"When I got there I put mics all around the drums," Nevison says. "But Bonham told me not to use them, to take them down. I said, 'Well, just in case', and he said, 'No, not just in case—take them down!' So I took them down and they showed me where to put the microphones, exactly where they had used them before. Two mics up on the first level, et cetera. They knew exactly what they wanted. There was very little of Ron Nevison in this recording, at least compared to other recordings I have done."

Nevison it was, however, who added the extra element that transformed the groove of *Graffiti*'s most fabled track—essentially the same groove Bonzo had fashioned for "When the Levee Breaks"— into something even more powerful: namely a new phaser unit built by a company called Eventide Clockworks and brought back from America by one of Zeppelin's road crew.

"I'd heard that these phasers sounded great on cymbals so I brought one in for 'Kashmir,'" Nevison says. "Up to that point, phasing could only be accomplished with tape: you would have an ►►

instrument and you'd put another tape machine up and record that instrument on it. Then you'd put the tapes together and speed up and slow down the machines to get the effect. The Eventide was a piece of equipment that actually did that for you—it was the beginning of the technology that led to all sorts of digital delay and reverb units and flangers. I only had two tracks for drums, so what I did was set up the phaser, put one of the tracks through it, and record it on a third track—just for the hell of it. And the band loved it and kept it in, and that's part of the whole sound of 'Kashmir' . . . it sounded cool, so I used it."

For Robert Plant, Bonham was at the absolute heart of what made the epic tracks on *Physical Graffiti*—"Kashmir," "In My Time of Dying," "In the Light," "Ten Years Gone"—so powerful. "Some of the great stuff came from Bonzo taking a hold of the thing and making it work from a drums point of view," Plant said of "Black Country Woman," in front of whom he'd now been singing on and off for a decade. "It was all riffs and rhythm tracks, not la-la songs. I would have to try and weave the vocal in amongst it all, and it was very hard."

"Kashmir" itself—originally "Driving to Kashmir"—came from a groove Bonzo and Page had worked up in October in Jones' absence. "One day when we were rehearsing for some album that we really didn't know too much about," Plant announced from the stage of Earls Court on May 24, 1975, "Bonzo came in with this really nice driving tempo. Really laid back sort of shoom shoom. And we thought, 'Mandrax? No.' And having been traveling a little bit to get the feel of foreign lands, the song developed from that shoom shoom . . . and with a touch of the East, a little bit of cholera on the arm . . . and what we had left was 'Kashmir.'"

"The structure of it was strange, weird enough to continue exploring," Page would tell Cameron Crowe, adding that he'd "worked on the riff with Bonham, Plant added the middle section, and Jones later overdubbed his bass and the string parts."

What most skeptics fail to grasp about Led Zeppelin is that they weren't just the greatest hard-rock band of all time: they were also the funkiest hard-rock band of all time. And funk is all over *Physical Graffiti*, sometimes in the unlikeliest places, not just on "Custard Pie" and "The Wanton Song," but on "Houses of the Holy" and "Sick Again," on the stunning uptempo passages of "In My Time of Dying" and those darkly dragging sections of "In the Light," and yes, on "Kashmir" too. There has never been a rock rhythm section like Bonham and Jones and there never will be again.

"[Bonham] might well have been the greatest rock drummer ever to draw breath; he certainly belted his kit with unmeterable force," Nick Coleman has written, wonderfully. "Yet it was his 'feel', the way his body related to the flow of time, that made him essential. Every note that Led Zeppelin ever played was indivisible from the pulse in Bonham's body—he swung against the click of time with a weight and suppleness that could not exist anywhere else in nature."

"We always had a choice of how we would play a rhythm, and we could do that as part of a musical dynamic within the same song," John Paul Jones told me in 2003 of the 12 years he worked with Bonham. "And that's what makes it musically interesting and musically exciting. To the listener who doesn't know what you're doing, it just sounds as if it's got texture and color and movement—and life." For Robert

Plant, Bonham was "a real thrifty player—it was what he didn't do that made it work."

"The essence to me of the whole Zeppelin thing was Bonham following the guitar," Ron Nevison adds. "He would take the riff and make that his drum part. If you listen to it from "Sick Again" to any other song on *Physical Graffiti*, instead of just doing them 4/4 and getting in with the bass player, he got in with the guitar player."

For Nevison, the *Graffiti* sessions really came to life after he made a decision not to sleep at Headley Grange. Tired of the group waking him at 3 a.m.—usually wired on cocaine and mistakenly convinced they'd struck sonic gold—he informed them he would henceforth be locking up the truck at the end of each day and driving back up the A3 to the guesthouse he rented from the Faces' Ian McLagan in the London suburb of East Sheen.

"I was pretty naïve," Nevison admits. "They kept saying, 'When's Charlie coming?' And I never met Charlie. There was a decided change of vibe after Charlie came. They realized in the end that I was doing the right thing. They didn't say, 'You stay here

or we'll get somebody else,' they didn't give me any ultimatum. They knew they were bad boys, and me going home improved the whole flow of the recording. So at least if they were staying up, they weren't keeping me up and at least there was somebody stable around."

Nevison says that notwithstanding the abuse he'd received earlier, relations with the band were cordial. "My biggest fan during the whole recording was Robert, who loved the effect I got on his vocals—probably because I wasn't a guy who looked at meters. A lot of engineers are afraid when the needle goes into the red, whereas I just went by my ears. I was taught early on, don't listen to the speakers, listen to the music."

Unsurprisingly, Page was more emotionally remote than Plant—or perhaps just more obsessive about getting the music right on the tape. When Zeppelin worked, they worked hard, none more so than the band's guitarist and putative leader.

"Jimmy was so well prepared," Nevison says. "He knew exactly what he wanted. He used to come into

the truck and listen to the whole thing. At the time I thought he just didn't like his guitar, but then I realized he was doing what I do now, which is to take the guitar down to make sure the drum track is solid. You have to remember, these tracks were cut without clicks and they were long songs and they had to be really solid."

The only time Nevison got close to Page was the evening of March 23, when the whole band—along with Peter Grant, road manager Richard Cole, and other members of the Zeppelin entourage—to Drury Lane to see a performance by Monty Python, in whose classic *Holy Grail* movie they had invested. "Jimmy was a lot of fun that night," says Ron. "I had a Bentley at the time and he came with me in it. In fact, we spent the night at the guest house in East Sheen and hung out. It was the only real one-on-one time I had with him, and we drove back the next morning to Headley."

Another night the band took a break was Valentine's Day, when their good friend Roy Harper—an iconoclastic folkie they wanted to sign to Swan Song—played north London's Rainbow Theatre with a motley backing crew that included Page, Ronnie Lane, and Keith Moon and featured a cameo appearance by Bonzo in a pair of black ballet tights (a picture of which would appear on the *Physical Graffiti* sleeve).

Aside from these occasional welcome interruptions, the Headley sessions were distraction-free; Nevison doesn't remember a single female setting foot in the place in the entire period he worked with Zeppelin. (The four members generally went home to their families for long weekends.)

"Over a period of a month we managed to spend at least three days a week recording," Plant reported after the fact, "in between various calamities and the Roy Harper Valentine gig. Some of the tracks we assembled in our own fashioned way of running through a track and realizing before we knew it that we had stumbled on something completely different."

If there was nothing quite as serendipitous as the impromptu Bonzo homage to Earl Palmer that triggered "Rock and Roll" at Headley three years earlier, the "run throughs"—a small portion of which can be heard on rehearsal bootlegs like *Tangible Vandalism*—reveal the changes that "In the Light" and "The Wanton Song" underwent. The former, for instance, featured a completely different A section—Plant singing over an anodyne keyboard phrase before the rhythm section kicks in to the descending B section link passage we know—while "The Wanton Song" was far less funky and syncopated than the final version on the album.

The bootleg recordings—a twenty-minute rehearsal of disco-metal hybrid "Trampled Under Foot," for example—reveal Bonzo to be in near-command of the sessions. "Ah, let's forget it," he mutters after trying a "Rock and Roll" lead-in fill to the hyperactive stomp of "Trampled Under Foot." At the end of a 12-and-a-half minute trial run through "In My Time of Dying," he talks over both Page and Jones as he tries to make one of Page's innumerable link sections fit with the beat.

It all turned out nicely, of course; at the close of "In My Time of Dying" on *Physical Graffiti*, we hear Bonzo cough and then yell, "Well, that's gotta be the one, isn't it!"

Listening to these voices today, you realize just how difficult Zeppelin's songs were to master—and how perfectionist they were about getting every aspect of a song's arrangement right before it was ➨➨

> "[BONHAM] MIGHT WELL HAVE BEEN THE GREATEST ROCK DRUMMER EVER TO DRAW BREATH; HE CERTAINLY BELTED HIS KIT WITH UNMETERABLE FORCE."
>
> —NICK COLEMAN

Jimmy Page
rocking the stage.

Playing "Stairway to Heaven" in 1975.

recorded.

"I hadn't been party to any of the rehearsals, which is totally different to how I've worked with other bands," recalls Ron Nevison. "Even with 'Kashmir,' when we cut the track there wasn't even a vocal on it—it was just bass, drums, and guitar. On other songs where they needed the feel thing, Jonesy would play the clavinet and then we'd put the bass on after that, and there was just a guide vocal. I was never party to any discussions about where to take the songs or what they had in mind. Jimmy never talked to me about any orchestrations for 'Kashmir' or anything."

Indeed, Nevison was astonished when—a year later—he heard the final mixes of the eight songs whose basic tracks had been cut at Headley. The overdubs recorded in May 1974 at Zeppelin's old haunt Olympic in Barnes—particularly the addition of Indian string players on "Kashmir"—had beefed up the songs and given them added majesty.

"Zeppelin had a history of not taking engineers with them," Nevison says. "I would love to have been involved in the recording of the orchestral stuff, but at Olympic they used Keith Harwood."

Harwood was one of the golden boys on the London studio scene and had worked on *Houses of the Holy* at Mick Jagger's home Stargroves—as well as on David Bowie's *Diamond Dogs* and the imminent Rolling Stones release *It's Only Rock 'n' Roll.* Three years later, after engineering Zeppelin's *Presence* in Munich, he was heading home from an Olympic mixing session for the Stones' *Love You Live* when his driver lost control of the car. Harwood

was killed and the Stones dedicated the album to him.

When Page and Harwood were finished at Olympic, they had eight stunning tracks to show for their labors. "Jimmy was a total perfectionist and he used to drive people mad with it," says Julie Carlo, who had been Harwood's girlfriend. "But Keith absolutely loved working with him because he was a bit like that as well."

"I remember Keith coming around to our flat with Jimmy," adds Phil Carlo, for whom Julie left Harwood (and who later took over from Richard Cole as Zeppelin's tour manager). "They had just mixed 'Kashmir' and Jimmy was absolutely thrilled to bits with it. He seemed to be more pleased with it than anything he'd ever done."

Above: Lori Maddox. Right: Her replacement, Bebe Buell.

It is a measure of the album's eclectic daring that *Physical Graffiti* starts not with a bludgeoning piledriver in the "Whole Lotta Love"/"Immigrant Song"/"Black Dog" mode but with a sizzling slab of Whiteboy funk. If "Custard Pie" was less of an explicit tribute to James Brown than *Houses of the Holy*'s "The Crunge"—closer in fact to the clavinet-gurgle floorfill of "Trampled Under Foot"—it nevertheless spun off the funkophilia that prompted Zep to cover Brown's "Licking Stick" and the Isley Brothers' "It's Your Thing" live.

Yet the song's blues provenance is there for all Delta scholars to hear, from Blind Boy Fuller's "I Want Some of Your Pie" and Sleepy John Estes' "Drop Down Mama," to Sonny Boy Williamson's "Help Me" and Bukka White's "Shake 'Em On Down," the latter already filleted for *III*'s "Hats off to (Roy) Harper." This is Plant the priapic Hunter, urging his female prey to "throw your man outdoor / Ain't no stranger, done been this way before" in his most raspy voice before topping things off with a righteous harmonica solo.

Also in a blues vein but closer to the dark dread of Robert Johnson's scarier recordings—and to "When the Levee Breaks," indeed—the dense gospel blues of "In My Time of Dying" is a desperate plea for redemption, complete with reference to R&B singer Benny Spellman's hit "Lipstick Traces (On A

Cigarette)": "I must have did somebody some good, yeah/ Oh, I believe I did/I see the smiling faces/I know there must be lipstick traces, oh God."

The track is dominated by the menacing swarm of Page's Danelectro, tuned to open A. It's Jimmy's guitar army in Mississippi/Chicago mode, the slide licks explicitly referencing Elmore James while also anticipating Jack White. There isn't enough on record of Page playing slide—perhaps he didn't rate himself highly enough as a practitioner of the bottleneck arts—but this more than makes up for the scarcity of it.

Listening to this monstrous meditation on mortality, based loosely on Blind Willie Johnson's "Jesus Make Up My Dying Bed," one could almost believe Zeppelin did sign a Johnson-style pact with the devil. Strutting into Clarksdale, the 11-minute epic takes the primeval chill of the Delta and infuses it with the lordly decadence of seventies rock—appropriating and colonizing it, for sure, but also updating and mutating it as a sonic template for the White Stripes, who covered it in 2002.

"I love the way Jack White says, 'Robert Plant is the thing I least liked about Led Zeppelin,'" Plant said to me in 2003. "And I think, 'Well, that's fine, boy, but if you're gonna play 'In My Time of Dying,' listen to the master—or even to 'Jesus Make Up My Dying Bed' from 1930. I tell you, there's no Blind Willie Johnson there."

The track includes passages of outrageous funk, ultra-syncopated but still awesomely heavy. The molten churn of the sound, with its ominous incantatory quality and Bonzo's brilliant pushes, suggests a kind of supercharged metal. "We were just having such a wonderful time," Page reflected of the track in 2008. "Look, we had a framework for 'In My Time of Dying,' okay, but then it just takes off and we're just doing what Led Zeppelin do. We're jamming. We're having a ball."

"Trampled Under Foot" can't be taken too seriously. It sounds exactly like what it is: a heavy rock band flirting with Black dance music à la the Stones on "Miss You" or Queen on "Another One Bites the Dust." At best a leaden-footed take on Stevie Wonder's "Superstition" via K.C. & the Sunshine Band, the groove is elephantine—and Jones' Hohner clavinet self-consciously choppy: Wild Cherry eat your honky heart out! Like "Custard Pie," it takes its cue from Delta blues, in this case the automotive sex metaphors of Robert Johnson's "Terraplane Blues." Unlike "Custard Pie," though, it's unsatisfyingly unsubtle. Still, Bonzo dug it. "When we first ran through it . . . we thought it was a bit souly for us," he told Chris Welch. "Then we changed it around a bit. It's great for me. Great rhythm for a drummer. It's just at the right pace and you can do a lot of frills."

Fortunately, redemption isn't far away. "Kashmir," the album's gilded centerpiece, is a

The third Swan Song launch party at the Chiselhurst Caves in Kent.

Plant talks to Lloyd Bridges and Mickey Dolenz at the LA Swan Song party.

Jimmy Page at the Swan Song launch party.

Do what thou wilt . . .
But know by this summons
That on the night of the Full Moon
of 31st October, 1974
Led Zeppelin
request your presence
at a
Halloween Party
to celebrate
Swan Song Records'
first U.K. album release
'Silk Torpedo'
by
The Pretty Things
in
Chislehurst Caves,
Chislehurst, Kent.
Celebrations will commence
at 8.00 p.m. . . .

Swan Song Records
Distributed by Atlantic Records

close cousin to "When the Levee Breaks," the Headley stairwell funk-thwack all but identical barring the swirling phaser effect Ron Nevison applied to it. Grandiose but entrancing, ascending and re-ascending through Page's favored modal DADGAD tuning, the song remains Zeppelin's Everest, their absolute apex.

"I wish we were remembered for 'Kashmir' more than 'Stairway,'" Plant has memorably said. "It's so right—there's nothing overblown, no

"I LOOK AT IT AS A DOCUMENT OF A BAND IN A WORKING ENVIRONMENT. PEOPLE MIGHT SAY IT IS SLOPPY, BUT I THINK THIS ALBUM IS REALLY HONEST."

—Jimmy Page on *Physical Graffiti*

vocal hysterics. Perfect Zeppelin."

"Along with 'Stairway,' that's probably the one that most people would think of if we were mentioned, although they were totally different numbers in terms of content," Page said in 1983. "The intensity of 'Kashmir' was such that when we'd done it, we knew that it was something that was so magnetic within itself, and you couldn't really describe what the quality was . . . it seemed so sort of ominous and had a particular quality to it. It's nice to go for an actual mood and know that you've pulled it off."

The drippy lyrical mysticism of "Kashmir"—inspired by a drive that Plant and Page had taken through southern Morocco—perfectly suits the music's occult majesty. "It was an amazing piece of music to write to, and an incredible challenge for me," he told Richard Kingsmill of Triple J radio. "Because of the time signature, the whole deal of the song is . . . not grandiose, but powerful: it required some kind of epithet, or abstract lyrical setting about the whole idea of life being an adventure and being a series of illuminated moments."

The song was also a major challenge to sing. Plant had had an operation to remove nodes on his vocal cords before the 1973 US tour, so hearing him strain to hit the high notes on "Kashmir"—particularly as he comes out of the Mellotron-driven middle section with the long bleeding-throat cry that commences at 4:13—gives the performance an added and very moving desperation. "It was like the song was bigger than me," he told Kingsmill. "I was petrified, it's true. It was painful. I was virtually in tears."

Another eight-and-a-half-minute epic opened the original vinyl Side Three of *Physical Graffiti*. "In the Light" had been transformed from its "In the Morning"/"Take Me Home" origins.

"We knew exactly what its construction was going to be," Page said of the song, "but nevertheless I had no idea at the time that John Paul was going to come up with such an amazing synthesizer intro, plus there's all the bowed guitars at the beginning as well, to give the overall drone effect. We did quite a few things with drones on, like 'In the Evening' and all➡

Plant belting at a show during Zeppelin's legendary five-night residency at Earls Court Exhibition Centre in May 1975.

that, but when he did that start for 'In the Light,' it was just unbelievable."

The song can almost be read as an unconscious tussle between Page's saturnine introversion and Plant's hippie faith in love. At a point when Zeppelin was about to enter their darkest years, Plant beseeches us to seek the light: "Just believe and you can't go wrong/In the light you will find the road." The song's mood keeps switching: after the dragging funk groove of the first verse proper ("Hey, oh, did you ever believe that I could leave you."), Jonesy's clavinet flips the feel completely on descending chords that echo The Band's "The Weight."

This in turn is followed by a return to the snaking eeriness of the intro, Page the magus in control again: "If you feel that you can't go on . . ." But next time around, Plant claims the song once and for all: "Everybody needs the light."

Though it was never played live, "In the Light" was rumored at one point to be Page's favorite track on *Physical Graffiti*, while Plant regularly inserted lyrics from it into the medley of "Calling To You" and "Whole Lotta Love" on the Page and Plant world tour of 1995-96.

"'Ten Years Gone" was yet another proggish epic whose basic tracks were recorded at Headley Grange. Again the music was based on an instrumental piece Page had worked up at Plumpton Place the previous year—a chiming, melancholic 12-string phrase followed by the punching staccato riff that brings in the rest of the band. It may even have formed part of the lost "Swan Song" opus he was planning—and that eventually formed the basis for the 1985 Firm track "Midnight Moonlight."

"'Ten Years Gone' was painstakingly pieced together from sections [Jimmy had] written,"

Plant recalled. "He goes away to his house and works on it a lot and then brings it to the band in its skeletal state. Slowly everybody brings their personality into it. This new flower sort of grows out of it." Page himself saw the track as a missing link between "Stairway to Heaven" and *Presence*'s "Achilles Last Stand."

The song's feel suggests a less dramatic "Kashmir," with another airy dose of mysticism in the lyrics: "Then as it was, then again it will be/And though the course may change sometimes/Rivers always reach the sea."

The inspiration here was the memory of the decade-old love affair with his wife's younger

"IT WAS LIKE THE SONG WAS BIGGER THAN ME. I WAS PETRIFIED, IT'S TRUE. IT WAS PAINFUL. I WAS VIRTUALLY IN TEARS."

—Robert Plant on singing "Kashmir" live

sister Shirley Wilson, a relationship that ended when Plant was forced to choose between her and his stop-start musical aspirations.

"I was working my ass off before joining Zeppelin," Plant said after the band relented in its long antagonism towards *Rolling Stone* and gave young Cameron Crowe the magazine's first Zeppelin cover story in January 1975. "A lady I really dearly loved said, 'Right. It's me or your fans.' Not that I had fans, but I said, 'I can't stop, I've got to keep going.'" He added, "She's quite content these days, I imagine. She's got a washing machine that works by itself and a little sports car."

Old wounds are sharply felt in the song's hoarse middle-eight outpouring of "Do you ever remember me, baby/Did it feel so good," followed by a gliding Page solo that's tonally close to the creamy mid-seventies feel of Don Felder on "Hotel California" or Pete Carr on Rod Stewart's "Tonight's the Night."

Juddering metallic funk with Page spitting out notes like little bullets, "The Wanton Song" is cut from the same cloth as "Custard Pie." Originally "Desiree"—possibly a namecheck for Desiree Serino, future spouse of Bad Company drummer Simon Kirke—the track nods too in the general direction of "Immigrant Song," its core riff similarly shooting back and forth between octaves. The song sounds superficially as yearning as "Custard Pie," but with a bit of dread in the lyric that brings it closer to "Black Dog": "With blazing eyes I see my trembling hands/When we know the time has come/Lose many senses, lose command…"

The last of the eight tracks recorded at Headley and completed at Olympic, "Sick Again," returns us—with an imperious swagger—to Zeppelin's primal blues-boogie ooze. A finger-

Main picture: Page had been working on the soundtrack for Kenneth Anger's *Lucifer Rising*. Inset: "The Wanton Song" was originally named "Desiree," possibly after Desiree Serino, who married Bad Company's Simon Kirke in 1978.

wagging song about El Lay and the tired circus of groupies on the band's 1973 US tour, it starts almost punkily before a virile and grinding groove sets in, complete with funky slide-guitar-and-cymbals pentatonic riposte to Plant's main vocal line.

"I just view it all with amusement," Page told Nick Kent of the groupie scene that swirled around Zeppelin at the Riot House and the glam-rock haven that was Rodney Bingenheimer's English Disco.

As a man who was happy to play girls off against each other, this smacks of mild disingenuousness on Page's part. Indeed, the line "One day soon you're gonna reach 16," almost certainly refers to Lori Maddox, the Valley girl Lolita whose heart he would casually break when he two-timed her with the older and more sophisticated Bebe Buell.

"I think he was obsessed with me because he loved that I looked kinda like him," Maddox told Pamela Des Barres, herself a former LA consort of Jimmy's. "Eighty pounds, hair down to here, skinny as can be."

As condescending and scornful as "Sick Again" is—"How fast you learn the downhill slide/Oh how you play the game/Still don't know your name."—it clearly made no appreciable difference to Zeppelin's ongoing exploitation of these willing vixens.

When the final Olympic sessions were completed before the summer of 1974, the band was rightly excited. "We got eight tracks off," Robert Plant said in the spring of 1974, "and a lot of them are really raunchy. We did some real belters with live vocals, off-the-wall stuff that turned out really nice."

But there was a small problem. They realized the eight finished tracks were, collectively, too long to fit on a single vinyl album. And not wanting to sacrifice any of them, they opted to make the album a double. It wasn't the first time they'd considered doing this. Ever since the release of *Led Zeppelin II,* it had been mooted that "the next album" might be a double—especially the fourth. Now the time seemed right.

"We had enough material for one-and-a-half LPs, so we figured, 'Let's put out a double and use some of the material we'd done previously but never released,'" Page said to Dave Schulps in 1977. "This time we figured it was better to stretch out than to leave off."

Inspirations included glorious sprawls like Dylan's *Blonde on Blonde*, The Beatles' 1968 *White Album*, and the Stones' *Exile On Main St.*, though the latter hadn't attained the vaunted status it enjoys today. The album would function as part pomp-rock statement, part *Basement Tapes*-style scrapbook, underlining Zeppelin's continuing willingness to branch out from their heavy blues base.

"There's a lot of variation of material," Plant would say the following year, "so it gives people a whole spectrum of style which is contained in one package, and I think that's very good." From the stage of the Long Beach Arena the following year he described the album as comprised of "parts of our consciousness."

The decision was therefore made to sift through the stockpile of recordings discarded from the previous four years and see what might work alongside the new material. "I had no way of knowing *Physical Graffiti* would be a double album," claims Ron Nevison. "It was only later, when it came out, that I realized they'd gone back to *Houses of the Holy* and before and dragged some other stuff up."

They went back further than *Houses*: back, in fact, to the unplugged pastorale of the visit Page and Plant had made to the Welsh refuge that was Bron-yr-Aur, a time, Plant once told me, when "my heart was so light and happy and—at that time, at that age—1970 was the biggest blue sky I ever saw."

Coming after "In the Light" on *Physical Graffiti*, "Bron-Yr-Aur"—occasionally played on Zeppelin's sixth US tour in the late summer of 1970—instantly takes us back to the hippie idyll of the third album. Recorded in July 1970 at ◆►

Island Studios during the sessions for *Led Zeppelin III*'s "That's the Way" and "Since I've Been Loving You," it's a short dreamy piece in open-C6 tuning for acoustic guitar, with shades of Page's earlier "White Summer"—and a world away from the thump of "Trampled Under Foot." Beautifully picked, with a rolling, unfurling circularity, it's reminiscent not just of Page's acoustic master Bert Jansch but of Nick Drake's exquisite playing on "Pink Moon."

Three of *Physical Graffiti*'s tracks—"Boogie with Stu," "Night Flight," and "Down by the Seaside"—came from sessions for the fourth album, recorded between late 1970 and early 1971. "Boogie with Stu" spins off from "Rock and Roll," which similarly featured Stones linchpin Ian "Stu" Stewart on battered upright piano, and exemplifies a casual *Exile/Basement Tapes* stance that says, "Hey, even though we're the biggest hard-rock band on the planet, what we really love to do is kick back at home with a little boogie-woogie." With a jokey working title of "Sloppy Drunk," "Boogie with Stu" was co-credited not just to Stu—whom Page had known since his teenage years in Epsom—but to "Mrs. Valens," mother of "La Bamba" legend Ritchie, whose "Ooh, My Head" it lifts from.

"Some of the things that happened [at Headley]—like 'Boogie with Stu,' where Stu turns up and plays a piano that's totally unplayable—were incredible," Page said. "That was too good to miss because Stu wouldn't record, he wouldn't do solo stuff. All of these things wouldn't end up on albums as far as other people were concerned, but they did with us."

A sub-Stonesy feel was also in evidence on "Night Flight," a slice of 4/4 bar-room raunch opening with hi-hat sixteenths from Bonzo. It's hard to imagine this Faces knockoff—about a young man conscripted to fight overseas—sitting alongside "Black Dog" and "Stairway to Heaven," so it's unsurprising it failed to make the cut on the fourth album; hard to believe, too, that it was initiated by Jonesy, whose Ian McLagan-style Hammond is a central feature of the track.

"Down by the Seaside," recorded at Island, is one of the most atypical things Zeppelin ever recorded. In essence, it's a Robert Plant stab at California country rock, featuring the man himself on guitar, Page on pedal steel, and Jones on slipnote electric piano. Bonzo could almost have played rimshots on it. It's not quite Neil Young but it's close, with an endearing back-to-the-country lyric: "Hear the people singin'/ Singin' 'bout the growin'/Knowin' where they're goin'," and a faster section that anticipates "Over the Hills and Far Away." Again, it's hard to imagine it on the fourth album, which in any case covered Plant's Laurel Canyon base with the gorgeous "Going to California."

Like "Down by the Seaside," "The Rover" had begun its life at Bron-yr-Aur. There is a short acoustic run-through of the song on various bootlegs, with little hint of the electric metamorphosis it would undergo when Zeppelin cut it at Stargroves during the *Houses of the Holy* sessions in May 1972 (and subsequently worked on it during soundchecks on their 1973

US tour). The track might just be the sub-metal prototype for all of eighties American rock—not to mention *In Through the Out Door*'s "In the Evening," The Firm, Coverdale-Page et al.—with its 4/4 stomp, sub-Frampton guitar phrase, and a chord sequence that bands like Van Halen and Bon Jovi and would emulate over the ensuing decade.

Page has long claimed that Ron Nevison accidentally erased the guitar tracks for "The Rover" at Headley Grange, forcing him to overdub several fat guitar tracks at Olympic with the aid of Keith Harwood. He was petty enough to insert "Guitar lost courtesy Nevison" and "Salvaged by the grace of Harwood" into the track details on *Physical Graffiti*'s inner sleeve; he's also referred to Nevison more than once as "Ron Nevermind," claiming that the engineer's response to his anger about the wiped tracks was precisely that.

Nevison disputes all of this, pointing out that the decision to include tracks from the *Houses of the Holy* sessions came some time after his work at Headley. "They never brought the *Houses* tapes or any other tapes down to Headley Grange, so there's no way I could have worked on that song," he says. "It could be that one of the other engineers erased the track and blamed me because I wasn't there. I don't know."

Lady in New York.

Stargroves was certainly where the final *Houses* outtake on *Graffiti* was done: or more accurately on the lawn outside the house. Originally titled "Never Ending Doubting Woman Blues," a phrase left off the final mix, "Black Country Woman" was a ramshackle helping of country blues closer in spirit to *Led Zeppelin III* than to *Houses of the Holy*. Opening with Zeppelin's very own "Is it rolling, Bob?"—Dylan's famous question to producer Bob Johnston on *Nashville Skyline*—engineer Eddie Kramer asks, "Shall we roll it, Jimmy?" before contending with the sound of a plane overhead.

"You wanna get this airplane on?" Kramer asks.

"Nah, leave it, yeah," Plant answers throatily.

Performed on Zeppelin's 1977 tour with "Bron-Yr-Aur Stomp"—with which it shares its metronomic marching band thump—the track features Page on acoustic, Jones on mandolin, and Plant on harmonica. Supposedly the lyrics again reference Shirley Wilson, the "sister" and a woman with whom Plant maintained an on-off relationship for some years, even having a son (Jesse) together in 1991. What we cannot quite know is whether it is addressed to her or to Maureen (who, logic would suggest, is the "blushing bride" of the song).

<blockquote>

"We had enough material for one-and-a-half LPs so we figured, 'Let's put out a double' . . . It was better to stretch out than to leave off."

– Jimmy Page

</blockquote>

Also from the *Houses* sessions comes "Houses of the Holy" itself—a droll conceit typical of the time. It shares a basic feel and production style with the midtempo "Dancing Days," which may be why it wasn't included on that album, but its cowbell strut suggests the Stones crossed with AC/DC.

The track's guitars, pushed through a Delta T digital delay unit, are dryly metallic and curiously reminiscent of Big Star's "O My Soul." Meanwhile, the lyrics boast at least one explicit reference to Satan ("Let the music be your master/Will you heed the master's call/Oh . . . Satan and man"), which is highly ironic given the absurd amount of time people have spent decoding backwards messages on "Stairway to Heaven." Recorded at Olympic rather than Stargroves, the finished version was unchanged from Eddie Kramer's original mix at Electric

Physical Graffiti was now complete, save for mixing sessions overseen by Keith Harwood at Olympic in October 1974. Coincidentally that month also saw the belated UK launch party for Swan Song Records.

The deal to distribute Swan Song had been agreed with Atlantic after the group's five-year contract with the label had come to an end in late 1973. "Initially it was a label without a name," says Danny Goldberg, who was promoted from being the band's US press officer to being president of Swan Song in America. "The only person signed to it was Maggie Bell, but the plan was that Zeppelin would put out their own next record on the label. So it was all about Maggie and then somewhere along the line Jimmy came up with the name Swan Song. Maggie's *Queen of the Night* album came out on Atlantic because there was no name for the label yet, though from an accounting and business point of view it was part of the ledger sheet of the Zeppelin label."

To *Hit Parader* on January 11, 1974, Page said Swan Song would be "a place where people who have talent will be able to be heard, for we can put ourselves behind it and try and pull it off," adding that it would be "a different kind of record company than some others that groups have formed because it isn't just involved with one group . . . it's really a family thing, not like Rolling Stones Records, which is really an ego thing right from the start."

"Swan Song was initially a great idea," says Simon Kirke, drummer with the label's breakout success Bad Company. "It had that Island Records vibe in that it was formed by musicians to look after their musical interests and those of other bands that would come on board. Of course it was a business and was run as such but it was not a shrine to capitalism by any stretch."

"The *Bad Company* album was the first release on Swan Song and it went to number one," says Danny Goldberg. "Led Zeppelin signed another band and it went to number one and that was an amazing differentiation for Swan Song—what a way to start! I think if they'd had a proper A&R department, Swan Song would have had a tremendous ability to sign artists. But it was really a vehicle for Zeppelin."

The label was officially launched on in May 1974, with lavish parties held in New York (May 7) and Los Angeles (May 13, two nights after the band met Elvis Presley). Maggie Bell, whose *Suicide Sal* was Swan Song's fourth release after *Physical Graffiti* itself, was at both.

"It was a great launch party, with pink flamingos and doves," she remembers. "Especially for a little girl from Glasgow who started in the Salvation Army playing the tambourine."

Six months later, ostensibly to publicize the Pretty Things' *Silk Torpedo* album, Peter Grant laid on a lavish Halloween launch for Swan Song at Chislehurst Caves in Kent. The scene was pure Fellini, with drinks served by nuns in suspenders and naked male wrestlers cavorting in the recesses of the caves.

"Everywhere that was accessible, they seemed to find something to put on inside of it," recalls Geoff Grimes, then a promo man for Atlantic in London. "There was a naked woman in a coffin, covered in jelly. When Nesuhi Ertegun [co-founder of Atlantic] walked by in this beautiful burgundy jacket he'd just bought, the girl leapt out at him from the coffin and covered him in jelly. He was not impressed."

For Robert Plant, observing the decadence with a wryly detached eye, the party had the effect of bringing Zeppelin themselves closer together after a year of—by their standards—relative inactivity.

"I'll tell you, at that Chislehurst Caves function I realized I really missed the unity of the four of us," he told Lisa Robinson, the New York journalist who'd become a confidante of sorts and who was herself at the party. "I realized that above everything else, above record companies, above films, we were Led Zeppelin—above everything. From that moment on we started rehearsing and getting into full gear."

Plant also told Robinson about the imminent new release. "We worked really hard, we worked ourselves almost into the ground," he said. "I mean, despite the fact that we don't see each other every day and Bonzo lives right down the road and half the time he's at Hereford Market selling

bulls, it still seems that at the right time we get together and we write something that keeps us all satisfied musically . . .

"I love the album. There are some real humdinger, roaring tracks on it—and then there are some others that are going to take a while . . . and then people will see. Some of the lyrics are a bit more 'groinal', if we can start using that phrase. We're really playing well now we're quite mature, you know."

The *NME*'s Nick Kent got a sneak preview of *Physical Graffiti* when he sat in on a rehearsal for the upcoming US tour at Ealing's Liveware Theatre on November 26. He called "Kashmir" "most impressive" and described Zeppelin as "quintessential doyens of the kamikaze dizzbuster game . . . still absolutely the best mainstream metal band around."

Physical Graffiti would already have been in stores by now had there not been predictable Zeppelin delays on account of the album's elaborate sleeve design. As far back as March, Plant had quipped, "we haven't yet got around to our six-month decision on covers yet. Question marks still hung over the design in late 1974, with Plant admitting to French mag *Rock Et Folk* that "what is delaying the album is the cover . . . Jimmy has an idea and I have another and we really can't agree."

Put together by Peter Corriston in New York and the late Mike Doud in London, the *Physical Graffiti* sleeve depicted two New York brownstones (96 and 98 St. Mark's Place) on an

"There was a naked woman in a coffin, covered in jelly."
– Geoff Grimes recalls the Swan Song launch party.

East Village block that had long been home to all manner of hippies and hipsters. Interchanging window illustrations revealed Zeppelin in drag and Bonzo in tights for Roy Harper's Valentines Day gig, plus a *Sgt. Pepper*-style array of legendary faces that included the Virgin Mary, Marlene Dietrich, Neil Armstrong, and Jerry Lee Lewis.

The title *Physical Graffiti* had been coined by Jimmy Page to illustrate the sheer slapdash energy of the album.

In the US, the album shipped a million on its first day. "No album in Atlantic history has generated so many immediate sales," said Jerry Wexler, who'd inked the deal with Zeppelin in September 1968. America had caught Zeppelin fever. The band soon had all six of their albums on the chart at the same time, an achievement augmented by the continuing sales of *Bad Company*, which the previous year had been the Warner-Elektra-Atlantic group's biggest-selling album.

The 1975 US tour got off to a difficult start when Page broke a finger in a train door at Victoria Station after warm-up gigs in Holland and Belgium. The band's old improvising

showcase "Dazed and Confused" had to make way for "How Many More Times" because Page couldn't bend his blues finger. Plant then went down with the flu after the sixth date in Indianapolis, forcing the cancellation of the next show in St. Louis.

There was also a heightened paranoia and security presence around the band, with ex-FBI roped in to shield them from the world. More than a little symbolic were the bowler hats and *Clockwork Orange* boiler suits that Bonham and his henchman Mick Hinton wore throughout the tour; at many of the tour's shows, Plant would introduce his Midlands mate as "Mr. Ultraviolence."

But by the tour's climax—in LA, naturally, with a three-night stand at the Forum in late March—everything was firing on all cylinders. Live versions of the new songs—especially "Kashmir," "In My Time of Dying," "Trampled Under Foot," and "Sick Again"—quickly endeared themselves to Zeppelin's fanatical followers, as indeed they would to the hoards of adoring fans who came to see the band's five-night stand at London's Earl's Court in May.

"I've never been more into a tour," Plant told Cameron Crowe in Los Angeles. "The music's jelled amazingly well. Everyone loved *Physical Graffiti*. That meant a lot. It's like we're on an incredible winning streak."

It was true: (almost) everyone did love *Physical Graffiti*. The album brought about a volte-face even among critics, a group of people who in Crowe's words had "continually kicked, shoved, pummeled, and kneed [Zeppelin] in the groin." Steve Clarke's review in *NME* was headlined, "Kiss Your Skull Goodbye" and concluded that "Hard rock lives, and how."

In *Melody Maker*, Michael Oldfield called *Physical Graffiti* "a work of genius." In *Creem*, Jaan Uhelszki wrote that Zeppelin "moves in strange ways . . . Sure, they're gutsy, ballsy, and flamboyantly aggressive, but they're also cerebral, by way of the glands." Even in *Rolling Stone* Jim Miller raved, describing the album as "*Beggars Banquet* and *Sgt. Pepper* rolled into one."

Concurring with these welcome hosannas was the enigmatic genius whose driving vision had—seven years earlier—brought about the musical miracle that was Led Zeppelin.

"I guess a good album where we'd matured—and where it's not a really condensed situation such as *Presence*—is *Physical Graffiti*," Jimmy Page told me in 2003. "Because it's a band working, and you can hear all the different things we were able to do . . . and other people can't do now." ❼

Trampled Under Foot, Barney Hoskyn's book on Led Zeppelin is published by Faber & Faber.

Crisis? What Crisis?

In August 1975, Led Zeppelin was about to begin rehearsals for another huge US tour. Then disaster struck, their very existence in a mangled heap. Yet out of the wreckage climbed *Presence*, an album that Jimmy Page rates as one of their best.

By: Mick Wall

Monday, August 4, 1975, another sweltering hot afternoon on the small Greek island of Rhodes. Maureen Plant, wife of Led Zeppelin singer Robert, is at the wheel of a rented Austin Mini, Robert beside her in the passenger seat, their three-year-old son Karac and six-year-old daughter Carmen in the back seat, along with their friend Scarlet, the four-year-old daughter of Zeppelin guitarist Jimmy Page.

Two months earlier, following Zeppelin's record-breaking five-night run at the 17,000-capacity Earls Court arena in London, the young Plant family had set off for Agadir, Morocco. Three weeks later they were in Marrakech where Page and his wife Charlotte and daughter Scarlet flew out to meet them. Together they took in a local festival "that gave us a little peep into the color of Moroccan music and the music of the hill tribes," said Plant.

From there they journeyed thousands of miles by Range Rover through the Spanish Sahara just as the Spanish-Moroccan war was breaking out. "There was a distinct possibility that we could have got very, very lost, going round in circles and taking ages to get out," said Plant. "It's such a vast country, with no landmarks and no people apart from the odd tent and a camel."

A month later, driving up through Casablanca and Tangier, they arrived in Switzerland for a meeting with Zeppelin manager Peter Grant at his lavish new base, renting promoter Claude Knobs' house in Montreaux, and spending a few days hanging out at the Montreux jazz festival, then in full swing. But by the end of July, Plant was getting itchy feet again, "pining for the sun [and] the happy, haphazard way of life that goes with it."

It was then that the idea of driving down to Rhodes came up. Plant arranged to meet Pretty Things vocalist Phil May and his wife, Electra, who had rented a house on the island from Roger Waters of Pink Floyd. Page, Charlotte, and Scarlet followed in a second car, with Maureen's sister Shirley and her husband. On August 3, Jimmy left the party briefly to fly to Sicily to visit Aleister Crowley's old Abbey of Thelema, which occult filmmaker Kenneth Anger had told him so much about and that he was now considering buying. The plan was to all meet up again in Paris a couple of days later where they would ➢

begin rehearsals for Zeppelin's next US tour, scheduled to begin with two shows, already sold out, on August 23 and 24 at the 90,000-capacity Oakland Coliseum in San Francisco.

Their most recent US tour had only ended in March, but with combined album sales and tour receipts estimated to have topped $40 million (more than $185 million in today's money) they wanted to keep momentum flowing. There was also the fact that they were now obliged to become tax exiles, unable to return to the UK for more than 30 days until April 1976. Most of the ensuing period would be taken up touring the world, it was decided, affording the band unusual opportunities to travel to territories they had never been able to before—South America was seriously discussed, as was India, Africa, and other previously thought out-of-the-way stops on the rock 'n' roll map.

This was Led Zeppelin at the very top of the mountain, able to look down on nearest rivals such as the Rolling Stones and Pink Floyd from a considerable height. Unstoppable, unbreachable, invulnerable, nothing could go wrong. Until suddenly it did. And nothing would ever be the same again.

Afterwards, nobody who was there could remember exactly what happened or why. Just that the car Maureen Plant was driving skidded and spun off the road, nosediving over a precipice and into a tree. When Robert had landed on top of Maureen, the impact shattered his right ankle and elbow and snapped several bones in his right leg. Looking at Maureen, who was bleeding and unconscious, he thought she was dead. The children were screaming in the back. Fortunately, Charlotte and Shirley, in the next car, were there to summon help, but it was still several hours before the family could be taken—on the back of a nearby fruit farmer's flatbed truck—to the local hospital. There it was discovered that Maureen had suffered a fractured skull and broken her pelvis and her leg. Karac had also broken a leg, while Carmen had broken her wrist. Scarlet was the only one to escape with just a few cuts and bruises.

Maureen had lost a lot of blood, and because she had a rare type, could only take Shirley's blood for immediate transfusion. The process was painfully slow, with only one doctor on duty at the Greek hospital.

That night a hysterical Charlotte called Zep tour manager and all-around fixer Richard Cole in London, begging him to do something to get everyone home. Cole flew into action, furiously calling around until he had co-opted two senior physicians—Dr. John Baretta, a Harley Street specialist who also acted as medical consultant for the Greek Embassy and spoke fluent Greek, and Dr. Mike Lawrence, a prominent orthopedic surgeon—into journeying with him immediately to Greece.

It was still 48 hours before they arrived, though, and even then hospital officials refused to release the

"This could be the end of Led Zeppelin. This might be the end of the line."

Peter Grant, following Plant's car crash

patients until a police investigation—searching for causes of the crash, specifically drugs—was completed, which might have taken weeks.

Again, Cole saved the day. He hired a private ambulance and arranged for two station wagons to be parked at a side entrance. He wheeled Robert, Maureen, and the children down to the getaway cars in the dead of night. Hours later, they were in the sky heading back to London.

Their return home was delayed still further, however, on the instructions of Zeppelin's own record label's accountants, who insisted Cole delay the plane's landing by 30 minutes so as to avoid using up a precious day of Plant's allotted tax-free time in the UK. Circling at 15,000 feet, Cole reflected that while it may have saved Plant thousands of pounds in taxes, "I still thought it was more important to save a life."

When the plane finally touched down, the Plants were transported via waiting ambulances to Guy's Hospital, where Maureen underwent immediate surgery. It would be several more weeks before she was well enough to leave. Robert, who was placed in a cast that ran from his hip to his toes, also faced sobering news from the doctors. "You probably won't walk again for six months, maybe more," he was told. "And there's no guarantee that you'll ever recover completely."

It was debatable who took the news worse—Plant or Grant. "This could be the end of Led Zeppelin," Grant complain—ed to Cole. "This might be the end of the line."

Jimmy Page was also devastated by the news. "I was shattered," he said. However, he had "always felt that no matter what happened, provided he could still play and sing, and even if we could only make albums, that we'd go on forever." Robert's fate, Jimmy

had no doubt, was tied inextricably to that of the band. "Just really because the whole aspect of what's going to come round the corner as far as writing goes is the dark element, the mysterious element. You just don't know what's coming. So many good things have come out of that, that it would be criminal to interrupt a sort of alchemical process like that." He added: "There's a lot of important work to be done yet."

To make matters worse, to preserve his new tax-exiled status, Plant would have to be moved out of the country again while his wife was still recuperating in the hospital. Temporary accommodation was arranged for him on the island of Jersey (exempt from punitive British tax laws) at the mansion home of millionaire lawyer Dick Christian, who sent a limousine and an ambulance to meet Plant and his mini entourage of Cole, Zeppelin soundman Benji Le Fevre, and band PA Marilyn. Christian kindly offered his guest the use of his Maserati and Jensen Interceptor cars, but a wheelchair-bound Plant would spend the next six weeks moping around the guest house, drinking beer and knocking back prescription painkillers. Occasionally he played the piano, but mainly he just sat and stared, his mood desperate. "I just don't know whether I'm ever going to be the same onstage again," he told Cole repeatedly.

Eventually it was decided that work was the best therapy. "The longer we wait," Page complained to Cole, "the harder it's gonna be to come back." With the band's ambitious touring plans put on indefinite hold, it was decided to get to work on the next Zeppelin album. By the end of September, Plant, his wheelchair, and his crutches were being boarded onto a British Airways flight to Los Angeles, where Page was waiting for him in a rented beach house in Malibu Colony. As with their stay at Bron-Yr-Aur five years before which produced the nucleus of the *Led Zeppelin III* album, the two planned to write together. There were no peaceful, flower-strewn valleys to enjoy this time, though, just the lights of old LA beckoning them onto the rocks.

Robert's mood was still predominantly black but, hanging out with Jimmy, writing again, he now had

Ready to rock and roll: (l-r) Page, Bonham, Plant, and Jones.

good days as well as bad, taking short, therapeutic strolls along the beach with his new cane, before collapsing back into his wheelchair. There were also trips to see Donovan perform at the Santa Monica Civic, and a catch-up with Paul Rodgers and Boz Burrell from Bad Company.

Jimmy also checked out his friend Michael Des Barres' band Detective, offering them a deal with Zep's label Swan Song. However, there was another factor about Plant's Californian rehabilitation that wasn't discussed: the plentiful supply of cocaine and heroin that Page's presence anywhere now demanded. Also staying at the Malibu house was Benji Le Fevre, who told Cole they'd nicknamed the place "Henry Hall"—slang for heroin.

Having used up their backlog of material on *Physical Graffiti*, with the exception of the riff to the unreleased "Walter's Walk," which Page now reused to create "Hots On for Nowhere," songs for the new album would have to be built from the ground up. One of the first to take shape was "Achilles Last Stand," the lengthy opus that would eventually open the next album. Built on the sort of strident, all-hands-on-deck guitar figure that Iron Maiden would later build a whole career out of—Page attempting to create something, he said, that reflected "the façade of a gothic building with layers of tracery and statues"—"Achilles Last Stand" also featured the first of a string of intensely autobiographical lyrics Plant now felt compelled to write.

Originally nicknamed "The Wheelchair Song," the subject in this instance was the enforced exile which had forced the band to become what Page later described as "technological gypsies," and led indirectly, Plant seemed to suggest, to their current malaise—"The devil's in his hole!" Page later described his guitar solo as "in the same tradition as the solo from 'Stairway to Heaven.'" In truth, few would now agree but, "It is on that level to me," he insisted.

Musically, "Tea for One," the equally lengthy blues showcase that would close the album "was us looking back at 'Since I've Been Loving You,'" Page would later tell me, "being in a very lonely space at the time and . . . reflecting accordingly."

Lyrically, it found Plant metaphorically wringing his hands, the loneliness of his separation from his wife and children—Maureen being still too ill to travel—juxtaposed against the artificial luxury of his drug-fueled life in Malibu. "I was just sitting in that wheelchair from beer stand to beer stand and getting morose," he recalled. "It was like . . . is this rock 'n' roll thing really anything at all?"

But that was as nothing compared to the venom he summoned up in "For Your Life" and "Hots on For Nowhere"; the former a vicious attack on the LA lifestyle he'd once eulogized, railing against "cocaine, cocaine, cocaine" in the "city of the damned"; in the latter he directs his anger this time towards both Page and Grant, and their insensitivity to his situation, only concerned for their own futures. Seemingly oblivious to Plant's ire, Page inadvertently colludes in the song's bitter denouement, using the tremolo arm on a Fender Strat he'd borrowed from former Byrd Gene Parsons, to produce a resounding twang in the

Robert Plant near his home in Wales, October 1976.

middle of his solo.

Naturally, there was also the almost obligatory pillaging of the blues, this time for a new cornerstone Zeppelin moment, another Blind Willie Johnson classic from 1928 called "It's Nobody's Fault But Mine," here shortened to "Nobody's Fault But Mine." Originally the story of Johnson fretting because his blindness prevented him from reading his bible, thereby incurring the wrath of God, it became a useful metaphor for Zeppelin's own fiery descent from heaven, Plant adapting the lyrics to include some revealingly stuttering lines about having "a monkey on my back," embellished by some suitably squalling harmonica. As usual, the only truly original parts were the strafing guitar lines Page concocted to which John Bonham added his most mercilessly cannon-like drum pummeling since "When the Levee Breaks."

It wasn't all bleak. "Candy Store Rock"—its genesis

"The main memory of [recording *Presence*] is pushing Robert around in the wheelchair from beer stand to beer stand."
John Paul Jones

traceable back to live performances of "Over the Hills and Far Away" where Page, Jones, and Bonham would frequently drift off into a similarly paced improvisation—was a jolly enough romp, with Page making a rare recorded return to his rockabilly roots, and Plant cheerfully following suit, "being Ral Donner," as he put it, "the guy who wanted to be Elvis."

"Royal Orleans"—named after the hotel at 621 St. Louis Street where Jones had had an unfortunate accidental encounter with a drag queen on the 1973 US tour—was another deliberate attempt to lighten the mood, its pleasingly staccato rhythms enlivened by the jokey lyric: "When the sun peeked through . . . he kissed the whiskers, left and right," and a jokey reference to talking "like Barry White."

With most of the material finished by the time Jones and Bonham arrived at the end of the month, time originally booked at SIR Studios in Hollywood for writing and rehearsal was used mainly to finesse what Page and Plant had already come up with. Work described by Page as "grueling" because, he said, "nobody else really came up with song ideas. It was really up to me to ▷

Page and Bonham onstage at Madison Square Garden in June 1977.

Calm before the storm. Plant at home in 1974.

come up with all the riffs, which is probably —why [the songs were] guitar-heavy. But I don't blame anybody. We were all kind of down."

In fact neither Jones nor Bonham were given a chance to participate. As Jones told Zep historian Dave Lewis in 2003, "It became apparent that Robert and I seemed to keep a different time sequence to Jimmy. We just couldn't find him." Jones added that he "drove into SIR Studios every night and waited and waited . . . I learned all about baseball during that period, as the World Series was on and there was not much else to do but watch it." Even when recording for the album had begun, "I just sort of went along with it all", he shrugged. "The main memory of that album is pushing Robert around in the wheelchair from beer stand to beer stand. We had a laugh, I suppose, but I didn't enjoy the sessions, really. I just tagged along with that one."

Hence the solitary co-writing credit Jones and Bonham receive on the album, for "Royal Orleans." Even when Jones did manage to contribute some solid ideas—such as the bass line he created with his distinctive Alembic eight-string for "Achilles Last Stand" and which he describes now as "an integral part of the song"—it went unacknowledged. "What one put into the track wasn't always reflected in the credits," he observed dryly.

It's clear that *Presence* was not one of Jones' favorite Zeppelin albums. In truth it would rarely become anybody's favorite Zeppelin album—except for Page, who still stubbornly rates it one of their best. As Dave Lewis says now, "It was the first album

all over again, with Jimmy in total control of everything and hardly anyone else getting a say. That's why there was no "Boogie with Stu" or "Hats off to (Roy) Harper" on that album, no Mellotrons, acoustic guitars, or keyboards of any kind—no Jonesy! It was all Jimmy. No one else really got a look in."

One person blissfully unconcerned with the niceties of songwriting at this point was John Bonham, whose enforced year away from home was beginning to have the anticipated effects. One night during the SIR sessions, he arrived at the Rainbow bar & grill, Zep's favored haunt on Sunset Strip, where he sat at the bar and ordered 20 black Russians (vodka and coffee liqueur), and polished off half of them in one go. Swiveling on his seat, he spotted a familiar face, Michelle Myer, longtime associate of producer and LA socialite Kim Fowley. Myer, sitting eating dinner, looked over and smiled. Bonzo did not smile back. Instead . . . he went over and punched her in the face, knocking her off her seat. "Don't ever look at me that way again!" he roared.

At the end of October, when the band finally left LA—Jimmy insisting they move at once, after an unusually thunderous storm which erupted over the Malibu coastline, which he took as a bad omen— they flew to Munich, where Musicland studios had been booked for them to complete the album. On the flight, Bonzo knocked himself out on several large G&Ts, a couple of bottles of white wine, and champagne, causing so much disruption that the other First Class passengers begged the steward not

> "Against the odds . . . we were still able to look the devil in the eye and say: 'We're as strong as you and stronger.'"
>
> **Robert Plant**

to wake him when the food was served. When he came to a couple of hours later he had wet himself. He shouted for Mick Hinton, his personal roadie, and forced him to stand in front of him while he changed his pants. Then he made Hinton sit in his urine-drenched seat while Bonzo took Hinton's seat in Economy.

Situated in the basement of the Arabella Hotel, Musicland was bright and modern, sparsely furnished, the accent firmly on the functional. The Rolling Stones were due in straight after Zeppelin. So tight was the scheduling squeeze that Zep had just 18 days to work in. No Zeppelin album since their first, seven years before, had been recorded so quickly, but Page was determined to make it work.

In the event, he would find himself calling Jagger, begging for more time. It was a request the Stones' mainman was happy to acquiesce to—up to a point. He could let Jimmy have three extra days, he said. Hardly any time at all in recording terms, but it was all Page needed to finish the job, laying down all his guitar overdubs in a frantic 14-hour session, including at least six for "Achilles Last Stand," quitting only when his fingers ached so much he could no longer manipulate them properly.

Outside, Munich was in the grips of a bitterly cold winter; inside the studio it was permanent midnight, Jimmy staying up for three days at a time, then sleeping on the floor of the studio.

"The band did the basic tracks and then went away," he recalled, "leaving me and [engineer] Keith Harwood to do all the overdubs. We had a deal between us: whoever woke up first woke up the other one and we'd continue the studio work."

As a result, Page remains inordinately proud of what at the time he initially referred to as simply "the Munich LP," its final title undecided until the cover had been finalized.

"It was a very, very intense album," he would recall, "Robert had had the accident, and we didn't know how he was gonna heal. He was on crutches, and singing from a wheelchair." Or as Plant said at the time, it was "our stand against everything. Against the elements and chance."

Only once during the Munich sessions did the weird momentum Page had created threaten to unravel, which was when Plant, still in plaster, pulled himself up from his wheelchair one afternoon to stretch, lost his balance, and fell onto his bad leg. A horrifyingly loud cracking sound filled the room.

"Not again! Not again!" he screamed. First to

reach him was Page, petrified that Plant had broken his leg again. "I'd never known Jimmy to move so quickly," Robert later recalled. "He was out of the mixing booth and holding me up, fragile as he might be, within a second. He became quite Germanic in his organization of things, and instantly I was rushed off to hospital again in case I'd reopened the fracture."

So worried was Page, in fact, that no more work could be done that day. Fortunately, after a call later that night confirming no further injury, Jimmy was back in the studio, putting in another all-nighter.

The album was finally finished on November 27, 1975, the day before Thanksgiving that year. The following morning, while Page was still sleeping, a delighted—and relieved—Plant put a call to the Swan Song office in New York to give them the good news, even suggesting they call the album *Thanksgiving*.

A week later, the entire band was back in Jersey, where, on December 3, Bonham and Jones made an impromptu appearance onstage with Norman Hale, resident pianist at local watering hole Behan's Park West and a former member of sixties chart-toppers The Tornados. A week later, the whole band joined Hale for a surprise 45-minute set at the club, where fewer than 300 people watched the band tear through their "Eddie Cochran and Little Richard repertoire," as Plant put it. "I was sitting on a stool, and every time I hit a high note I stood up, but not putting any weight on my foot." By the end of the set, Plant was "wiggling the stool past the drums and further out. Once we got going we didn't want to stop."

In Paris three weeks later, celebrating New Year's Day, Plant took his first steps unaided since the crash five months before. "One small step for man," he joked, "one giant leap for six nights at Madison Square Garden . . ."

In January 1976, the whole band was in New York, staying at the Park Lane Hotel on Central Park South. While Page began tinkering again with the mix of the live soundtrack to the long-delayed "road movie" which would later become *The Song Remains the Same*, Plant was hitting the town in the company of Benji Le Fevre and an English bodyguard called David. Although the plaster cast had now been removed, he still walked with a cane or crutch.

Less conspicuously but more worryingly, Bonzo was also intent on getting the most out of his enforced stay in the city. When Deep Purple arrived in town for a show at Nassau Coliseum, a drunken Bonzo walked onstage in the middle of their set, grabbed a free mic and announced, "My name is John Bonham of Led Zeppelin, and I just wanna tell ya that we got a new album comin' out called *Presence* and that it's f****** great!"

The album's eventual title, *Presence*—irritatingly revealed ahead of time by Bonzo—was inspired by the sleeve it came in, a typically incongruous Hipgnosis creation, from an idea Storm Thorgerson, Aubrey Powell, and friends Peter Christopherson and George Hardie (who had worked on the first Zeppelin sleeve) were already tinkering with. Reminiscent of the sleeve

Like 1975 never happened. Page onstage at Tampa Stadium In Florida in 1977.

the same team had come up with the year before for Pink Floyd's *Wish You Were Here* (which included images of two suited businessmen shaking hands, one of them on fire, a swimmer crawling through sand, and others of an ilk), the front of *Presence* was a photograph of a "nuclear" family (mom, dad, and two children) seated at a restaurant table. Positioned at the center of the white tablecloth is not a candle, as might be expected, or some floral arrangement, perhaps, but a twisted black oblong shape mounted on a plinth, dubbed "The Object" by Hardie and co.

In the background to this central image, shot in a studio in Bow Street, London, are photographs from that year's Earls Court Boat Show. The rest of the gatefold sleeve includes similarly contrived images: on the back of the outer sleeve, a schoolgirl (modeled by Samantha Giles, previously one of the children on the *Houses of the Holy* sleeve) is seen with her teacher and another pupil at a desk on which stands another image of The Object. Eight more similarly enigmatic images (many taken from the archives of *Life* and *Look* magazines) furnish the inner sleeve, while the inner sleeve containing the vinyl carried unvarnished images of The Object on its own. ▷

GETTY

Later copyrighted by Swan Song, the object in question was a 12-inch black obelisk, designed by Hardie as "a black hole" then completed by model maker Crispin Mellor. It was nicknamed "the present," says Hardie, as "a play on the fact that the actual object—a hole, in fact—wasn't present at all, but absent."

Storm Thorgerson recalled "contaminating" the deliberately dated images with what he describes as "the black obsessional object," which he maintained "stands as being as powerful as one's imagination cares it to be . . . We felt Zeppelin could rightfully feel the same way about themselves in the world of rock music."

According to Page "they came up with 'the object' and wanted to call [the album] Obelisk. I held out for Presence. You think about more than just a symbol that way." And of course, the acknowledgement of a "presence" had more occult resonance than a mere "object." And unlike their previous two albums, this time they did allow the band's name and the album title to appear on the sleeve, albeit embossed on the white sleeve, similar to The Beatles' White Album. (The original UK shipment of Presence added a shrink-wrapped outer package with title and band name in black with a red underlined

The cover of Presence.

border. In the US the shrink-wrap also included a track listing.)

To launch the album, Swan Song had 1,000 copies of the obelisk made which they planned to place simultaneously outside a wide range of iconic buildings across the globe, including the White House, the Houses of Parliament, and 10 Downing Street. The idea was not dissimilar to how, a year later, Pink Floyd would launch their Animals album by floating a giant pig over London's Battersea Power Station. But the idea was canceled when Sounds magazine got wind of it and leaked the news. Instead, models of The Object were eventually gifted to various favored journalists, DJs, and other media professionals, and are now highly collectible artifacts.

When Presence was released on March 31, 1976, it was another instant number-one hit, going gold in the UK (platinum in the US) on advance sales alone, and becoming the fastest-selling album in the Atlantic Records group's history. Reviews were generally good too. John Ingham, in Sounds, called it "unadulterated rock and roll" and described "Achilles Last Stand" as the song to "succeed 'Stairway to Heaven,'" while Stephen Davis in Rolling Stone said it confirmed Zeppelin as "heavy-metal champions of the known universe." He add the caveat: "Give an Englishman

50,000 watts, a chartered jet, a little cocaine, and some groupies and he thinks he's a god. It's getting to be an old story"—a more piercingly accurate comment than even the writer probably knew.

But sales soon tailed off, just as they had for Led Zeppelin III and Houses of the Holy, initial excitement failing to translate into wider general interest among non-partisan record buyers as what was perceived as the album's generally depressing ambience became known.

Undeterred, Page and Grant dismissed the lack of a strong following wind for sales of the album as a side effect of the band's inability to promote it with a world tour. But the fact is that Presence remains one of Zeppelin's least satisfying musical confections; the story behind it of more lasting interest than the often rather turgid music that resulted, despite the fact that both Page and Plant regarded it as a personal triumph.

"Against the odds, sitting in a f******chair, pushed everywhere for months and months, we were still able to look the devil in the eye and say: 'We're as strong as you and stronger, and we should not only write, we should record,'" Plant told a reporter from Creem. "I took a very good, close scrutiny of myself, and transcended the death vibe, and now I'm here again, and it's mad city again."

Page's affection for Presence was more to do with fond reminiscences of the nights he spent alone, with just recording engineer Keith Harwood for company, doodling away to his stoned heart's desire, than with the end product in itself.

Not that Zeppelin's overall popularity was particularly affected. Promoters, eager to tempt the band back onto the road, told Peter Grant that demand for Zeppelin tickets would be greater than ever—if and when the band decided they were able to return.

With time on their hands and interest in Presence flagging, plans were already in place for Led Zeppelin to make a full-on return to America the following year. When things would surely improve for the band. Wouldn't they? ❼

Bonham, Plant, Page, and Jones during the 1977 US tour.

In Through the Out Door

It would be great to say that their final studio album saw Led Zeppelin light the blue touchpaper in a fireworks factory. Sadly their sign off was more like a match burning out in an ashtray.

By: Geoff Barton

Sometimes nothing less than a good old-fashioned cliché will do. So here goes: with *In Through The Out Door,* their eighth and final studio album, Led Zeppelin went out with a whimper rather than a bang. Zeppelin didn't disintegrate spectacularly in an explosion of fire, Hindenburg-style. Instead, the superinflated rock monster, the titanic of the skies created by Messrs Page, Plant, Jones, and Bonham just quietly expired. Hiss. Pffft. Shhh. . .

Whichever way you look at it, when *In Through the Out Door* was released in August 1979 the musical climate was plain wrong. In the big wide world outside the closeted confines of Zep, disco, punk, and new wave held sway. The advent of Spandau Ballet, Visage, Gary Numan, Duran Duran, and the electronic movement that would initially be dubbed "futurist" was also just around the corner.

As well as the release of *In Through the Out Door*—a number-one album on both sides of the Atlantic, let us not forget—in 1979 Zeppelin would enjoy massive live success at Knebworth. In many ways they were still untouchable. But the world was changing. Had already changed. The Ringwraiths had tethered their demonic steeds. There was precious little magic in the air. Fairies, goblins, and gremlins were nowhere to be seen. Despite their perceived stature, Zeppelin weren't really kings of the world any more.

Within Zeppelin, trouble was brewing. Page's heroin addiction was becoming increasingly problematic and debilitating. When John Bonham wasn't chasing the dragon like Jimmy, he was chasing the vodka bottle. Robert Plant was still coming to terms with a tragic event in his personal life: the death of his five-year-old son, Karac, from a respiratory infection in summer 1977. Robert sought solace in flagons of the finest Black Country ale. It was down to the ever-stoic John Paul Jones to hold it all together.

After the best part of a year-and-a-half of confusion and uncertainty—which had all kicked off in July 1977 with the band's infamous security guard bust-up in Oakland, California—Led Zeppelin defied the rampant breakup rumors and reassembled in London in December 1978. It was a brief but surprisingly productive meeting. Almost immediately afterward they began work on the album that would become *In Through the Out Door*, in the

unusual location of Stockholm, Sweden—at Polar Studios, a pristine new complex owned by ABBA. It was high tech, and had lots of new electronic gizmos that the band was itching to try out. The temptation to twiddle was to prove part of *In Through the Out Door*'s downfall.

Sweden is bleak and forlorn in winter. As a result, Led Zeppelin didn't hang around and the album was recorded in quick-fire fashion. There was no wild partying, and a strict Monday-to-Friday working routine was established, with the band flying back home to Britain on the weekends. It took just three weeks.

John Paul Jones plainly felt it was his duty to rescue the project. You have to admire his dedication, but the appeal of *In Through the Out Door* is severely diminished by his simplistic synthesizer playing.

This problem wasn't so much in evidence on the original vinyl pressings, which were thick-sounding in the finest Zeppelin tradition. But listen to the CD version—amazingly digitally remastered by Page himself—and Jones' contributions are much more to the fore.

In the cold light of today what immediately strikes you about *In Through the Out Door* is the paucity of tracks: just seven, with a total running time of 42:37.

The album begins well enough with "In the Evening," and the atmosphere of a steaming Moroccan souk is accurately evoked—typically Zeppelin. The track has a fine hook, but overall it's too sloppy and scatological. There's an unusual moment about halfway through when everything collapses. Just as you feel as if the song could go on forever it simply fades away.

"South Bound Suarez" has a honky tonk feel, and Page, again, dashes off a few notes and leaves the building. Bonham is the same; his familiar steamhammer style is superseded by a sly shuffle. Plant's vocals are authoritative but somewhat gruffer and more rough-edged than

you might expect. *In Through the Out Door* had the first real signs that he was losing his distinctive high-pitched wail and moving toward the more measured vocal mannerisms evident on his 1982 solo album *Pictures at Eleven.* The Caribbean feel of "Fool in the Rain" (the US single) is initially reminiscent of "D'yer Mak'er" played backwards. For a moment, guitar and keyboards link up to follow the stumbling-but-progressive riff in tandem, and the results are charming.

"Carouselambra" is one long jam. Epic and keyboard-fueled, again it's too loosely structured. You wait and wait for it to develop into something massive, brooding and *Physical Graffiti*-like, but it never happens. Just when you think the song is about to reach a climax it reverts to being laid back and genteel.

By contrast, "All My Love" is plain beautiful. With Page notably absent from the songwriting credits, Plant offers a paean to his deceased son in a song steeped in fond remembrance. Plant is on top form as he whispers the emotion-charged line, "all of my love . . . to you now." A lavish psuedo-blues number, "I'm Gonna Crawl," closes the album, and Page wakes up belatedly with some guitar playing that stabs and draws blood.

The original vinyl was released in six different sleeves, but the results are not Hipgnosis' best. The photos are rather stiff and too obviously staged. It's nowhere near as iconic as, say, *Presence*, with its mysterious black obelisk.

The album was also encased in plain brown wrapping paper, so buyers didn't know which of the six sleeves they were getting. And if you sprinkled the sleeve with water, it changed color in the manner of a child's magic painting book.

The title *In Through the Out Door* is reminiscent of more innocent times, when one would wait for the start of the main feature at the local cinema and then sneak in through the exit to see the film for free. Looking at what happened to Zeppelin after its release, the exit theme is entirely appropriate.

> "The climate had changed. Disco, punk and new wave held sway. Eddie Van Halen was doing stuff with a guitar that had never been done..."

Days of Thunder

John Bonham's explosive drumming powered Led Zeppelin like the engine of a battleship. Bonzo was irreplaceable, and his death in September 1980 following a massive vodka binge also killed the band. Here, we remember the man whose playing sounded like an earthquake, but who always secretly yearned for a quieter kind of life.

By: CHRIS WELCH

Drummer John Bonham was the heartbeat of Led Zeppelin. When his great heart stopped, the life went out of the band. It was a tragedy for rock music as well as for friends and family when he died at the age of 31 on September 25, 1980. After several personal tragedies had rocked the band in the mid-seventies, it seemed as if Zeppelin was poised to make the ultimate resurgence. Instead, it all came to a dramatic end when John died in the throes of rehearsals for what would have been the band's biggest tour in years.

To understand why Bonham died so young, we must also understand the pressures of life with the greatest rock band in the world. Being in Led Zeppelin brought him great rewards, fame, and success, but it also undermined his personality and health.

It was a wonderful, life-changing day when the lad from the Midlands agreed to join Jimmy Page's new band in 1968. Down to earth, jovial, and generous, John Bonham was the last person many thought would succumb to the rock 'n' roll circus. A former builder and carpenter who taught himself to become a powerhouse drummer, he had to be convinced that The New Yardbirds, as Page's new band was originally known, would ever amount to much. He agreed to join only after a deluge of pleading telegrams from manager Peter Grant, originally telling his then employer Tim Rose, "No way [am I leaving]. Not only do I love this life, but the money's too good."

Yet Bonham didn't get to become the drummer in Led Zeppelin by being the shy and retiring type. He attacked his kit with gusto. But despite his image as a wild man of rock, his attempts to emulate the manic destructive intensity of his pal Keith Moon of The Who did not come naturally. He was hardworking and had a huge appetite for life. When he became hugely wealthy from the success of Led Zeppelin, he indulged in his passion for fast cars but also spent wisely, creating a happy home for him and his family at The Old Hyde in Worcestershire.

For John Bonham, there was no place like home. He hated flying and sitting around all day waiting for a gig. The endless Zeppelin tours he had to go on became a drain on his stamina and confidence. There was the adrenaline rush of playing explosive music every night to thousands of screaming fans, but after that came the need to unwind—usually in a succession of faceless hotels and bars. Life became a blur of rioting fans, speeding limos, booze, and groupies. It was fun at first, but powering up the Zeppelin machine soon became a daunting task.

John Henry Bonham was born in Redditch, Worcestershire, on May 31, 1948. His father Jack ran a building company and employed both of his sons, John and Michael. Aged five, John began to show interest in music. At home he began drumming on a bath salt container fitted with strands of wire on the bottom to make a crude snare drum. After adding pots and pans to his armory, when he was 10 his mother got him a real snare drum. Then his dad bought him a complete kit. As well as working for his dad as a builder, John drummed with local bands.

The Beatles era was dawning, but Bonham had a taste for jazz drummers like Gene Krupa, Joe Morello, and Sonny Payne; he loved their stick-twirling showmanship. He took drum lessons, but developed his own hard-hitting rock 'n' roll style.

"Drumming was the only thing I was any good at and so I stuck at it," he said later. "I always worked hard all the time. When I was 16 I went into full-time music, but I'd have to go back to the building sites to earn money to live. If there were no gigs, there was no money."

He began playing with his bare hands (a technique he would use on his showpiece Zep song "Moby Dick"). He also developed a fast bass-drum pedal technique inspired by Carmine Appice, with whom he would form a strong friendship, helping hook Appice and bassist Tim Bogert up with Jeff Beck in Beck, Bogert & Appice. "It was John who told Tim and I that Jeff Beck wanted to form a band with us," Appice recalls. "That was after he'd played with Jeff at the Singer Bowl and had taken all his clothes off while playing, which was really wild as my parents were backstage watching the gig. I had to explain to them why! What a night."

As he gained confidence, he would go up to a bandleader and say, "Your drummer's not much good, is he? Let me have a go. I'll show you." He would then take over the hapless drummer's kit, pound it completely to bits, and take the guy's job.

In 1965, at the age of 17, he married his girlfriend Pat Phillips. As money was tight, they lived in a caravan that was owned by John's father. Later they moved into a high-rise flat in Dudley (where they were actually still living when the first Led Zeppelin album was released).

He joined A Way Of Life, who recorded some demos in a Birmingham studio. The band also included Dave Pegg, who would later go on to play with Fairport Convention. Bonham played so loudly that he was told he was "unrecordable." He was also told there was no future in playing so loud. Some years later he sent the manager of that studio a Led Zeppelin gold disc with a note saying, "Thanks for your advice."

In 1965, he joined The Crawling King Snakes, where he met Robert Plant, who thought Bonham was a flash whiz kid. Despite much banter and rivalry, the two of them became firm friends. Bonham left the Snakes after a few months to rejoin A Way Of Life. Plant and Bonham were then reunited in the third and final lineup of Plant's group Band of Joy in January 1967, wearing the new hippy fashion for kaftan, beads and bells.

At one memorable gig at the Queen Mary Ballroom in Dudley, as the Band of Joy encored with Tim Hardin's "If I Were a Carpenter," Plant performed a blueprint of what would become his trademark libidinous performance of "Whole Lotta Love," wrapping his leg around the mic stand and simulating a sexual act. It proved too much for Bonham's mother Joan, who strode to the front of the venue demanding at the top of her voice: "John, you get off those drums now! You're not playing with that boy, he's a pervert!"

The drummer quit again in May 1968 to back visiting American singer Tim Rose on a UK tour, performing songs including "Morning Dew" and "Hey Joe" and earning fifty pounds a week. "The sad thing about it," says Tim today, "was that we never managed to record anything together. When John started with me his timing was a bit erratic. His 4/4 timing could vary between 3 and 3/4 and 4 and 1/4."

John Bonham: the greatest rock drummer of all time.

Jason Bonham filled in for his dad at Zeppelin's 2007 reunion.

FATHER FIGURE

Jerry Ewing talks to Jason Bonham about his illustrious dad.

You must be immensely proud that so many years after your father's death, he remains one of the most revered and successful rock musicians we've ever known.

It still feels like yesterday to me. But for me, the fans still talk about dad in the present, never the past. It's always, "When he does this," and never, "When he did that." And that I find that really endearing. Even now, with these Foreigner shows I'm playing and there's all these 20 to 25-year-old people wearing that Zeppelin '77 T-shirt that's become very popular these days. My kid goes to school over here in America and he's suddenly realized how cool granddad was.

The thing was the whole band. Dad's playing was a part of it, but he did have one hell of a canvas to work on. It was the space they all had to work with as well as being such a tight unit. It was legendary—put it on today and it still doesn't sound dated. Who would have thought that today Zep would still be as big, if not bigger than ever?

That really comes through watching Zeppelin's DVD.

Oh yes. I'd seen a few bootlegs and obviously the Knebworth show, but never with such great sound. What got me at the premiere was no matter what the drum solo, you could tell it was John Bonham. No matter what kit he was on. Even when he played my small kit at home it sounded like him.

What's your best memory of your dad?

It would have to be when I was a kid and doing the motocross stuff. And dad would drive me all the way to Machynlleth near Aberystwyth. He would get up at six in the morning to make egg sandwiches, so the whole house would stink of boiled eggs. And then we'd head off in his Land Rover. A red Land Rover with silver side pipes. I ask you, who ever had a red Land Rover? And I've really got back into listening to Fleetwood Mac's *Rumours* album, because that's what he would love listening to in the car. On eight- track. No, I think it was cassette by then. We had this lovely brand new Pioneer player in the car with a graphic equalizer in the glove compartment. That's my best memory of dad, not Bonzo the rock animal, but being a dad away from all that. And me moaning at him for smoking a cigarette and making me feel ill in the car!

One person decidedly more impressed was a youthful Phil Collins, who caught Bonham with Rose at London's Marquee. "Within the first few minutes I was dumbstruck by the drummer," he says. "He was doing things with his bass drum that I'd never seen or heard before. He then played a solo and again I'd never heard or seen a drummer play like that. He played with his hands on the drums—I later found out that as a bricklayer he had very hard hands, and it was obvious from seeing him solo that night. I vowed to keep an eye on this guy Bonham and I followed his progress. He was, even then, a major influence on my playing."

Meanwhile, down in London, Jimmy Page, John Paul Jones, and Peter Grant were putting a band together from the ashes of The Yardbirds. They persuaded Robert Plant to join, who in turn recommended Bonham for the gig. The drummer took some convincing, but within weeks he had joined Page, Jones, and Plant in the studio. He told astonished friends back in Birmingham that he had just earned £3,000.

The new band proved a magical team. John Paul Jones said, "The first time I ever met John was in a tiny basement room we had rented in Lyle Street. We just had loads of amps and speaker cabs there that had been begged, borrowed, or stolen. The first thing to strike me about Bonzo was his confidence, and you know he was a real cocky bugger in those days. Still, you have to be to play like that. It was great, instant concentration. He wasn't showing off, but was just aware of what he could do. He was rock solid."

At first Bonham's playing was too busy however, and he ignored warnings from Page to "keep it simple." Peter Grant strode over to Bonham and asked, "Do you like your job in this band?" The drummer nodded. "Well do as this man says. Behave yourself, or you'll disappear. Through different doors."

With Bonham on board, The New Yardbirds, as they were still called, played their first gig in Copenhagen on September 14, 1968. The way in which Bonham had galvanized the band on those early gigs had a lasting influence throughout the recording career of Led Zeppelin (as they had now become). His dynamic playing perfectly suited such arrangements as "Communication Breakdown," "Stairway to Heaven," "Kashmir," "Achilles Last Stand," and "Trampled Under Foot," while his thunderous backbeat on "When the Levee Breaks" influenced a new generation of drummers.

Meanwhile, the flow of hit albums and sold-out concerts for Zeppelin meant that his world changed virtually overnight. The once poverty-stricken Bonhams could afford flash cars, a big house, and a champagne lifestyle. But he still had to work for a living. Out on the road, the 21-year-old Bonzo delivered a 20-minute, blood-spattered drum solo every night. And being the powerhouse of the energy sapping Led Zeppelin show left him on the verge of collapse. He hated flying, which made him physically sick.

Holed up in hotels, the only way for a traveling musician to immunize himself against the routine was to take a drink or two, and perhaps experiment with drugs. Right from his teenage years, Bonham had enjoyed a beer. But he got boisterous after a few pints, which led to his reputation for mayhem. His pranks soon rivaled those of Keith Moon for outrage and destruction. Anyone getting too close found their clothes ripped and sprayed with lager.

Back home, Bonham returned to normality, and raised son Jason and daughter Zoë. He busied himself with running his farm and breeding Hereford cattle in the calm peacefulness of the Worcestershire countryside. The real John Bonham preferred the bricklaying and decorating he'd learned from working with his father to carousing in California. Yet, he also harbored a love of danger—epitomized by driving his drag-racing car at 240mph in Zeppelin's movie *The Song Remains the Same* and his evident pride at son Jason's performances for the Kawasaki Schoolboy motocross team.

Despite all the bravado, he confided to friends that he suffered from panic attacks before every concert. "I've got worse," he said in 1975. "I have terribly bad nerves all the time. Once we start into *"Rock and Roll,"* I'm fine. It's worse at festivals. You might have to sit around for a whole day, and you daren't drink because you'll get tired and blow the gig. So you sit drinking tea in a caravan with everybody saying: 'Far out, man.'"

After earning a fortune, Zeppelin became tax exiles, which meant living abroad. Then came a series of mishaps that dogged the group and undermined the drummer's confidence still further. Bonham's boisterous good humor began to give way to dark brooding and fits of anger.

Surrounded by hired security, he may have felt invulnerable. But he overstepped the mark when he joined Peter Grant, tour manager Richard Cole, and crew member John Bindon in a vicious assault on an American security guard at the fateful concert at Oakland Coliseum, California, in July 1977. Afterwards Bonham, Grant, and the two Zeppelin henchmen were arrested.

Despite his sometimes gruff demeanor, John Bonham was shy and would get nervous before Led Zep gigs.

The real John Bonham preferred the bricklaying and decorating he learned from working with his father to carousing in California.

Later, it led to fines and suspended sentences—and to Led Zeppelin never returning to America after this tour.

It was all turning sour. Then came the death of Robert Plant's son back in England. Suddenly it seemed like the group was close to breaking up. Bonham was left with more time on his hands, and his behavior became unpredictable. Said his friend, drummer Bev Bevan of ELO, "He was an extrovert, a friendly, huggable bloke. But unfortunately the drink just got too much for him. He overdid it and could become quite aggressive. He was similar to Keith Moon. They felt they had to live up to their reputations."

When Led Zeppelin played Knebworth in 1979, Bonham played well enough on the two landmark UK shows. But while on a German tour, he began to exhibit signs of fatigue. At a show in Nuremberg, after three numbers he got sick. He then appeared unwell for the rest of the tour.

In September 1980, rehearsals for the scheduled North American tour were about to start at Jimmy Page's home in Windsor. On the way there in a car with Robert Plant on the morning of the 24th, John suddenly said, "I've had it with playing drums. Everybody plays better than me. I'll tell you what, when we get to the rehearsal, you play the drums and I'll sing."

That day at Page's house, John started drinking at lunchtime and carried on until midnight. He allegedly got through 40 shots of vodka during a marathon 12-hour session. After falling asleep on a sofa, he was put to bed by his assistant and laid on pillows for support.

The following morning, there was no sign of him anywhere. John Paul Jones and road manager Benje LeFevre found him apparently unconscious. They tried to wake him, but then realized he was dead. Everyone was saddened, and even angry, at the waste of life. Peter Grant went into a depression that lasted several years.

Rumors suggested Bonzo had been taking drugs, but it was drink that had caused his death. Said John Paul Jones, "It was just at the point where we had all come back together again. We had high hopes it was all coming right. Bonzo had been getting a bit erratic and he wasn't in good shape. There were some good moments, but then he started on the vodka. I think he had been drinking because

there were some problems in his personal life. But he died because of an accident. He was lying down the wrong way."

John's death left the Bonham family devastated. "It didn't take long to work out when I arrived, because security guards stood at either side of the gate and Robert Plant was waiting for me," revealed John's younger brother, the late Michael Bonham, of how the news was broken to him. "He told me to leave my car and walk up the drive with him. As he did so, he gently broke the news to me that John had died some time during the previous night. I don't know enough words to describe the impact his words had on me in that split second. But as I sat with my family the only thing I knew was that the brother I loved so much, my lifelong hero, was gone."

It was revealed at the inquest that he died from inhalation of vomit during his sleep, "due to consumption of alcohol." The verdict was accidental death.

The funeral took place at Rushock Parish Church in Worcestershire on October 10, 1980, attended by mourners including family, friends, and his bandmates. Tributes poured in from stars such as Paul McCartney, Phil Collins, Cozy Powell, and Carl Palmer.

Said Bev Bevan, "The funeral was the most traumatic I had ever been to, because he was so young and had so much in front of him. His family were utterly distraught. Who knows what more he would have done as a drummer?"

Led Zeppelin could have carried on with another drummer, as The Who had done after the death of Keith Moon, but realistically no one could replace him. Led Zeppelin had officially broken up. Other drummers, including Phil Collins and Jason Bonham, have played on Zeppelin "reunions" since. None could hope to match the power, magic, and presence of the much-loved man who once told Robert Plant he was the greatest drummer in the world.

"He was definitely the greatest rock 'n' roll drummer that ever lived," Jimmy Page once said. "And that's all there is to it, really." ❼

• Additional information from *Late Nights, Hard Fights: My Brother John* by Michael Bonham and Jerry Ewing.

Peter Grant—
In His Own Words

In 1990, Paul Henderson sat down with late Led Zeppelin manager Peter Grant
for a conversation that looked back over the band's career.

By: Paul Henderson

Copenhagen, Denmark, September 1968. A former Yardbirds guitarist, an in-demand session bass player, a jobbing drummer, and a big-in-the-Midlands vocalist begin a 10-date Scandinavian tour. Billed as The New Yardbirds for contractual reasons, these are the band's first gigs after getting together only three weeks previously.

With them on the trip is their manager, a large, bearded, imposing man with an unconventional sense of style; ex-coffee bar and club doorman, ex-wrestler, bit-part actor (doubling for Anthony Quinn in *The Guns of Navarone*, and some small parts in TV programs), and former manager of sixties chart-toppers the Animals, Jeff Beck, and others.

On returning to England, the band go into a London recording studio and polish off their entire debut album in just 30 hours at a cost of £1,800 including the cover (seven years later the record would have grossed more than £3 million), and change their name.

The band became the biggest rock band of all time and legendary; the manager became the most effective manager in the history of rock music and something of a legend himself. The manager was Peter Grant. The band was Led Zeppelin.

Cut to London, summer 1990. Outside a plush Chelsea hotel, the sun shines down on a vista of elegant, white new buildings that look for all the world like the South of France. Several floors up, in one of the hotel's suites overlooking the marina in which a handful of expensive cruisers bob gently, a semi-"retired," trimmed down, suited, and still-bearded Peter Grant sits back in a chair, draws heavily on a cigarette, and smiles as he casts his mind back to the birth of a rock 'n' roll legend of which he was very much—if largely unseen and often unsung—a major component.

What thoughts about the band went through your head when you watched the New Yardbirds, as they were then billed, playing those first shows in Scandinavia in 1968?
Oh, I remember everything about that first show in Copenhagen. I remember everything Jimmy Page had told me about the drummer, Bonzo. And the whole performance. It was so . . . exciting! Just to be part of it was fantastic. There

was never a thought of, God, this is going to sell X amount of records.

I thought it could be the best band ever. Remember that I'd been to America a lot of times, with the Animals, the Yardbirds, and different other bands. And I just knew that Jimmy would come through. I knew it would be the best.

I remember the first time we played the Fillmore East, in '69, for three nights, with Iron Butterfly, who were a big, big, band in America at the time. When you're a new band you have to go on first. But I said to Bill Graham, the promoter, who I'd known for years, "Bill, you've got to put Zeppelin on second for me." Which he did, with Delaney and Bonnie as the opening act. When Iron Butterfly's management found out, they wanted Zeppelin off. They didn't want them near them.

> ## "I thought [Led Zeppelin] could be the best band ever . . . I just knew that Jimmy would come through. I knew it would be the best."

And they were right. Zeppelin did a fantastic set. The audience was still going: "Zeppelin! Zeppelin! Zeppelin!" when Iron Butterfly had started their set. Good band, not a bad band, but no match for Zeppelin. But then nobody ever was.

Jimmy Page has said that the first time he knew Zeppelin had really broken through was when they played San Francisco on that first '69 tour. Page said: "There were other gigs . . . where the response was so incredible that we knew we'd made our impression. But after the San Francisco gig it was just—bang!"
Yeah. That was the first night he played the Les Paul guitar onstage. He was playing a Fender before that, the one that Eric Clapton had given him. He'd had it for years, from being with the Yardbirds. There was something the matter with the pickups, and I remember every night Jimmy was there with the soldering iron, soldering the guitar.

Can you remember a time when you first thought: "This is really it"?
The first big gig they ever did, at Boston Gardens, to 20,000 people. It's a sweat-box, that place. And they absolutely pulverized them. I mean, they had it musically, and their performance was like . . . People in the audience used to tell me it was like a "force." It was in their heads for three or four days. And I thought, "There's no holding them, now. There's no holding back."

Rumor has always had it that you returned from a trip to America with a worldwide deal with Atlantic that included an advance of $200,000—the highest fee ever paid to a new group. Is that rumor actually true?
Yes. And I mean, that was a big deal with Atlantic in those days—$210,000 for a band for three years was a hell of a lot of money.

Is it also true that Atlantic hadn't even seen the band when the deal was done?
That's right. But Atlantic believed in Jimmy Page as a musician—believed in his craft, in John Paul Jones, in Robert Plant, who was the third one to come in, and in John Bonham. Atlantic knew. And I suppose my enthusiasm rubbed off on [Atlantic executives] Ahmet Ertegun and Jerry Wexler. They were a fantastic label. I suppose they still are.

Was that the best deal you ever made for Zeppelin?
The best deal I made—not in terms of money, because I never did anything for money, and which I sensed in 1968 nearly stopped Atlantic signing the band—was "No soundtracks." Atlantic couldn't have the rights to any Zeppelin film soundtracks. So when it came to *The Song Remains the Same* . . . Atlantic said to me, "Oh, that's great. It's a live album." I said, "No it's not, it's a soundtrack album." And they said, "Well, it's still ours." I said, "No. If you go back to page 38 or 39, from 1968, you'll find it's not in there." I think that was pretty good. Plus, we made the film.

We had a lot of offers from people all wanting to make films of Led Zeppelin—just a concert film, which of course *The Song Remains the Same* wasn't. And when we were talking about doing it, I said, "Well let's do it, but let's put our own wedge up, let's put our own money ⏵

Peter Grant in his office, 1970.

Peter Grant was known as being one of the most ruthless managers in rock history.

Peter Grant, Robert Plant, and John Paul Jones at Knebworth House, Hertfordshire, England in August 1979.

up." Which we did, so we weren't beholding to anybody. But if it had been a pile of crap it would have been the most expensive home movie of all time."

You established an unprecedented amount of independence for Zeppelin by setting up production and publishing companies that gave the band extensive control over their creative career. By doing that you started something of a music business revolution. Promoters in particular weren't happy when they suddenly found themselves being offered the short end of a 90 percent, take-it-or-leave-it deal for Zeppelin.
I did that on them, yes . . . The thing was, there were so many of them that were cheating bands. There were a lot of good promoters, I mean some fine promoters: Mel Bush comes to mind straight away. Bill Graham. I mean, I don't get on with Bill Graham. We fell out in '77 [when Grant, John Bonham, and a bodyguard infamously hospitalized one of Graham's security men], but he's a fine promoter. You can't take that away from him. Those people don't cheat you.

Were you hated by the promoters for starting this "revolution"?
By the agents. Because when I went straight to the promoter I found a way of saving the bands 10 percent. Oh yeah, I'm well aware that I'm not exactly liked. But that doesn't matter. I don't care if they hate me. What you've got to do is what's right for your artist. Always remember, it's the band and the manager versus the rest.

What do you think was your greatest strength as a manager?
Being able to say no. That's very important.

I'll give you an example. Some American people wanted us to do a TV satellite broadcast on New Year's Eve, 1970. They wanted Led Zeppelin to do a concert in West Germany, and it was going to go over to America . . . into cinemas. They said, "We'll give you half a million dollars." I said, "Oh, I dunno. . ." you know. Anyway, it eventually came to a million dollars.

But I found out that satellite sound can be affected by snowstorms . . . so I thought, well that's no good. What do I want to blow that for the band for? It's their arses that are on the line . . . So I said no.

They thought I was crazy. A million dollars was a hell of a lot of money in 1970—it's a hell of a lot of money any time. I mean, it's more money than I'd ever heard of in my life.

Was it because of poor sound quality in those days that Zeppelin also never did much TV?
Oh yeah. They did a pilot program for the BBC once. I was up in the control box. Oh, it was dreadful. And I thought, no, never.

And them not turning up for [seventies and eighties UK music TV program] *The Old Grey Whistle Test*. When I saw that queue in Wardour Street [outside London's Marquee club], that convinced me. I thought, that's it—no singles, no television . . . Because, if the people believe in the band, they're gonna come. And that was proved at Knebworth [1979]—210,000 people for the first week, with no other bands advertised.

Did you ever have problems with bootleggers at the big festivals, such as Knebworth, and the famous Bath appearance in 1970?
Somebody tried to bootleg [audio] the Bath festival. That's when I threw the water in the machines and all that. I caught them under the stage. Freddie Bannister was the promoter, and I couldn't find him, so I thought, f*** it, and went and did it myself. I kicked the s*** out of them and all the equipment. You know they have

"I don't care if they hate me . . . Always remember, it's the band and the manager versus the rest."

buckets of sand and water and all that, and an axe? I pulled the axe off the wall and steamed in and chopped it all up. Did a machete job on the machinery. I didn't get heavies to do it, I did it myself. Then at least I knew it was done.

I had a hell of a battle at the Bath festival. I'd researched where the stage would be and when the sun would set behind it, and Zeppelin had to go on dead on eight o'clock. It was running late, and other people wanted to go on, but I said, "No, Zeppelin are going on at eight o'clock, and that's it."

What happened was that they went on in daylight, so you get that "broad" view, then as the sun set and it got darker we could bring the lights up so that it was the focal point.

I'm not sure that Robert's idea worked, though—throwing the tambourines out to the audience. They were bouncing on Hells Angels' heads! But they were alright, because I'd made mates with them.

With the benefit of hindsight, are there any things you would have done very differently?
No, I don't think so.

What about setting up Zeppelin's own record company, Swan Song? Was that . . .
. . . A mistake? No it wasn't . . . The idea was to get even better artistic control, and give them the creative space. I regret setting up Swan Song, because there wasn't the time. It was Led Zeppelin, then Bad Company came along . . . You can't do it.

I mean, that's half of the reason I passed on Queen. They came to see me to manage them—I guess this would be the end of '74 or early '75—and we had a couple of meetings. And I said to them, "Fellas, I would love to do it, but I haven't got that many hours in the day." I loved the band, but I knew somebody would have to suffer, and it's not fair. I never wanted to be an empire builder.

Could your style of management be called "aggressive"?
I would say so. Call it what you like—as long as it works. If somebody had to be trod on, they got trod on. Too true.

Were Led Zeppelin easy to work with?
Easy? I wouldn't have said easy. But something that successful is never easy. The hardest thing was always making sure the tours didn't clash with the children's holidays. Yes, really. That was hard, because more or less everybody had families.

They were never difficult. I sat down with them

Peter Grant, John Paul Jones, and Jimmy Page leaving the House of Lewis.

in October '68 and said, "Listen, you can start on Boxing Day for 10 or 12 dates in America with Vanilla Fudge, which means you've got to go on Christmas Eve." And I was s****** myself having to tell them, "And incidentally, fellas, I'm not going." It was one of the few times I never went. And I regretted it so much I thought, I'm never going to not go with them again. And they did it.

If you laid it out, explained the reason why, they were never difficult.

And they never missed shows. Of all that "excess" that's been written about—and I emphasize written about, they never missed a concert. They weren't goody-goodies by any means, but they were always there.

Talking of "alleged" excess, what was life like aboard the "Starship" that Zeppelin used to travel between gigs in the US?
Wonderful! Before that we had a nine-seater Falcon jet, which was a tremendous plane. We used to fly to every gig, into the limo, police escort, do the gig, do the encore, and then—no changing, bang!—to the plane. I mean, it's wonderful isn't it, having your own plane?

But they had to sit opposite each other all the time. And of course, there were rows, but they never lasted more than two or three hours a night. Somebody might get chinned by one of the others, having punch-ups between themselves. I mean, Bonzo and Robert were famous for that.

The first time in Japan, in 1970, Robert went on with a split lip for the encore every time. And this was an argument over something they did in the [pre-Zeppelin band] Band of Joy—Robert wouldn't pay Bonzo £37 for petrol or something.

The thing is, in all seriousness, on that small plane you were too in that "cocoon." And then the "Starship" came along. Which was only $14,000 more, because they [Boeing] wanted the publicity and that kind of thing. And we ▷

thought, well why not? We'll have a 720.

And I do get lucky. The first day, in Chicago, they'd parked it next to Hugh Hefner's plane, hadn't they? And all the press were there, and somebody said to me, "Well how do you think it compares to Mr Hefner's plane?" I said, "It makes his look like a Dinky toy." Boomph—press everywhere. Headlines everywhere.

I mean, it's pretty good: here's a rock 'n' roll band from England flying around with a plane that they said was better than Air Force 1. . .What do they take—130 people? We had 35 people in it.

There was a wonderful Hammond C3 organ built into the bar and all that—Jonesy playing it. We used to do the hokey-cokey coming off the plant and all that! Terrific!

It was during the "Starship" days, of course, that the now legendary allegations of "excess" in the Zeppelin camp got on a real roll.

We're hardly gonna wreck our own plane, are we? And despite what you might have read, there were no passengers with Led Zeppelin. No passengers at all. No entourage. Everybody had a function.

I mean, sure, there were birds. What am I gonna say, that there were no birds around? There were birds around, of course . . . Some of the stories [of excess] were blown up. But, as Bonzo said in the *Observer*: "You can't come off stage and go back to your hotel and have a cup of hot chocolate and watch telly."

Presumably, then, most of the stories of excess were at least based on elements of truth?

Yes, of course. [His grin broadens into a wide smile] The excess was fantastic!

What events from the Zeppelin history stand out in your memory?

I'm quite fond of all of the things, which is why it's quite hard to single any things out. I think

getting the Ivor Novello Award in '75 or '76 was a big thing. Oh, that was terrific. That was for "contribution to British music," which wasn't like all those disc awards. That's the one thing that I have on my mantelpiece at home. That really meant something.

Did you ever discuss musical direction with Zeppelin and have any input on that side of things?

No. It was totally up to them. I don't know anything about music. I know what hits me here [bangs a fist against his chest]. No, it was totally their creation.

They'd go off to recordings and all that. I'd get a call from Bonzo: "Oh, you've got to come down. We ain't half done something today." I remember particularly "Kashmir": "Come down! Come down! Get down here. Get in the Porsche and get down here," sort of thing. And I'd get down and hear it.

I didn't spend much time in the recording studios. None of that: "Well, I don't think you should do that, lads," . . . While you're sitting there ligging and being groovy in the control box you could really be putting your mind to thinking about other things.

How do you see each of them in terms of individual personality?

Jimmy Page is absolutely the master craftsman. And probably a nicer person you couldn't wish to meet. He can also be very trying—or rather very stubborn.

Robert was a tremendous showman, and well suited to his star sign, Leo—I'll leave you to read the rest of it.

John Paul Jones is probably the understatement of all time, because he is a phenomenal craftsman and musician. Never mind his bass playing and his keyboards, look at the strings he arranged—"Kashmir" and things like that.

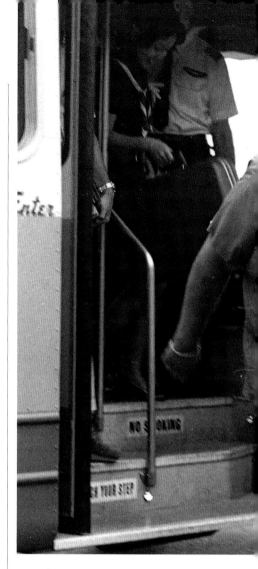

As far as Bonzo's concerned, he's probably the best mate I've ever had in my life. And as a drummer—unbelievable drummer. And all that's been said about him . . . Yeah, I've seen him wreck hotels—I helped him. But he was always there. He was always there for the band, he was always there for his family. And I really admired that.

Where were you when you heard the news that John Bonham had died [on September 25, 1980]?

I was at home in Sussex when I heard. Ray Washburn, who worked for me, came up to me and said, "Come downstairs." He sat me down, handed me some Valium, and said, "Take these." I said, "Why do I want to take them?" And he said . . . "John Bonham's died . . ."

I was shattered . . . Somebody said to me that I mourned too long for John Bonham. There's no such thing as too long.

After John's death, did you ever feel that Zeppelin might have continued, with a new drummer?

No! It's as clean cut as that. There was no question of it. Never any thought. The group went off to Jersey and they made their mind up. We met in the Savoy Hotel and I said, "It can't be."

It could never be the same. It was those four people—they were Led Zeppelin. The music and the mind—singular—of Led Zeppelin was those four people. When those four guys were on stage . . . total magic.

John Bonham and Peter Grant, February 1970, Copenhagen.

Peter Grant and Jimmy Page getting off a bus in Honolulu, 1970.

four years. I couldn't have done it.

I've spent the last six years in regaining my health. I used to be [400 pounds] and I've lost [140 pounds]. I'm probably fitter and healthier now than I have been since the early seventies.

The main thing I'm doing now is a film with Malcolm McLaren which has been in the air for five or six years.

It's based on my life story and all the things I've done, going right back to when I first started, when Mickey Most and I worked in the 2 Is coffee bar [London rock 'n' rollers' hangout in the sixties] and the first important thing I did, which was when I went off to America to meet Chuck Berry and making a deal for him to come to England.

Presumably there might be a few things you'd prefer to leave out?
Yes, there may well be a few bits I might leave out!

And a few bits added?
Who knows? But they tell me it doesn't need spicing up. Barrie Keefe, who wrote *The Long Good Friday*, is going to write the script, and it's going to be shot in England, and maybe some of it in Los Angeles, starting in spring next year. The idea is that it will be released Christmas 1991. [The film never got made.]

Do you expect it to include any footage of Led Zeppelin?
No, there won't be any footage of Zeppelin in it. But there'll be some Zeppelin in the soundtrack. Malcolm's idea is to use twelve songs that meant something . . . to me. And I've got a lot to draw from.

How would you sum up Peter Grant?
I'd like to think that what ever I get involved in, I really give my best for it. That's what I input —the best I can do for those people, regardless of the way I have to go about it.

I'm very proud of Zeppelin, I'm very proud of

You're obviously aware of the constant rumors of Led Zeppelin regrouping, with John Bonham's son, Jason, tipped to occupy the drum stool. Can you see it happening?
It could well happen. But I'll tell you something. For me, it would never be like it was. Zeppelin was those four guys. That was Led Zeppelin. Yes, I do think it would be a mistake. And it would be going back on everything that everybody said when we lost John—"Never again."

Prior to Zeppelin ceasing to exist at the point of John's death, was there any time when a split really looked on the cards?
In 1974. They were recording at Headley Grange, and John Paul Jones turned up unexpectedly and said he'd decided to leave the band. I said, "What are you gonna do, John, if you leave the band?" Because if he'd wanted to leave the band he would have left the band. You can't stop people doing what they really want to do.

He said, "I'm going to be the choirmaster at Winchester Cathedral. I'm fed up with all the touring." He was just generally . . . "peeved"—I think that was his word—with things. I said, "Have you told anyone else?" And he said, "No, I came straight to you." I said, "Well, you're gonna be 'not too well.' Take some time off and think about it."

That's how Bad Company got to record their first album at Headley Grange. It was all so fresh and all that. Boomph! In there and recorded it.

Eventually I think he just decided he was doing something he really loved. Maybe he just was missing home. Anyway, it was never really discussed again. I don't even think the other members of the band knew.

That was the nearest they came to splitting. And there was of course the time after Robert

went through unbelievable . . . I mean, how he ever handled that, when his son died. At that time I think he wanted to walk away from everything. And I really understood that.

What brought about the end of the your involvement with Led Zeppelin?
Well, the band was no longer, and there was no way I could manage three different people. I started doing a few things with Robert—I made the deal for him, in '81/'82, for his existing solo recording career.

But it couldn't go on. And, to be honest with you, I wasn't in any shape health-wise to do it. Really, from after we lost John and for various reasons, I had a period of blackness for three or

all the artists I've been involved with, and I'm proud of myself—especially for my dear old mum. I mean, I was born illegitimate, and in the late thirties that must have been horrendous.

I never knew my father. I'm proud for my mum and for my own children that I've done what I did. Very proud.

And how would you sum up Led Zeppelin?
I'd say the greatest band of all time, and there'll never be another one like them. And I'm very happy to have been associated with them.

Do you think they would have been as successful if they'd had a different manager?
That's an impossible thing to answer. I hope not. ❼

"[After Bonham's death] I was shattered . . . Somebody said I mourned too long for John Bonham. There's no such thing as too long."

MOTHER

The inside story of Led Zeppelin—as told by their friends and contemporaries.

Led Zeppelin is known as one of the greatest rock bands of all time, and many things have been written about them. However, it's time to let the stars themselves tell us what Zeppelin and their music meant to them—whether they caught them on tour, lived vicariously through their albums, or came to know them in latter years.

CAST OF CHARACTERS (in alphabetical order)

Ian Anderson – vocalist, Jethro Tull

Michael Anthony – bassist, Van Halen

Carmine Appice – drummer, Vanilla Fudge

Paul Barrere – guitarist/vocalist, Little Feat

Rodney Bingenheimer – Hollywood personality/DJ

Ritchie Blackmore – former Deep Purple/Rainbow guitarist

Joe Bonamassa – guitarist/vocalist

James Dean Bradfield – guitarist/vocalist, Manic Street Preachers

Don Brewer – drummer, Grand Funk Railroad

James Burton – guitarist, Elvis

Richard Cole – former Led Zeppelin tour manager

Jaz Coleman – vocalist, Killing Joke

Phil Collen – guitarist, Def Leppard

Alice Cooper – frontman extraordinaire

Michael Corby – keyboard player, The Babys

Cherie Currie – vocalist, The Runaways

Roger Daltrey – vocalist, The Who

Elliot Easton – guitarist, The Cars

Duane Eddy – guitarist

Rik Emmett – guitarist, Triumph

Ace Frehley – former Kiss guitarist

Jay Jay French – guitarist, Twisted Sister

Billy Gibbons – guitarist/vocalist, ZZ Top

Danny Goldberg – PR for Led Zeppelin 1973-76

Tom Hamilton – bassist, Aerosmith

Roy Harper – singer-songwriter

Taylor Hawkins – drummer, Foo Fighters

Glenn Hughes – former Deep Purple/Trapeze vocalist

Tony Iommi – guitarist, Black Sabbath

John 5 – former Marilyn Manson guitarist

Andy Johns – engineer on *Led Zeppelin IV*

Kelly Jones – guitarist/vocalist, Stereophonics

Mick Jones – guitarist, Foreigner

Phill Jupitus – DJ

Simon Kirke – drummer, Free/Bad Company

Eddie Kramer – engineer on five Led Zeppelin albums

Joey Kramer – drummer, Aerosmith

Jim Lea – former Slade bassist

Ric Lee – drummer, Ten Years After

Steve Lukather – guitarist, Toto

Luke Morley – guitarist, Thunder

Dave Mustaine – guitarist/vocalist, Megadeth

Ron Nevison – engineer on *Physical Graffiti*

Jimmy Page – guitarist, Led Zeppelin

Carl Palmer – drummer, ELP

Les Paul - guitarist

Joe Perry – guitarist, Aerosmith

Steve Perry – former Journey vocalist

Ricky Phillips – bassist, Styx

Robert Plant – vocalist, Led Zeppelin

Don Powell – drummer, Slade

Marky Ramone – drummer, Ramones

Kid Rock - singer

Gary Rossington – guitarist, Lynyrd Skynyrd

Claudio Sanchez – guitarist/vocalist, Coheed and Cambria

Joe Satriani – guitarist

Neal Schon – guitarist, Journey

Slash – guitarist, Velvet Revolver

Stephen Stills – singer-songwriter

Mark Tremonti – guitarist, Alter Bridge

Steven Tyler – vocalist, Aerosmith

Leslie West – guitarist/singer, Mountain

Brad Whitford – guitarist, Aerosmith

Ann Wilson – vocalist, Heart

Nancy Wilson – guitarist, Heart

James Young – guitarist/vocalist, Styx

Led Zeppelin factoid
Led Zep IV has sold 23 million copies in the US alone, making it the best-selling UK studio album in America

LODE

ROBERT PLANT
Golden God, golden tonsils.

ROGER DALTREY:
"Robert's got one of the best voices of any rock singer. The quality of his voice made him special. He's a singer's singer."

PAUL RODGERS:
"Robert interpreted the blues very very accurately and took it to another level. He took it out of the smaller blues clubs and into the arenas, which is a beautiful thing to do. I think even the blues people appreciated that. He was your ultimate front man and probably still is."

ANN WILSON:
"Vocally, Robert Plant influenced me as a sexy, philosophically powerful blues singer."

CARMINE APPICE:
"Robert's range was amazing. And just the way he uses his voice as an instrument. Sometimes he didn't even sing lyrics, he sang something and it became a hook of a song."

STEPHEN STILLS:
"There's just one of him. No one else sings like that. It fits with the Zep. It's really hard to carry on like that, just stand there with nothing to play. I don't see how it's done actually. . ."

EDDIE KRAMER:
"Look at all of the attributes of Robert Plant—the swagger, his wavy blonde hair, his physical presence—he was the proto-typical rock god lead singer. It was very nice for a lead singer to have the ability to make women swoon."

By: Ken Sharp, Steven Rosen, Siân Llewellyn, Geoff Barton, Paul Elliott, Philip Wilding, Jerry Ewing

THEIR TIME IS GONNA COME

The story of the good times and bad times of Led Zeppelin—as seen through the eyes of rock's biggest stars.

Led Zeppelin performing in 1972.

In early 1968 there were two session musicians doing the rounds in London—one was Yardbirds guitarist Jimmy Page, and the other a bass player named John Paul Jones. At the same time, a singer named Robert Plant and a drummer called John Bonham were playing in a pub band called Band of Joy. Ultimately, the quartet would hook up and create a popular beat combo called Led Zeppelin.

PAUL RODGERS The first time I heard about Jimmy Page was just around the time that Free had first gotten together. There was a big blues boom going on at that time. I met Robert [Plant] up in Birmingham. Free were touring with Alexis Korner and Robert got up to jam. He came back to the hotel for a cup of tea and a sandwich and we had a chat. He told me that he'd met this guy named Jimmy Page and they wanted to put a band together. Robert asked me if I had heard of Jimmy Page and I said yes, that he was a hot session musician down in London that everyone was talking about. Robert added that he had been offered a gig with him and they've suggested 30 quid a week or a percentage. I said, "Take the percentage." Years later when I told this to Peter Grant—who by this time was also my manager—he looked down his nose at me, breathing heavily and said, "Oh, so that was you, was it?"

DON POWELL In the mid-sixties we used to play the same places as Robert Plant and John Bonham. They were playing in bar bands [The Band of Joy]. Robert came to one of our gigs and said he'd been offered this job in The Yardbirds by Jimmy Page. And he said, "I'm not too keen on the music but it means I'll get a chance to go to America and see the States." So that's why he took the job. And the next thing we see is Led Zeppelin and Robert's the lead singer.

STEVE PERRY There's a story that circulated that when Led Zeppelin came to San Francisco to do some trial gigs before they had made their first record, they came to the Fillmore to play. Big Brother & The Holding Company were opening and Robert Plant watched Janis Joplin sing. And if you listen to Robert Plant closely you'll hear Janis. I love Robert Plant's voice. Robert was one of the first vocalists who had the idea of absolute power and just laying it down [imitates Plant's voice]. That whole thing he did was just primal.

EDDIE KRAMER I remember John Paul Jones played me the first Led Zeppelin record in 1968 just before they left for America and I

said, "Jesus, what is this? It's pretty heavy." And I asked him, "Well, what's the name of the band?" And he said, "Led Zeppelin," and I laughed and said, "That's a terrible bloody name." But boy was I ever wrong.

LESLIE WEST The first time I heard *Led Zeppelin I*, I had just gotten busted the night before and I had to go to court. I was living in Forest Hills. I put on the record and listened to it and I said, "Wow!" I didn't even know who those guys were. I knew who Jimmy Page was, but I didn't know who the band were. Mountain hadn't formed yet and I had just finished my first solo album. And I listened and said, "Oh boy, I'm in big trouble if that's who we got to compete with!" I was really impressed with the sound of the band—I said I'd love to sound like that.

To this day you put that first Led Zeppelin album on and it puts most other stuff to shame. It sounded more than a three-piece band. First of all, John Bonham played so big, it sounded like four drummers. And Jimmy Page was a great session player. And all of a sudden now he was playing with a group. I thought everybody had a unique sound in the group. Jimmy Page had a unique sound. He wasn't like Clapton, but the songs were really knockout songs, just great songs. Led Zeppelin had everything.

STEVE LUKATHER The sound of Jimmy's guitar and the band was like nothing like I've ever heard before. It's also memorable to me because the first time I had a sexual experience with a girl I was listening to *Led Zeppelin I*. Not only musically was it a great record, but there's such sexual energy to that album. The blues is very sexual. And Zeppelin was so intense. I played that album 'til I wore it out. I'd lift up the record needle over and over again to try and figure out Jimmy's solos. Amazing stuff.

PAUL BARRÈRE It was recorded in about 36 hours, so I believe. But the strangest thing is that is that . . . it still

The Pop Proms program.

sounds amazing. Recording has come on so far during that time, and music sounds cleaner and cleaner, but one thing that technology can't replicate is feel. Led Zeppelin sounded monstrous for the time—the drums and guitar in particular—it still does.

CARMINE APPICE The first time I heard Zeppelin was when our attorney gave us the Zeppelin album 'cause they wanted us [Vanilla Fudge] to take them on tour with us as our opening act. And I was just blown away. I mean, I said "Wow!" Being a drummer, my attention went to John Bonham and his foot thing that he did on "Good Times Bad Times," which was at the time totally unique. Upon meeting him he said to me, "I got that from you." I said, "I don't do that." And he pointed out on the Vanilla Fudge album where I actually did it one time. He said, "You did it on 'Ticket to Ride.'" He told me exactly where it was. I said "You're kidding me?" So, when he said he got it from me I didn't believe him until I went back and listened and I said "Wow." So, next time I saw him I said, "Hey, I listened to that but you just took it to the extreme." He goes "Yeah, but I got it from you." I said "Okay, I won't argue with you." And he took it to the extreme. And that blew me away.

ZEP UNDERTAKES THEIR FIRST US TOUR IN LATE 1968

With their debut album just released, Zeppelin hit the road for the first time in the US, playing to support to the likes of Vanilla Fudge, Iron Butterfly, and a four-night stint in Los Angeles with the Alice Cooper band.

RODNEY BINGENHEIMER I was at the Whisky a Go Go and it was Alice Cooper and Led Zeppelin and I emceed the show; I introduced them. I remember afterwards backstage at the Whisky, Jimmy had a really bad case of flu and he was practically turning green.

ALICE COOPER We did a show with Led Zeppelin at the Whisky a Go Go which holds maybe 300 people and nobody had heard of either one of us, we were just local bands as far as LA went. It was really a fun night. They all had the flu, so everyone was throwing up backstage. But the fact that Jimmy Page was in The Yardbirds was a big deal for us, and I'd just met Robert Plant and these guys. They were great, we really got along, but we had to flip a coin to see who was going to go on first. Nobody had any say over it because we were both unheard of, so we kind of condescended and said, "No we'll open for you guys because Jimmy Page was in The Yardbirds."

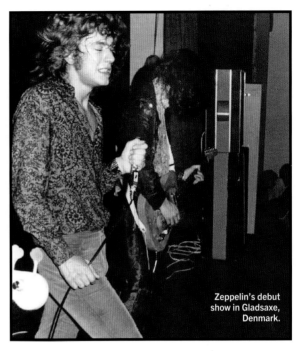

Zeppelin's debut show in Gladsaxe, Denmark.

CARMINE APPICE We were sort of waiting for a band to come along to blow us off stage. We'd go on stage and say, "Let's try and blow 'em off," you know? Led Zeppelin were the first band to really blow *us* off the stage. The very first gig we did with them was in Denver, Colorado at the end of December 1968. So, it was Led Zeppelin, Spirit, and Vanilla Fudge. The show was sold out.

Right at the beginning we went down to see them 'cause we heard the album. We had the same attorney. And when we saw them, we thought they were great but the audience was saying "Bring on the Fudge." And we thought that was pretty funny at the time, especially later when they got big. Nobody knew them at the time. They were great musicians and they were versatile. They could play anything. You know, some of their things sounded country. Some of their things were reggae and some of their things were pure rock. Some of them were heavy . . .

Whole Lotta Guitar

In 1974, The Babys guitarist Michael Corby was living in London when he happened to cross paths with Led Zeppelin. Little did he know he'd end up selling his favorite guitar to the day's biggest guitar hero. Corby takes up the story.

"I was living in Battersea, South London, I was engaged in putting together a rock 'n' roll band which subsequently became known as The Babys. An associate of my manager, the late Adrian Millar, called Noddy Mackenzie was friendly with Raymond Thomas who was Jimmy Page's guitar roadie. After informing Raymond that I was the custodian of a three pick-up original Gibson Les Paul 'Black Beauty' I found myself commanded to appear at the court of Led Zeppelin at their rehearsals in a disused cinema in Fulham, owned by Emerson Lake & Palmer.

"Little did I know that I would find myself jamming with the godfathers of rock on and off for the next two weeks while Jimmy and I argued over the price of another guitar that I had not had the least intention of selling when I set out.

"The instrument in question was to become Jimmy Page's now

celebrated red, bastardized, 1952 Les Paul. How I managed to end up parting with it and how I spent so many hours jamming with Jimmy and the entire lineup of Led Zeppelin is something I still have difficulty in coming to terms with to this day.

"After about ten days of attending endless arguments regarding the price of

my own favorite Les Paul and having reached a point where the matter was almost settled, I was more than surprised when Jimmy asked me if I would show him some of the licks I had been jamming with him. Here was a man whose life and style had enriched my very being, what chance did I have of keeping my guitar?

"I made less than no protest at all and Jimmy lead me to a small ante room where I dutifully showed His Royal Musicalness my sacred library of chord structures. It was at that moment and in private that I had the most remarkable, intimate and memorable insight to his playing. What had taken me months to learn he had learned in hours.

"My ego was crestfallen but I had expected nothing less. God knows, I was still in shock that he had even spoken to me let alone played with me, allowing me to play his treasured '59 Tigerstripe in an old Marshall Major 200 amp that he had acquired from Jimi Hendrix while Bonzo, Plant, and John Paul Jones joined in."

The original receipt for the red 1952 Les Paul guitar that Corby sold to Jimmy.

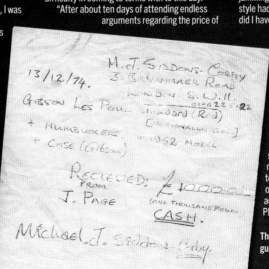

PHIL COLLEN:
"I still get chills when I hear 'Whole Lotta Love.' It's so dynamic—it builds up to this incredible climax and you just go with it. That weird, hippie bit in the middle of the song is really cool, too. And then when Jimmy hits those chords at the end, it's like Pete Townshend on 'Won't Get Fooled Again.' He's just hitting those strings really hard, and you can feel it."

KELLY JONES:
"Led Zeppelin II was the first album I ever had on vinyl. It's still my favorite Zeppelin album. Even now, it amazes me how many great songs are on there. It was all blues and songs about women and sex and all that: 'The Lemon Song,' all that stuff about squeezing my lemon till the juice runs down my legs . . . It's all very tongue-in-cheek, like the old blues records."

JOHN 5:
"The first record I got was *Led Zeppelin II*, because I heard it on the radio all the time, and my guitar teacher was always talking about it. I remember hearing 'Whole Lotta Love,' and that solo, and I was hooked."

EDDIE KRAMER:
"Zeppelin II had the *sound*. It's the sound that all the kids today try to emulate. 'What Is and What Should Never Be' is a great track. I have great memories of 'Livin' Loving Maid' and 'Heartbreaker.' You start digging into it and they're all your favorites."

One of their pivotal dates on the East Coast proved to be at Bill Graham's legendary venue the Fillmore East. Much to the chagrin of headliners Iron Butterfly . . .

RICHARD COLE They hadn't done many shows. I don't think they knew 100 percent how Robert was gonna hold up. Because America is also a different territory, altogether. The first few shows were a bit shaky and the press wasn't good to them. Robert used to sing in his bare feet in those days. He was always a f***** hippie. But by the time we got to New York, the whole thing had gotten so solid that it became the one unit that it was to be for many years.

JAY JAY FRENCH I was there when they headlined the Fillmore East [in New York] on January 31, 1969. I was only there to see Iron Butterfly, the headlining band. I had a front row seat. Believe it or not, the opening act was a gospel group called Porters Popular Preachers. And then out comes Led Zeppelin. It was one of the most startling performances I ever saw. Page was playing a Telecaster and they played the entire first album, from start to finish. At one point the band stopped playing and Robert put the microphone aside and sang just through the strength of his lungs and basically filled the Fillmore. It was insane. I ran out and bought Zeppelin's album on the way to school the next day.

I ended up burning those Iron Butterfly records. I had the honor of having dinner with Robert Plant in 1988, and we spoke about that show. He asked whether I remembered a burst of laughter during Ron Bushy's drum solo during "In-A-Gadda-Da-Vida." I didn't hear it but apparently there was a dressing room-come-balcony that hung over the stage, and Bonham was doubled over in hysterics at how bad the solo was. Zeppelin knew they'd eaten the headline band for breakfast, lunch, and dinner.

MARKY RAMONE I first saw Zeppelin play live at the Fillmore East. I was 13, 14. I knew an usher and he let me in for free. I was just blown away. Outrageous. They were the ultimate band at that moment. They blew away everybody that came before them: Hendrix, Cream . . . Bonham's quadruples around the drum set and his triplets and Page's triplets. Plant's range was just amazing. And the bass tones that John Paul Jones used were incredible. They played seven-minute songs. They didn't do two-minute songs.

ACE FREHLEY That show at the Fillmore East changed my life. I was 16 when I saw them. A lot of people didn't know who Led Zeppelin were, although the "in" people did. The lead singer in the group that I was playing with at the time, who was a couple of years older than me told me, "There's this great new band called Led Zeppelin that's gonna play at the Fillmore East and you've gotta see them." I think I got their first album a week or two before the show and I fell in love with it.

I was real excited about going to the show. I remember it like it was yesterday. They were using Rickenbacker amps, which you can't find anymore. Back then Page wasn't using a Les Paul, he was using a Telecaster. Between him and Robert Plant they destroyed. They took over the Fillmore East to the point where, after they went off and the headliner was coming on, half the people walked out and didn't come back. I still think about that first time I saw Led Zeppelin at The Fillmore from time to time. God, I wish somebody had a video camera back then, it was incredible.

Later in 1969, after a brief tour of Scandinavian and British clubs (including a gig at London's Roundhouse on April 5), Zeppelin returned to the US in the spring. This time around, they shared the stage with the likes of The Who, Grand Funk Railroad, and Three Dog Night.

CARL PALMER I went to see them play at The Roundhouse in London, a very famous place where Jimi Hendrix played, The Crazy World of Arthur Brown, The Doors . . . It was a railway station that was turned into a large, 2,500 seater psychedelic rock club. It was massive. And I enjoyed their show. All of the members of Led Zeppelin are great musicians. They gelled together as a band and it was exciting.

ROGER DALTREY When Zeppelin first came out I thought they were fantastic. They supported us on one of their first gigs in the States in Maryland. I stood on the side of the stage and watched their set and I thought they were brilliant. I was impressed with the whole band. We

obviously knew the guys and I knew Jimmy from way back. He played on The Who's first single. They were Cream derivative but with a lot more weight. Robert was a rock 'n' roll singer. Jack Bruce was really a jazz and blues singer. But Robert knew how to rock.

Throughout our early history, we used to do load of gigs with Hendrix and Cream, so this kind of formula with a three-piece band and a singer—although Cream was just a three-piece—we were well schooled in that. But Zeppelin took it to another level. There was a power there. All of a sudden this was a new form of music. The music scene was starting to get a little bit tired. Even Hendrix was starting to get tired then and he was moving on into jazz. Zeppelin regenerated it.

ANN WILSON We saw Zep several times. Maybe most notably was at a local Seattle amphitheater, Greenlake Aqua Theater, in '69. They were closing the show for Sonny & Cher and Three Dog Night! At the amphitheater show, Nancy and I were still so young that "The Lemon Song" was a bit scary for us—the level of sexual arousal of the older girls in the audience was an eye opener. This was no Three Dog Night show we were attending!

Once again, Zeppelin returned to the UK for dates throughout the summer, which included their performance at the Pop Proms at the Royal Albert Hall on June 29, 1969. Shortly theraffter, and for their third tour in the space of about eight months, Zep returned to the US to hit the festival circuit.

BACK IN THE US—SUMMER '69

DON BREWER Grand Funk played the Atlanta Pop Festival with Led Zeppelin in 1969. We hung around to catch Led Zeppelin's set. They preceded us by maybe a year or two as far as getting the big recognition. We did play another show with them at Olympia Arena in Detroit, Michigan. We were supposed to do a series of dates for them. We were gonna open the show. We were both being booked by Premiere Talent, Frank Barsalona, and all of the old New York mafia music business guys. [laughs] They put us on as the opening act and we came out in Detroit at Olympia and we just started tearin' the place down. The audience was going crazy. Peter Grant, their manager, was furious because we were getting such a good response. He came to our manager, Terry Knight and said [imitates Grant], "I want that f***** band off the stage RIGHT NOW!"

Terry said, "No way, they have two more songs to go." Well, they ended up pulling the plug on us. They actually shut the electricity off and that was the end of our show and that was the end of our run opening for Led Zeppelin. We were kicked off the tour!

RIC LEE We played the Singer Bowl Music Festival with Led Zeppelin in July 1969. Vanilla Fudge were headlining and The Jeff Beck Group with Rod Stewart were the main support act. When they went on for their encore I was standing backstage and Bonzo came running by and said, "Come on," and we ran onstage. When we got there, there was Rod Stewart and Robert Plant, Jimmy Page and Jeff Beck, and three bassists. Bonham was beating out a riff on the kit. I grabbed a floor tom tom and started thrumming hell out of it. The crowd were going apes*** as we banged out a blues standard—I can't remember which one exactly—and it went down a storm, so we started another one.

Bonham, who had been drinking and was already stripped to the waist, took off his trousers and underpants. He was standing there naked, playing away. And the police saw it. And I saw Richard Cole and Peter Grant spotting the police. The number fizzled out and Peter and Richard ran onstage, each grabbing one of Bonzo's arms and you could see his bare arse disappearing as they carried him off. But they got his trousers back on before the police arrived.

RICHARD COLE It must have been the second or third tour. We were in the Villa Roma in San Francisco. Bill Graham threw this big party for the band. This hotel was like built in a circle so the rooms were on the outside, and then you could look down into the lot—there was only two or three floors high and there was a waterfall. The manager was screaming and shouting.

What happened was at the party they used to bring us all these weird things—we'd have ducks in the room for some reason or another. And one of these ducks got sucked down the waste pipe, and of course the water had

GETTY

The world in the palm of their hand
Robert Plant and Jimmy Page
onstage in Germany, 1973.

" I still think about that first time I saw Led Zeppelin at the Fillmore . . . God, I wish somebody had a video camera back then, it was incredible.
—Ace Frehley "

JOHN PAUL JONES
The quiet bassist.

MICHAEL ANTHONY: "He's the classic example of a really underrated bass player. To this day, I'll put on 'The Lemon Song' and John Paul Jones' bass playing just blows me away. What I loved about him was he was good without trying to play lead guitar on a bass, which a lot of bass players do today."

RICKY PHILLIPS: "He's not just a bassist, he's a composer, and an amazing keyboardist. He knew how to lay down a tight groove with John Bonham, but he also had a way to do it with his note choices and his phrasing, which is so unique. He does more with the blues scale that I've ever heard anyone do."

MICK JONES: "He could play anything—he'd play organ, keyboards, and he's an amazing bass player. He was the first bass player to pick up that sort of a funky American style."

TOM HAMILTON: "JPJ started out with a profound talent. It does exist. If you combine that with someone able to focus and combine that with intense desire, it results in someone as high caliber of a musician as JPJ."

JOE BONAMASSA: "John Paul Jones really doesn't get enough credit for holding the whole thing down. I mean, 'Good Times Bad Times,' that alone should put him in the Rock and Roll Hall of Fame."

Zeppelin perfects their bad boy poses in 1968.

flooded and gone all around this balcony, and come down like a shower or a waterfall, around the rest of the hotel. Hence we didn't stay there again.

PAUL STANLEY: I saw Zeppelin live in the summer between the release of their first and second album. I saw them at the New York State Pavilion at the Old World's Fair. My guess was that there were well under two thousand people there. They were the most astonishing band I've seen to this day. There's nothing that comes close to what I witnessed that night. I remember watching them and when it was over my friend and I left the concert. We walked out and looked at each other and said, "Let's not say anything, it'll only cheapen it." And we never spoke about it because it was the perfect marriage of all the elements that made great rock 'n' roll. It was sexy, it was ruthless, it was dangerous.

BRAD WHITFORD: I got to see Zeppelin for the first time not long after I first heard their debut album. I saw them in August of '69 at the Frank Connelly's Carousel Theater in Framingham, Massachusetts. I drove all the way down to the show, but when I got there it was sold out. The beauty of the show was it was being held in a tent, a theater in-the-round tent. I knew I could at least listen to the show because it was a canvas tent. My girlfriend and I walked up to the police line, which was all the way around the theater and asked one of the officers where the bathrooms were. So he points behind him and said, "The bathrooms are right over there," and he let us walk right past him. So we walked in, sat down, and got to see the bulk of the show. They didn't have any fancy clothes on. They were

wearing dirty jeans and dirty T-shirts. They were these hippies up there. Their hair was really long. You could barely see their faces half the time. They looked unkempt. It was just so pure and they delivered.

At one point the PA went down and the band kept on playing and you could still hear Robert singing. He just kept on singing. Something had broken down temporarily and they didn't stop. Jimmy was playing through two stacks and it was loud . . . I was dumbfounded. They were that good . . . I was on an adrenaline high from that show for like 12 months. That was the best I ever saw them perform. It was still so fresh and new to them and they were just nailing it.

GARY ROSSINGTON I saw Zeppelin live twice in Jacksonville, Florida at The Jacksonville Memorial Coliseum. We had a band then, I think we were called Lynyrd Skynyrd but we could have been still going by the name The One Percent. I remember Jethro Tull opened for them and they were great, but everybody kept in their seats. When we saw Zeppelin they blew our minds because all of the girls ran up to the stage. Until then everybody stayed in their seats and just listened to bands. Zeppelin were just unbelievable. They came out and played so good. Page broke out the violin bow and started going . . . [imitates sounds]. We thought that was so cool.

IAN ANDERSON We were the opening act. We played arenas across America and did our 35 minutes every night. It was a great opportunity to go nuts for half-an-hour, give a good account of ourselves, and make it back to the hotel before the bar closed.

It was their first arena tour and they had a crew, just like us, only larger. But there was no big production. They just went on and did it, like we did. It was great for us because we were being introduced to a more rock 'n' roll audience.

It's easy to forget that Zeppelin were, like us, very much rooted in folk music and acoustic music which played a small but significant part of their set. I mean, "Stairway to Heaven" is a long, elaborate piece with a number of different sections but it's very much an acoustic performance with some big rock 'n' roll moments. That was something that imprinted itself on me. It's too grandiose to call it symphonic writing but you try to create some musical moments, some drama.

You learn these things through working with your peers and working with *Zeppelin I* used to watch them play. Some nights they could be unstoppable and beyond belief and the next night they could lose the plot. Because if anything went wrong with the audio—feedback, tuning problems—it became very evident in the performance. Particularly from

The New Yardbirds: the first gig, Denmark, 1968.

LED ZEPPELIN III

JAMES DEAN BRADFIELD: "I got *III* cheap in Woolworth's I think, I got it on cassette, I couldn't be bothered with all that artwork they had going with the vinyl, it reminded me of an advent calendar. It was a strange album for me because when you're 14 or 15 you think you know what Led Zeppelin are, this rock leviathan, and then you hear *III* and realize how subtle they could be. 'Tangerine' did it for me straight away, and 'Since I've Been Loving You' has to be their best blues translation ever by a mile. You can hear the bass drum pedal squeaking on it."

LUKE MORLEY: "When I watched the film *Almost Famous*, it had all these lovely, almost pastoral acoustic songs from *Led Zeppelin III*— and it really made me think about how this element of Zep's music is so often overlooked. So many rock bands are two-dimensional: they can play fast or slow. Zeppelin had an enormous dynamic range and they played it all so effortlessly."

ROY HARPER: "I remember 'Immigrant Song,' 'Celebration Day,' and 'Since I've Been Loving You' being played at gigs. And they became staples of the Zeppelin set. 'That's the Way' was probably Robert finding himself, right at the beginning of his own real writing. If you stand back and look at that album, it really is like their first record."

Jimmy Page. When he was having a good time he was having a *really* good time, but when he wasn't you could see how depressed and upset he was.

For us it meant that if Zeppelin weren't so good that night then people might remember our little 35-minute spot, but if they were brilliant then nobody would remember us. You had to take your chances when you could get them.

RICHARD COLE The band was in Seattle and we were staying at the Edgewater Inn. And the hotel manager is there and Peter [Grant] and I are standing there, and I've got the cash, and we're going through the bill. And the manager says, "Do you know you had these rooms, and you threw that out the window, and that?" And we said, "Yeah, we f***** know what we done, just give us the bill. How much do you want?" And he gave us the bill. I got out the money. And the guy looked, and we said, "Well, at least we f***** paid you, what's wrong with you?"

He said, "It's not that. I just can't imagine what it must be like for you guys. I work in this f***** hotel, I'd love to smash a room up." So Peter said, "Oh, is that all it is? Well, take one of the rooms, go and smash it up and bring me the bill. We're leaving in 15 minutes." The guy smashed the room to smithereens. And he came back, gave us the bill, and we paid it.

LED ZEPPELIN II IS BORN

Amid the to-ing and fro-ing across the Atlantic throughout the second half of 1969, the members of Zeppelin remarkably managed to sneak in writing sessions in hotel rooms and at soundcheck, and then undertook recording sessions for tracks for *Led Zeppelin II* in London, Los Angeles, and New York when they could.

MICK JONES I was with Glyn Johns in Olympic Studios and was called into a little mix room and heard "Whole Lotta Love" for the first time and it just blew me away completely. I thought, Wow! That is the toughest, nastiest rock song I've ever heard, just the power and the darkness of it. They just nailed it.

I think that's when I recognized the magic of Zeppelin. They opened a huge door. And while a lot of people tried to, nobody could ever could even

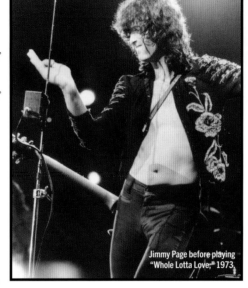

Jimmy Page before playing "Whole Lotta Love," 1973.

get close to what they accomplished. And today, I still listen to Zeppelin, it's just one of those timeless things.

LESLIE WEST "Whole Lotta Love" is one of my favorite, favorite songs of all time. I think part of "Mississippi Queen" I stole from that. I tried to grab a riff from that song. Everybody is a thief, you know, it's just how you disguise it.

PAUL RODGERS John Bonham added so much to Led Zeppelin. I remember Jimmy Page telling me that "Whole Lotta Love" started out with his drum beat. And it was such a cool beat that Jimmy just jumped right on it with that great riff and the song became born. There was an incredible creative flow between all of them.

With *Led Zeppelin II* riding high in the charts (it knocked The Beatles' *Abbey Road* from the top spot), once again the quartet hit the road to take their new material to their ever-increasing audience.

RICHARD COLE The band was flying somewhere from England, and we're all up there in first class and Bill Wyman was there with his girlfriend at the time, Astrid. And she was talking to Bonzo. We were getting off the plane and Astrid pulled me to one side and said, "Richard, why do they bring a farmer on the road with them?" I said, "What are you f***** talking about? He's the f***** drummer!" "Oh," she replied. "All he was talking about was his cows and sheep and goats he owns."

ROY HARPER: I first met Jimmy Page in 1970 at the Bath Festival, although I didn't know who he was at the time. This guy came up to me and said "You know that instrumental on your first record, *Blackpool*? Can you play it?" So I played it for him and he said "Thanks very much." We exchanged pleasantries and then he walked away. And the only thing I thought as I watched him leave was "That guy's pants are too short for him."

So then I did my bit onstage—it might have been the night before— then these guys got up there. I remember looking up and thinking "Oh, there's that guy who asked me to play the instrumental. He's in a band. And

Bonham and Page out on the tiles, Denmark 1973.

LED ZEPPELIN IV

DAVE MUSTAINE: "'Four Sticks' has probably since become my all-time favorite song of Zeppelin's."

KID ROCK: "With Zeppelin, I always go to *IV*, the old man with that thing on his back. Not only was it that they were such popular songs, but 'When the Levee Breaks,' I used to DJ that at basement parties. It's at the end of side two on the vinyl, isn't it? I mean, if you've got a song that good at the *end* of your album, what does it say about the rest of your record!"

STEVE LUKATHER: "'Stairway to Heaven' is one of the greatest guitar solos of all time. It's perfect. The way it builds, the choice of notes, it's the ultimate. I couldn't imagine that solo being any other way, it's *that* good. It was a mind f***. It's still every bit as good today as it was then. And that's the sign of a true classic."

MARK TREMONTI: "I wouldn't call Page heavy metal, not like Tony Iommi or someone. Page wrote "Going to California"—that's not a metal song. He was from the school of hard-rock."

NANCY WILSON: "'Black Dog' has the riff that kinda skips the bar, which was a mistake when they recorded it that they left in. So now it's one of those iconic moments where everybody has to learn it 'wrong' to play it right."

Zeppelin at the peak of their live powers in 1972.

isn't that singer the guy I used to see around Birmingham with all the chicks following him around? This should be interesting." They played the first song and it was brilliant.

And during the second song, all the young women in the crowd started to stand up involuntarily, with tears running down their faces. It was like, "Jesus, what's happening here then?" It was one of those moments where you just got into it and became as moved as they were. In the end, you knew you'd seen something you were never going to forget.

After a significant amount of touring on both sides of the Atlantic, Led Zeppelin would begin work on their third album. It would be a departure from their previous releases, with its heavy focus upon their acoustic side. Jimmy Page had been listening to a lot of British folk music, and Robert had been exploring Celtic folklore and history. The pair spent time songwriting at Bron-Yr-Aur Cottage in Machynlleth in Wales.

JAMES DEAD BRADFIELD You can tell *Led Zeppelin III* is the album that gave them the confidence that allowed them to go on and create songs like "Going to California" [from *Led Zeppelin IV*] and the stuff they did on *Physical Graffiti*. It also gave other musicians, even people like Steve Marriott when he was in Humble Pie, free range to go to different places, it brought a more bucolic edge to things. There's also a simplicity to the album even with things like "Immigrant Song," that two-string riff Page is playing, these really simple phrases. He could be incredibly complicated in his playing, but then that song is so straightforward.

The thing with *III* is that all the things that set Led Zeppelin apart came from that album, it was their FA Cup that would eventually let them go on and win the Championship.

ROY HARPER I used to go up to their office in Oxford Street, where Peter Grant and Mickie Most would be. And one day, Jimmy was up there and gave me the new record. I just said thanks and put it under my arm. Jimmy said, "Look at it." So I twirled the little wheel around and put in back under my arm. Very nice and all that. So he went "Look at it!" Then I discovered "Hats off to (Roy) Harper." I was very touched.

SLASH "Tangerine" from *Led Zeppelin III* was the very first song I mastered. I had a teacher at school who had a Les Paul and he was always playing Cream and Zeppelin licks and whatever. And when I heard him do that I said, "that's what I want to do."

Despite their continued massive success (the band played their first date at Madison Square Garden on September 19, 1970), Bonham and co continued to jam with friends when they were playing locally.

GLENN HUGHES Trapeze were playing in a club in Erdington, Birmingham—a very famous club called Mothers. Floyd played there, Zeppelin played there. It was a major venue in Birmingham in the early seventies. I was playing there with Trapeze in 1971 and Sabbath would show up sometimes, The Move would show up with Roy Wood . . .

One night I'm singing along, and I can see the door and who's coming in. And I noticed John Bonham walk in with his assistant. Matthew. He walked pretty much straight up to the stage, walked on, and wanted to play. He'd heard about my band apparently and he was checking it out. So he walked on to the stage and we're playing the song "Jury" from *Medusa*. He loved that track and he wanted to play along with us. So we played the song again and later that night he commented how much he loved the band, the sound, the vibe . . . And from that point we became very close friends. He would sit in with Trapeze very frequently. We'd play "Jury" twice—once without him and once with him. We'd jam along, he'd be on for about half an hour.

WORK ON *LED ZEPPELIN IV* COMMENCES

ANDY JOHNS I was 20 years old when I worked on *Led Zeppelin IV*. I think I finished the mixing just before my 21st birthday. *Led Zeppelin IV* was recorded at two studios—Island Studios and Headley Grange. I'd been working with the Rolling Stones mobile. They were the first people in Europe to have a proper recording truck. I'd done a couple of projects at Mick Jagger's house. Mick had a house where we'd roll the truck up to and it worked very well there. I'd done the Stones and some other acts.

So when Jimmy asked me to do another record with them, I said, "Why don't we try the Stones truck and Mick's house because it has so many intriguing different spaces as opposed to being confined to one room in the studio?" Jimmy said, "That sounds great, how much does it cost?" I told him that Mick's house would cost £1,000 a week. He said, "I bet I can find something just as good that doesn't cost a thousand a week. Good Lord, I'm not giving Mick Jagger that kind of money." So Jimmy had his people find this place called Headley Grange, which worked great. It even had furniture, which was something that Mick's house lacked.

BATH FESTIVAL OF BLUES & PROGRESSIVE MUSIC '70
BATH & WEST SHOWGROUND - SHEPTON MALLET
SATURDAY 27th JUNE SUNDAY 28th
FREDERICK BANNISTER PRESENTS

Canned Heat
Steppenwolf
Johnny Winter
It's a Beautiful Day
Fairport Convention
Keef Hartley
Maynard Ferguson big band
LED ZEPPELIN
John Mayall
Pink Floyd
Jefferson Airplane
Frank Zappa and the mothers of invention
Moody Blues
Flock
Colosseum
Santana
Byrds
Dr. John-the night tripper
Country Joe
Hot Tuna
Continuity by JOHN PEEL & MIKE RAVEN

Robert Plant performing at Madison Square Garden on Led Zeppelin's 1977 North American Tour.

LED ZEPPELIN

JOHN BONHAM
Drummer
extraordinaire.

JOEY KRAMER:
"I love John Bonham. It's about what he doesn't play. And it's about his finesse and his feel. He was one of those few guys when you heard him behind the drums, you knew it was him because he had a very distinctive sound."

MARKY RAMONE:
"Bonham could do anything. He could do rock. He could do jazz. He had a heavy blues sound. He was extremely powerful and never let up. His showmanship was unbelievable but his playing was tight."

CARL PALMER:
"He had a definite sound, which he would capture on whatever drums that he played. As far as I'm concerned, he was probably one of the most original-sounding players of that time."

GARY ROSSINGTON:
"My God, he's one of the best drummers that ever lived! What made him great was that he was so solid and straightforward."

TAYLOR HAWKINS:
"He had a great almost pop feel to his drumming. He was inventive and he cross-pollinated a lot of styles."

KELLY JONES:
"Let's not forget there's a f****** drum solo on *Led Zeppelin II*! 'Moby Dick'—brilliant!"

Robert Plant and the band's road manager Richard Cole get comfy.

IAN ANDERSON We recorded *Aqualung* in the brand new, but not quite technically sorted out, main studio at Island Studios in Basing Street which was actually a converted church. We were in this big cavernous room that was horrible to work in. It was acoustically awful. But down below us Led Zeppelin were working away on the tracks for *Led Zeppelin IV* in a much smaller studio. But even though it was really cramped, it had a very friendly atmosphere and sounded a lot better than our studio. Even for Zeppelin, size wasn't everything.

ANDY JOHNS I remember Jimmy had a little bit of trouble with the solo on "Stairway to Heaven." As for the solo, he hadn't completely figured it out. Nowadays you sometimes spend a whole day doing one thing. Back then, we never did that. We never spent a very long time recording anything.

I remember sitting in the control room with Jimmy, he's standing there next to me, and he'd done

quite a few passes and it wasn't going anywhere. I could see he was getting a bit paranoid and so I was getting paranoid. I turned around and said, "You're making me paranoid!" And he said, "No, you're making me paranoid!" It was a silly circle of paranoia. Then bang! On the next take or two he ripped it out.

Led Zeppelin IV was released in November 1971, and went straight to the top of the chart in both the US and the UK. Consequently, much of 1972 was spent on the road, including a jaunt to Australia and New Zealand. It was also in this year when Zep played the LA Forum (on June 25) and the Long Beach Arena (June 27). 2003's *How the West Was Won* live album was an amalgamation of these two shows.

RODNEY BINGENHEIMER I used to have a nightclub called Rodney's English Disco and they hung there frequently. In fact, there were times when they'd arrive in Los Angeles and have the limousines pick them up; the luggage would still be in the limousines and before checking into the hotel they would go directly to my club. Because there was English beat there and English rock 'n' roll and of course, that's where all the chicks hung out. Every girl you could ever imagine was in there—it was like a neon jungle.

DANNY GOLDBERG The days at the Hyatt House [the Continental Hyatt House, a hotel on Sunset Boulevard in Hollywood, later dubbed "the Riot House"] were pretty crazy. It was that feeling of, "We can do absolutely anything." There were no rules. It was just that feeling of, "Anything we do, we can get away with because we're Led Zeppelin." And the whole phenomenon of having an entire floor, it was kind of like one big playground. So it was not so much crazy in terms of the actual incidents which happened. I mean, so what if [tour manager] Richard Cole drove a motorcycle through a hallway in the Hyatt House? What was notable about it was it epitomized the "We can do anything we want" kind of attitude.

And so there was an attitude of great anarchy. Bonham would play his records very, very loud at three or four in the morning and somebody downstairs called the hotel and complained. And they moved the person who complained. This was the type of attitude they got from the hotel and the hotel realized this would make them the favorite hotel for rock groups. So it gave the group a feeling of omnipotence that was unique.

Jimmy never rode through hallways or threw TVs out the window, but he loved it when other people did. He was more the kind of person who would manipulate someone into doing those kinds of things. And then laugh to himself

LA, June 1972 at Rodney Bingenheimer's English Disco. Inset: Jimmy Page with Lori Maddox.

JIMMY PAGE
A true guitar magician.

DUANE EDDY:
"Jimmy's a brilliant player, just brilliant. He's one of the few guys that blazed away on the guitar and still has something to really say with it. It was about soul, feeling, technique, and skill, he blended it all together. There's only a few guys that I know of who've done that."

MARK TREMONTI:
"I learned early on that Page was probably the best guitarist ever. The vibe he put forward was so different. I love his dark and twisted stuff, but I was a bigger fan of his pretty stuff; the airy open tunings, and all the clever little licks."

NANCY WILSON:
"Guitar- wise, Jimmy is my musical poet."

NEAL SCHON:
"One of the most important things is when a player arrives on a style and people know who it is the second they hear it. And that applies to Jimmy Page."

PHIL COLLEN: "The real genius of Jimmy Page was that he didn't do anything that was simply run-of-the-mill. He always played with imagination."

TONY IOMMI:
"The way Jimmy plays, the riffs he comes up with, is unbelievable. He came up with a great style of playing, the off-timing stuff. He's got a great mind and is a great writer."

LES PAUL:
"Jimmy's phrasing was great, he didn't play to show off, he played for a reason."

watching everyone make fools of themselves.

GARY ROSSINGTON We ran into Zeppelin at the Hyatt House in LA. That's when everybody was drunk and partying and throwing TVs out the windows . It was a crazy party, the whole floor would be partying. Like the movie *Almost Famous*, we were in some room on that floor with everybody. We didn't meet them formally. We never really got that close to them. We were younger than everyone and kind of in awe. We'd see them in the hotel coming in and out, getting in their limos. That was real exciting because we were fans. We didn't want to bother them and run up to them because they had so many fans around them.

As a matter of fact, Cameron Crowe who was a great friend of ours and wrote *Almost Famous*, was with us back in those days. He was amazed at it all. We were all just kids.

RODNEY BINGENHEIMER Anything you ever read about in books about the Hyatt House was true. Those were the days. And Zeppelin were real nice to me—they treated me with respect. I was up there on the higher floors of the "Riot House" when they would take guys and hold the guy over the balcony by his heels. Page was quiet; he'd observe everything. He was into a lot of girls like Lori Maddox and he liked Bebe Buell. The wild guy, of course, was Bonham. Robert was a little crazy but okay. And John Paul Jones never participated; he was always in a different room.

SIMON KIRKE Bonzo always seemed to have a new car every other week and he'd drag me out of my room at 3 o'clock in the morning, and drag me down to the garage, saying "You got to see this car, man." I think it was a Corvette. Then he started it up and all the car alarms went off. We shot out of this ramp from the underground car park onto Sunset Boulevard and made an illegal turn. We were doing 90 mph within 10 seconds. And sure enough the cops

John Paul Jones performing onstage, 1975.

HIPGNOSIS BANNISTER IN ASSOCIATION WITH PETER GRANT
PRESENTS

LED-ZEPPELIN
AT
KNEBWORTH 1979

OFFICIAL PROGRAMME 90p

were behind us. And it's like John knew what was gonna happen because the cop said, "Pull over and let me see your hands."

Thank God it was a young cop and he recognized us. He says, "I know you." Bonzo said, "Yeah, I'm with Led Zeppelin, we're appearing at the Forum." And then John said, "I got some tickets here, bring your girlfriend." And then the cop said, "Look it, I'm gonna let you off the ticket. I'm gonna stop the traffic and you're gonna take this thing back. You're gonna park it and you're gonna go to bed and I don't want to see it again on this street." And John said, "Hey, you're the boss."

As seemed to be the Led Zeppelin way, while they were traversing the globe in 1972, the band somehow managed to squeeze in recording sessions for their fifth album, *Houses of the Holy.* Upon its release in March of 1973, Zeppelin hit the road in Europe and followed this with yet another tour of the US. It was on this trip that their shows at Madison Square Garden (July 27-29) would be recorded for their film, *The Song Remains the Same.*

SIMON KIRKE The first time I saw Zeppelin in concert was at a gig in Texas. And we were in the wings and during "No Quarter," which had this piano thing that went on for ages, John Paul saw me and he winked at me and said, "It's easy, it's easy." And he had a little Wurlitzer piano going through the PA and he was weaving these wonderful arpeggios and scales while all the lights were going. He's a very soft spoken guy, a real gentleman, very mild mannered, just an all around great guy and he complimented Bonzo's drumming wonderfully.

MARKY RAMONE I saw them later on at Madison Square Garden. They were still very good but not as good as at the Fillmore. It was

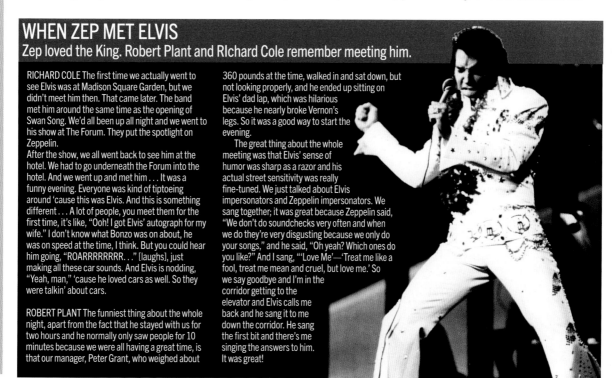

WHEN ZEP MET ELVIS
Zep loved the King. Robert Plant and RIchard Cole remember meeting him.

RICHARD COLE The first time we actually went to see Elvis was at Madison Square Garden, but we didn't meet him then. That came later. The band met him around the same time as the opening of Swan Song. We'd all been up all night and we went to his show at The Forum. They put the spotlight on Zeppelin.
After the show, we all went back to see him at the hotel. We had to go underneath the Forum into the hotel. And we went up and met him . . . It was a funny evening. Everyone was kind of tiptoeing around 'cause this was Elvis. And this is something different . . . A lot of people, you meet them for the first time, it's like, "Ooh! I got Elvis' autograph for my wife." I don't know what Bonzo was on about, he was on speed at the time, I think. But you could hear him going, "ROARRRRRRRR. . ." [laughs], just making all these car sounds. And Elvis is nodding, "Yeah, man," 'cause he loved cars as well. So they were talkin' about cars.

ROBERT PLANT The funniest thing about the whole night, apart from the fact that he stayed with us for two hours and he normally only saw people for 10 minutes because we were all having a great time, is that our manager, Peter Grant, who weighed about

360 pounds at the time, walked in and sat down, but not looking properly, and he ended up sitting on Elvis' dad lap, which was hilarious because he nearly broke Vernon's legs. So it was a good way to start the evening.
The great thing about the whole meeting was that Elvis' sense of humor was sharp as a razor and his actual street sensitivity was really fine-tuned. We just talked about Elvis impersonators and Zeppelin impersonators. We sang together; it was great because Zeppelin said, "We don't do soundchecks very often and when we do they're very disgusting because we only do your songs," and he said, "Oh yeah? Which ones do you like?" And I sang, "'Love Me'—'Treat me like a fool, treat me mean and cruel, but love me.' So we say goodbye and I'm in the corridor getting to the elevator and Elvis calls me back and he sang it to me down the corridor. He sang the first bit and there's me singing the answers to him. It was great!

GETTY IMAGES/IAN DICKSON/REDFERNS

Earl's Court, May 1975
Robert Plant and Jimmy Page
performing onstage.

" f anything went wrong with the audio — feedback, tuning problems — it became very evident in the performance. Particularly from Jimmy Page — you could see how depressed and upset he was. "
—Ian Anderson

HOUSES OF THE HOLY

CLAUDIO SANCHEZ: "Houses of the Holy is probably my favorite Led Zeppelin record. It's the first proper album that I discovered and I enjoyed without my father's guidance."

NANCY WILSON: "Not unlike 'Stairway to Heaven,' 'The Rain Song' really incorporates a lot of sophisticated musical theory and change, and also builds into an epic rock song. It's everything—the words, the melodies, the track itself. And it's in a tuning that every guitar player has a different idea about what it is! It's a Holy Grail for me."

JOEY KRAMER: "I can't really pick a favorite album but I have some favorite Zeppelin songs. I really like 'The Crunge' and 'The Ocean.' I'm about the funk and the space and those tunes have it. That's what Bonham brought to those songs."

Led Zeppelin with their private plane, The Starship.

Life onboard The Starship, 1973.

more glitzy. There was more stage stuff. They were dressing more rock star-ish. At the time, glitter was big—New York Dolls, Mott The Hoople, David Bowie, Alice Cooper . . . Sothey started wearing satin things. And, you know, Page with the "granny takes a trip" rose black on black satin that he wore on the Madison Square Garden show. And their set got longer. "Stairway to Heaven" was out already. The reason why I liked the song was because of Jimmy Page's lead guitar playing and Bonham's drum fill in the middle of Jimmy's break, which is very hard to duplicate.

STEVEN TYLER We got to be quite close to the band because Ray Tabano, who used to play in Aerosmith before Brad, used to get this red Lebanese hash and when they played the Garden, Jimmy invited us down. So we sold Jimmy and the gang a pound of Red Lebanese with a stamp of a camel and a half moon . . . It was good s*** and a good night.

I'll never forget this as long as I live, I lay down on the stage and looked around the place just to get a feel. It was huge, awesome, like looking over the Grand Canyon, and I'm thinking, "I'm going to do this place one day man. I'm going to sell this motherf****** place out." Five years later, we were here playing Madison Square Garden, so some of Zeppelin's genius must have rubbed off on me.

DANNY GOLDBERG Lee [Solters, publicist] and I flew to Paris to see them at the Palais de Sports. To stand on the side of the stage and watch Jimmy was very impressive and it was that period [*Houses of the Holy* tour] when he still did an acoustic break during the middle of the show. I was particularly impressed with how good he was on the acoustic guitar because it was different than the image you were expecting with "Whole Lotta Love."

The meeting was fairly formal. It was with the whole group and Peter Grat, Lee, and myself. Really, Robert Plant and John Bonham did most of the talking. And Peter. Jimmy was pretty quiet. In general, Jimmy was the kind of person who was more open in a one-on-one situation rather than with a large group of people. He tended to lay back and see what everyone else was saying. A lot of the power over the group came from these moody silences. And then in a one-on-one situation he would tell you what he really thought. He could be intimidating through these moody silences. He had a very, very specific sense of himself. He definitely would be the center of the decision-making of that group.

Good boys when they're asleep: Bonham, Plant, and Jones.

1974—A YEAR OF RECORDING

Following the last five years of relentless touring, 1974 was something of a quieter year for Zeppelin. Much of it was spent working on their double masterpiece *Physical Grafitti*, with only the occasional live guest appearance.

JIM LEA We went to see Led Zeppelin in London in about 1974, and John Bonham came up to me. He said, "Hey, I really like that record of yours, "Thanks for the Memory," and I wanna play to that riff but what I'd do is I'd go [imitates drum beat]." He started mouthing the drumming. But that was quite a compliment because John Bonham and I had had a fight in America about six months before.

That particular week, there were was only about 23 pages in the *NME*. And we had adverts for our Earl's Court shows and we had adverts for our new single, and we had three full-page interviews. So out of the 20 pages I think Slade had about 20, and Led Zeppelin had just a tiny little review on their album. And he was talking to me about it, and I was saying "I really like Elton John and I like the Stones . . ." I don't know why he took exception to me. I loved Led Zeppelin as well, they were fantastic and Bonham was probably the greatest rock drummer that's ever been. He was great when I saw him playing in a cabaret band.

And I was really quite upset that he took umbrage and came at me with a walking stick. So somewhere in the conversation I had upset him and to this day I don't know why that was. Then we went to see the band and he was as nice as pie.

RON NEVISON Recording at Headley Grange was interesting. It brought character to the sessions. You're living and working there and there's total concentration. Everybody's together and there's a camaraderie. Also, you can experiment with different sounds in different places.

They were pretty rowdy. They stayed up late and partied. I had to stop staying at Headley Grange at one point because we would work from noon to midnight, and then at three in the morning they'd wake me up and want to start all over again. I didn't want to hang with them when they were partying. So I'd drive home from Headley Grange and I'd lock up the studio so they didn't do any damage and I'd come back in the morning.

PAUL RODGERS John Paul Jones is a very clever musician. He writes classical pieces and ensembles. Like Jimmy, he's another session musician who could handle everything. But with Zeppelin you could tell he really loved what he was doing, especially when playing with Mr. Bonham. I love what he did in "Kashmir" with the strings; I thought that was just fantastic. He was a very adventurous bass player, very creative and out there but also controlled. Again, it comes back to having a lot of technique but getting beyond the technique. You might be getting into the area where you have a lot of notes you can hit, but you're thinking about them, and you're placing them, and you're using it wisely. He did lots of that. He also understood his role in the band. He was a great foil for the rest of them. He was that sort of perfect backdrop, really. When you take the time to listen to his work, I'm constantly astounded by what he achieved.

I can still put "Kashmir" on and it sends shivers down my spine. I remember when it first came out. Bad Company got together with the Zeps in LA for a launch party and that track just blew the doors off. Robert and Jimmy told me they'd spent a lot of time on holiday in Morocco, and they would hear this amazing music on the street corners. And it really seeped into their consciousness, probably a little like how George Harrison was influenced by the Maharishi and the Indian influence, which I really appreciate because it brought that over to the west. There's a lot there that people can dig into in terms of meditation and Eastern philosophies. So Robert and Jimmy were standing on street corners hearing this amazing music, and they allowed it to seep into what they were doing.

PHYSICAL GRAFFITI

RITCHIE BLACKMORE: "'Kashmir' and 'When the Levee Breaks' were probably my favorite Led Zeppelin songs. 'Kashmir' inspired me to write 'Stargazer' for Rainbow incorporating the Turkish element."

ROGER DALTREY: "I sang a Zeppelin song for a project (*British Rock Symphony*) with an orchestra and it was interesting to do it, but I found 'Kashmir' tricky. The reason it was tricky was just for the sentiment of it. I just found it hard to put myself into a Led Zeppelin lyric."

RON NEVISON: "I never knew that *Physical Graffiti* was going to be a double album. When we started out we were just cutting tracks for a new record. I left the project before they started pulling in songs from *Houses of the Holy* and getting them up to scratch. So I didn't know it was a double until it came out!"

LUKE MORLEY: "'In My Time of Dying' is the supreme statement. It's simple out-and-out blues, and you can tell that it's developed from the band just jamming, but it's beautifully pieced together. Every time I play it I always think, 'Well, there goes another 12 minutes of my life . . .' It still amazes me."

GARY ROSSINGTON: "'Kashmir' is my kind of song. It's very exotic-sounding. When it comes on I just can't turn that one off."

John Paul Jones backstage at the Fillmore East.

1975 saw the quartet return to the road on both sides of the Atlantic for some of their biggest shows—most notably, an unprecedented five-night stint at Earl's Court.

PHIL COLLEN: I saw Zeppelin at Earls Court in '75. In a way they were pretty awful. Robert Plant was singing a lot of songs in a lower octave, which was disappointing, even though I understand now how hard it is for a singer to keep screaming all that "Been a long time since I rock and rolled!" stuff night after night. The overall sound was terrible, and the playing wasn't that great. But I had THE BEST time in the world! It was amazing—it was Led Zeppelin! Abysmal as it was, it was f****** great!

Unfortunately, fate would also deal Zep a nasty hand in 1975. On August 4, Robert Plant and his wife Maureen were involved in a nasty car accident, enforcing a brief sabbatical for the band. However, by the time 1976 rolled around, Plant was back on his feet and raring to go, with a new album *Presence* ready for release in March.

CHERIE CURRIE: Robert was instrumental in getting The Runaways signed to a record deal. He loved the band and was a big supporter. He came to our show at The Starwood. There's photos that exist where he's wearing a Runaways T-shirt, which says "The Runaways," and

IN THROUGH THE OUT DOOR

JIMMY PAGE:
"In Through the Out Door was done in three weeks, so I can't see why people have to take so long to do an album. I don't know why people take two years to do an album. I really wouldn't have the patience."

TAYLOR HAWKINS:
"I'm just going to be that guy that pisses everybody off and say I love *In Through the Out Door* and 'Casa Hombre' is my favorite track. I love that record; I love the weirdness of it. I don't really have time for Zeppelin doing the blues. I love the fact that there's tons of weird keyboards all over the place. That's like almost their prog rock record in a way."

ANN WILSON:
"In Through the Out Door was transitional for Zeppelin and everyone. They rose, as always, to the pure and shifting hungry nature of their unique, singular voice."

underneath it says "Robert." Those weren't T-shirts we sold, these were our stage costumes at the time, and we had one made for him because he was Robert Plant. We never even thought he would show up but he did and put the T-shirt on right away. There were a lot of stars there that night, but I don't remember any of them except for him.

Robert was hanging backstage with us at The Starwood and was very supportive of the band. I can't explain how kind he was. He was using a cane at the time and was recovering from an automobile accident. He was married at the time and I was only 16, and I really wanted him bad. And I'm not a groupie, never been a groupie. He kind of got the vibe that I wanted him and he turned to Kim Fowley and said, "I'm married to a wonderful woman and if she wasn't in my life I'd think about it but, no." That's integrity. He had beautiful women falling at his feet all night, including me, and he passed. This is a good, good man.

He really liked our show and then he invited us to see Led Zeppelin play at the Forum. Oh my god, it was amazing! We had amazing seats, stage left, third row.

Talk about seeing God . . . Robert is a rock 'n' roll god. He's the absolute shining star of rock 'n' roll. The show was spectacular and it was one of the greatest concerts I've ever seen.

GLENN HUGHES When Deep Purple played two nights at New York's Radio City Music Hall in January 1976, the first night Plant showed up, and the second night Bonzo was there. We come out to do the encore and before it starts, John comes out onstage—and he shoves a gun in my ribs from the back. And he whispered, "You're coming with me." And he took my microphone and before we started playing, he started ranting on about *The Song Remains the Same*, and how the movie was going to be coming out in a few months, basically took over the microphone.

He stood onstage while we were playing the encore and when we came off he shunted me into his limo. He was waving around this gun, he'd had a few cocktails, so I hung out with him at the Purple party and we went back to the Plaza where we were all staying . . . And finally he fell asleep. And I legged it. That was one of the last times I saw John. I saw him a few more times . . . But it was kinda scary.

DAVE MUSTAINE *Presence* didn't reflect the period at all. For me, it was a really interesting hippy record. There was a heavy use of the phasers, for example on the guitars at the start of "Nobody's Fault But Mine," and those sounds really appealed to me because I was so into drugs at that point. You'd listen to that album while stoned and think, "Hell-ooo?" And that sleeve with those mysterious obelisks—what was that about?

JOE PERRY Jeezus! I think it was 1977. It was one of the times they played Madison Square Garden five or six nights in a row. One thing that disappointed me was that they jammed a lot because I liked hearing the shorter versions like on their records. It wasn't so much the jamming that disappointed, I love listening to them play, but it meant that they had to leave out a bunch of other songs. But that was what *de rigeur* at the rock shop in those days, it wasn't just them, everybody was playing like that. Of course, nobody could play like them.

Sadly, Zeppelin's end was drawing near. Dogged by tragedy (Plant's young son died unexpectedly), the band would go on to release one final album—*In Through the Out Door*, and play a massive show at Knebworth Park. Their penultimate show, however, would take place in Munich on July 5, 1980.

SIMON KIRKE I was at a low ebb in my marriage. Bonzo called me and he said, "Come on over and hang out with us for a few days." I flew over to Germany, and Bonzo said, "Well look, would you like to play drums on 'Whole Lotta Love'?" I said, "I'd love to, man, you kidding?" No other drummer had ever played with Bonzo so I considered it a high honor. But I was a bit nervous because I knew that "Whole Lotta Love" went into all these different time things. And then came the show. I think it's on tape somewhere. Robert mentions, "Well, a good friend of ours, Simon Kirke from Bad Company . . ." And the roadies put up another kit next to John's—and it was great harmony, it sounded like an artillery attack when the both drums came in. Jimmy gave me a wink and Robert gave me a thumbs up and I managed to do it—I'll never forget it.

With John Bonham's tragic and unexpected death on September 24, 1980, Led Zeppelin called it a day. And with only two fairly dodgy exceptions—Live Aid in 1985 and Atlantic Record's 40th Anniversary in 1988—the band has never reunited. Until 2007, when Led Zeppelin (with Bonham's son Jason on drums) played London's O2 Arena.

TAYLOR HAWKINS They got bashed for Live Aid. Phil Collins got blamed for that and I think that was bulls***. Phil Collins is one of the solidest, best drummers in the world. It wasn't Phil's fault. First of all they were under- rehearsed; Robert Plant didn't sound good, and I think Jimmy Page may have been in a bad way.

JASON BONHAM It's not a God-given right for me to play the drums for Led Zeppelin today, but we did some rehearsals back in June and I have to say that once we got started, it was amazing. Jimmy's playing like a young man again. ❷

Presence of Mind

A lot of people presume that *Presence* is your favorite album.

JIMMY PAGE: I don't know why they think it's my favorite album; I don't have any one favorite album because they all mean different things from the whole journey of Led Zeppelin. *Presence* was recorded in real stressful circumstances, Robert was in plaster with his leg and we didn't know what the outcome was going to be of all that at the time. It's a very dark album, it's really intense. That's the one where it took three weeks to record and do overdubs.

We did it in the Musicland Studios, Munich, and after us were the Rolling Stones. I called them up and asked if I could get a couple more days, because they were busy trying out various guitars, and they said OK. The tracks were done and Robert's vocals were done and I was going to do what I had normally done and still do—the overdubs and production.

There was me and the engineer Keith Harwood, and whoever woke first would get the other up and we'd get straight

into the studio and do the guitar overlays. It was the same with the mixing. Jagger was staying in the same hotel and I went up to see him to say thanks for letting us use the studio in their downtime. He said, "What have you done?" I said "I've done an album, do you want to hear some?" I put on "Nobody's Fault But Mine," which he sort of knew as a blues song and he was quite startled by it.

Although doing an album in three weeks was an exception, I never worked slowly, nor did anyone else. We were all very fast and to the point. If we were recording something and it wasn't happening, we would stop that number and do something else, there was no point laboring it. That's something I brought with me from the session days—you know when the spark's there and you know when it's gone, and there's no point proceeding, especially if you have other numbers to do.

When *Presence* came out, everyone thought it was the direction Zeppelin would be taking in the future.

JIMMY PAGE: Yeah, for example, "Tea For One" is exceptional. It was to the point, recorded in a couple of takes. Roberts' vocals are tremendous. He was doing that when his leg was in a cast, miles away from home.

Weren't you particularly out of it during the recording of *Presence*?

JIMMY PAGE: I was into it. [laughs] I was seriously focused. You don't make music like that in such a short amount time falling about in the street drunk. You do it when you're one hundred percent focused.

Phil Carson (left) with Ronnie Wood and Ahmet Ertegun, head of Atlantic Records, in 1976.

WHAT IS AND WHAT SHOULD ALWAYS BE

Led Zeppelin rewrote rock's rulebook, especially when it came to dealing with their record company. Former Atlantic Records Vice President Phil Carson explains all.

By: Hugh Fielder

It wasn't just the sound of rock music that Led Zeppelin changed forever. The music *business* was never the same again either. The contract that Zeppelin signed with Atlantic Records in late 1968 included not just the biggest advance yet handed to a new group, it also gave them unprecedented control over every aspect of their music and image.

What made the deal even more remarkable was that nobody at Atlantic had seen Led Zeppelin play live before they signed them. In fact, the band had only played a handful of gigs, and most of those were as The New Yardbirds. But Atlantic *had* heard the tapes of the first Led Zeppelin album.

"It was [producer] Jerry Wexler who wanted to sign them. He'd recognized the enormous talent of Jimmy Page," says Phil Carson, who was in charge of running Atlantic Records' international operation at that time and later became a vice president of the company. "It was then handed over to [Atlantic's founder] Ahmet Ertegün who finalized the deal with [Zeppelin manager] Peter Grant."

Carson continues, "The deal changed the way things were done because Led Zeppelin demanded a massive measure of control. They controlled what singles would be taken from an album, they controlled the artwork. They controlled the mastering process—Jimmy Page mastered every album personally. Atlantic had no say in any of that whatsoever."

How was Led Zeppelin able to do this?
Because it was clear to Ahmet immediately what he was dealing with—the talent of the band and the talent of the management team. Peter was running the thing

with the assistance of [leading New York music business attorney] Steve Weiss. And Ahmet realized there was something extraordinary in the way that Peter Grant and Jimmy Page had created Led Zeppelin. He knew it would be the very best. He also knew that The Yardbirds, the band Jimmy had been with previously, had a following in the States so they would be able to tour even though they had no record out when the first tour was booked. Jimmy already had a reputation, even though it was fairly low-key. No one knew any of the others, but the impact was instant.

Why did Led Zeppelin approach Atlantic?
The fact that Atlantic had been so successful with Cream probably had something to do with it. Plus, I think Jimmy had a respect for the music coming out of Atlantic. The catalogue of music that Ahmet and Jerry had built up at Atlantic was hugely respected among British musicians. And Atlantic still had the air of an independent label even though it was a pretty big company by then. It certainly wasn't a corporate record company.

They also had this edict about signing bands—"Only sign a band if there is a virtuoso musician in it." Because virtuoso musicians don't play with good musicians, they only play with excellent musicians. And if you think about Led Zeppelin, there are four virtuoso musicians in that band.

Led Zeppelin could veto singles, but they couldn't control what radio played, could they?
But that was the point. Jimmy's whole idea was that you should play an album in its entirety. And in those days I would go into a radio station like [pioneering New York station] NWEW with Jimmy and [DJ] Scott Murray would put on side one of *Led Zeppelin II* and play the whole f****** thing. Other DJs would pick up on different tracks. Sometimes there would be a consensus about a particular track, and then the record company would go to the band and say, "Hey, we've gotta put that track out as a single." That was how "Whole Lotta Love" came to be Zeppelin's first big single. There was an edit done to bring it down to a reasonable length that caused all kinds of mayhem. In the end they agreed that the edited version could be played on radio but not sold in the shops.

My first experience with Peter Grant was over "Whole Lotta Love" when I decided to put it out as a single in England. I had it pressed and ready to go out, when I was summoned to Peter Grant's office and told, "You can't do that." I said, "What do you mean? I'm running the record label over here." And he said, "You speak to Ahmet right now." So I rang him from Peter's office and he said, "Get get the damn thing back." Which I did at once. But about 1,200 copies leaked out from our Manchester distribution center, and now of course they're huge collector's items. I just wish I'd kept a few.

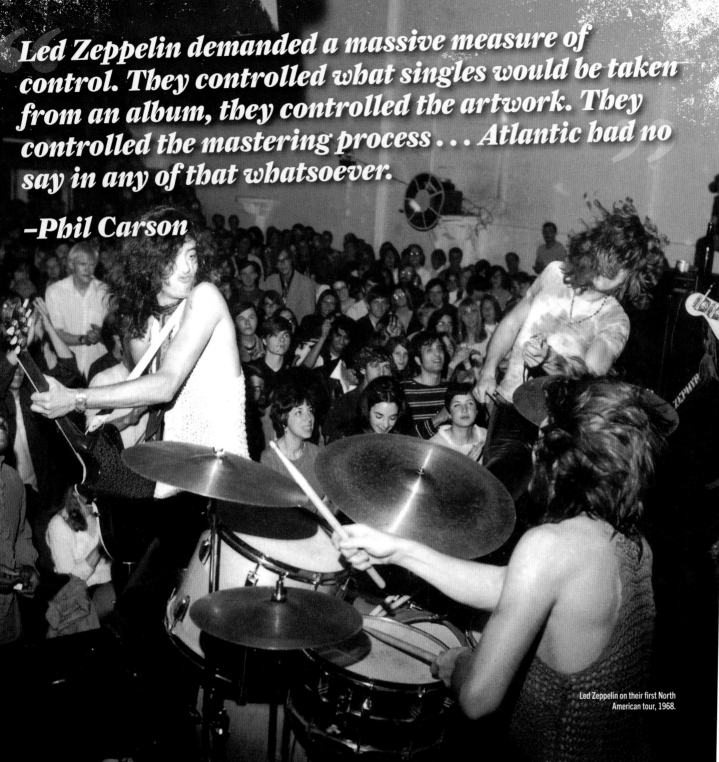

> **Led Zeppelin demanded a massive measure of control. They controlled what singles would be taken from an album, they controlled the artwork. They controlled the mastering process . . . Atlantic had no say in any of that whatsoever.**
>
> **–Phil Carson**

Led Zeppelin on their first North American tour, 1968.

Didn't this deprive Atlantic of a major promotional tool?
That's what we all thought. But we were proved wrong because any airplay simply made people search out the album. After a while you wondered whether rock bands really needed singles. And in Zeppelin's case they certainly didn't.

Other bands, like ELP and Yes, released singles. Even The Rolling Stones.
The Stones were always a singles band. They never really sold a lot of albums until they joined Atlantic. It was just the concept of marketing that Atlantic had was different. Which is one of the reasons the Stones signed with Ahmet.

Why did Led Zeppelin refuse to appear on television?
They did a few right at the beginning but they were not happy with how they sounded on television. Their feeling was that if you wanted to see the band you should go to a concert. And at the start they toured relentlessly. By the middle of 1970, a year-and-a-half after they'd signed to Atlantic, they'd already done five tours of America, and found time to record their second album. It was incredible.

So what was Atlantic's role?
More or less innocent bystanders! All we had to do was keep our heads down and make sure the records were in the stores. Of course we also got the radio play. But we were nothing to do with the live side of things. Zeppelin concert tickets would go on sale without even an advertisement. Sometimes it would just be an announcement on a radio station. It was mostly word of mouth. And the interesting thing is that it still is, only now it's the internet generation. So you had 1.2 million people applying for 16,000 tickets to see them at the concert [in November] they're doing for Ahmet.

Were you worried that after Led Zeppelin other bands would come along and demand the degree same control?
Yes, but we were able to say, "We made a special case for Led Zeppelin because they sold three million albums. Your album may be great, but we don't think that it's that great." And Zeppelin were the only band that had that measure of control for many years. We gave it to other acts like Crosby Stills & Nash because we felt that they deserved it, but it wasn't in the contract the way it was with Zeppelin.

THE AFTERLIFE OF
LED ZEPPELIN

Led Zeppelin didn't end with John Bonham's death in 1980—instead, it limped on through a series of big plans and botched reunions.

By: Mick Wall

Although the story of Led Zeppelin ostensibly ended that bleak day in September 1980, new chapters have been added on a regular basis. The first—the posthumous release in 1982 of the odds-and-sods *Coda* album—was meant to have closed the book. Despite modest sales (a million in the US, compared to seven million for Zep's final album *In Through the Out Door*, and only 60,000 in the UK where *In Through the Out Door* had sold over 300,000), it added to the curiosity, combing the band's back catalogue for leftovers and finding plenty to suggest they were far from the spent force that punk-obsessed critics claimed at the time of their demise.

The early eighties were not kind to the memory of bands like Zeppelin, with long hair as unfashionable as flares, and machines taking the place of bearded, bad-tempered drummers. It didn't become clear quite how much Zeppelin was missed until July 1985, when the surviving members took to the stage in Philadelphia for their part in the Live Aid concert. While their playing that day was inarguably sloppy, the crowd reacting with uncontrolled hysteria was something none of us who were there will ever be able to forget. There could not have been many more screams and tears if Jesus had come down from the heavens and decided to walk among them.

Even the band admitted they were shocked by the force of the reaction. So much so, they were even prepared to countenance what had previously been considered unthinkable: a full-on Led Zeppelin reformation, with the redoubtable Thompson taking Bonzo's place. Rehearsals took place down in Bath a few months later. But it all came to naught as Plant began to have second thoughts about working again with Page, who was off drugs but drinking heavily. "The first day was all right," John Paul Jones recalled. "I had all sorts of ideas for it." But Plant's doubts grew; when Thompson was involved in a serious car accident, he took it as an omen. "It just fell apart from then," said Jones.

Three years later they were all back onstage again, this time with Bonham's son, Jason, occupying the drum stool. The occasion was the televised 40th-anniversary party for the band's label, Atlantic. But instead of being a "dream ticket," Page told me, "It became like my worst nightmare." The problem, he said, was that the band's scheduled performance was delayed by several hours, "by which time I'd peaked and I just . . . lost it." Certainly his performance has gone down in history as one of his worst. As he admitted, "People saw that and just assumed I couldn't play anymore."

It wasn't true, and by 1990, with the four-CD *Remasters* box set to promote, Page, Plant, and Jones were sitting around a table together discussing the possibility of a Zeppelin reunion, albeit on a strictly temporary basis. Much to his chagrin, Jason Bonham was excluded from these discussions, with Plant pushing for the more fashionable Mike Bordin

of Faith No More to be offered the job. Once again, however, the plan started to unravel, with Plant getting cold feet when the others expressed reservations about using the young, dreadlocked FNM drummer. "What you've got to remember," an insider told me, "is Robert is used to having his own way now. He can't bear to go back to the days when Jimmy and Jonesy made the major decisions about the music."

Be that as it may, Plant seemed more than pleased to team up again with Page for their MTV *Unplugged* performance in 1994. With Jones not even on the guest list, the notion of this being a Zeppelin reformation in disguise was easily denied. Page, who would have been equally happy bringing Jones in and simply calling the band Led Zeppelin, merely shrugged. If that's what it took to get Robert on board again, so be it. For as Plant had declared, "I don't want to go backwards, I only want to go forwards." But Jones noted with disdain the posters for the subsequent Page and Plant tour which boasted the slogan, "The Evolution of Led Zeppelin"; "I felt that was a bit too close for comfort." He was also miffed at the title given to the accompanying album: *No Quarter* was taken from one of his own Zeppelin songs. Jones, who was touring with Diamanda Galás, was asked for his reaction "constantly, and it hurt to have to deal with it. It was a great shame, after all we'd been through together."

Page would find himself on the wrong end of Plant's wriggling insistence on not reigniting the Zeppelin flame when he announced he would never sing "Stairway to Heaven" again. "Robert's probably got a perfectly adequate and eloquent reason for all of that," he sighed, "but . . . I don't know. All I do know is that when we were in Japan [with *Page and Plant*] we were on a TV talk show and we did a bit of it then, which was unusual. We just did a little bit of it, the opening part of it."

Since then there have been at least two more occasions when Page and Plant have set aside their differences long enough to discuss the possibility of playing together again as Led Zeppelin. The first time, in preparation for the release of both DVD and *How the West Was Won* in 2003, a plan—to undertake a brief but intensely lucrative US summer tour—was scuppered, insider sources claim, when Plant became more interested in the coincidental release that year of his *Sixty Six to Timbuktu* solo compilation. The second time, when a brace of shows at Madison Square Garden were mooted to mark the 25th anniversary of Bonzo's death, the plan was scrapped when Plant could not decide whether it would be a good thing to do or not.

In 2006, Led Zeppelin was inducted into the UK Music Hall of Fame, but both Plant and Jones declined to attend. Jimmy Page was the only member at the ceremony. In 2007, however, the band created a concert film and live album, recorded at the O2 Arena in London called *Celebration Day*. Any future reunion has not been announced at the time of publication. ❶

The Live Aid reunion
in 1985.

Robert Plant photographed in London, 1983.

ROBERT PLANT

The 1999 interview from *Classic Rock* of Robert Plant and former bandmates Jezz Woodroffe and Robbie Blunt.

By: Jeff Collins

Robert Plant is back at the Rockfield Studios in Monmouth for a reunion with the band that helped him make those first post-Zeppelin albums, 1982's *Pictures at Eleven* and the following year's *The Principle of Moments*. Sitting to his right in the living room at the studio's Coach House accommodation is former Black Sabbath keyboard player Jezz Woodroffe, while guitarist Robbie Blunt hovers nearby, lost amid his own memories, on the other side of the room. Unfortunately, at the last minute, bassist Paul Martinez has been unable to make it to the studio due to a family bereavement.

Phil Collins was one of two drummers on those albums, the other being the late, great Cozy Powell. And the reason for Collins' absence today is simply that he's 3,000 miles away, in New York, promoting *Tarzan*, the Disney musical for which he did the music, that has just opened on Broadway. But he's sent us an email ahead of this reunion to read to his former colleagues: "Dear Lads. Oh, the memories. I remember it like it was 25 years ago! If you ever want to do it again, call me. I can still play drums, but I'm better on the slower songs! Wish I was there, Phil Collins. XXX"

At the end, they nod and smile in unison at the memories of the longtime Genesis drummer's contributions to Plant's albums and the subsequent tour of America.

They all agree that Phil Collins enjoyed his time at Rockfield, even if he sometimes couldn't take the pace. "One of my favorite memories," says Robbie Blunt, "was watching Phil throw up in the bedroom next to mine after he'd been on a night out with us. That was amusing."

"I thought it was great when he played on the road with us," Jezz says of Collins. "It just got better and better. And I loved that old plane we

toured on; the five of us rumbling across America in this sixties prop plane."

"Phil arrived with a different attitude," Plant recalls. "He was so professional, whereas we were ambling around slowly, saying things like: 'Oh yeah, this is nice.' Phil only had four days with us, as his first solo album, *Face Value*, was just breaking and he had to leave to go and promote that. It meant we had to be really effective."

Collins played on six tracks on *Pictures at Eleven*. Former Black Sabbath, Rainbow, and Whitesnake drummer Cozy Powell's powerful signature is on the remaining two songs.

When putting the band together, Plant's first call was to his longtime friend Robbie Blunt, who had played guitar in Stan Webb's Chicken Shack and the glam rock band Silverhead.

"I first met Robert in 1967 when we were both mods," says Blunt. "He was in a band in Kidderminster, where we both lived. I also remember seeing John Bonham in a band called The Way of Life. You had to see them, because he drummed the same way as he later did with Zep. It was incredible. I've known Robert that long."

The two friends hooked up briefly for Plant's fifties style band The Honeydrippers, in 1980, before deciding to write new material together.

Next, the pair got hold of Jezz Woodroffe. It was a convoluted route, too. Having left Black Sabbath in 1976, Jezz recorded a solo album, which was heard by a friend of Plant's, who then recommended the singer to snap him up.

Robert Plant performing onstage in the early eighties.

"I was based then at my dad's music shop in Birmingham," explains the keyboard player. "Robert came in one day and invited me to his house. Robbie was there playing some riffs in Robert's home studio, and we forged a special understanding straight away."

After initial rehearsal sessions at ▷

GETTY IMAGES

Robert Plant posing in London, 1983.

Robert Plant sitting on a truck cab, 1985.

the former Zep singer's home, the three musicians decamped to Rockfield, staying at the Old Mill House—the studio's rehearsal space.

"It was brilliant," Jezz enthuses. "It was a massive old place. Once there, we tried to get a drummer and a bass player to complete the band. We had quite a few interesting things happen. Simon Kirke—from Free and Bad Company—came down, but that didn't work out too well. We had some young bass players, who played a kind of Level 42 style, which also didn't work. Then Cozy Powell finally arrived and it all clicked. What a smashing bloke he was. We became great friends."

Cozy Powell's enthusiasm and sense of humor endeared him to the band straight away. Sadly, 15 years later, the drummer died in a car crash near Bristol. There's a lull in the conversation as Robert, Jezz, and Robbie reflect on the time they spent working with him. And it seems the drummer's stint at Rockfield fulfilled a personal dream.

"One of the funniest things was when Cozy listening back to the drums on [*Pictures at Eleven's*] 'Slow Dancer,'" says Jezz. "It was the first time he'd heard it back. So he pushed up every single fader of every single drum as high as they would go.

"I think that was one of Cozy's happiest moments ever, because he'd always wanted to work with Robert. Always. And now here he was doing his spectacular, powerful drumming, and smiling from ear to ear."

"I was stood on a chair at the back of the control room, pinned against the wall by the noise," Robbie continues. "It sounded ridiculously loud but great. We had so many good times here."

The band spent August and September 1981 in the studio. It was less than a year after the death of John Bonham, and Robert Plant was making the most of his new start—a complete break from the behemoth that was Zeppelin. He'd turned

PICTURES AT ELEVEN

By: Mick Wall

Robert Plant's first solo album, released in June 1982—his last recording to be issued on the rapidly disintegrating Swan Song label—was a transitional work, at best; an exercise in treading water, at worst. Although in later years he would bend over backwards to unshackle himself from the legacy of his time in the world's most extravagantly gifted—and most over-the-top—rock band, *Pictures at Eleven* found him never straying far from the sound he was then best known for.

In ex-Steve Gibbons Band guitarist Robbie Blunt, Plant had found someone he felt immediately comfortable writing with (check out the "trad" rock guitar on album closer "Mystery Title"). As a result, of the eight tracks, five can safely be characterized as straightforward rockers, two as entirely irony free ballads, and one that somewhat too self-consciously occupies the space somewhere between that Zeppelin really did make their own. Inevitably, then, the best of the bunch are the most Zep-like. Of the rockers, "Burning Down One Side" features portentous drumming from Phil Collins, in his rather too obvious attempt to fill the shoes of Plant's behemoth previous drummer, while "Like I've Never Been Gone," the best of the two ballads, is again spoiled only by its obvious self-reference; as is the commendable but rather too "Kashmir"-like "Slow Dancer."

The baffling "Pledge Pin" relies too heavily on saxophonist Raphael Ravenscroft for its appeal; "Moonlight in Samosa" sounds like "Stairway to Heaven" without the ascent. That said, if *Pictures at Eleven* proved anything, it was the weight of the creative role the singer had occupied in Zeppelin. Co-written, sung, and produced by Plant at a time when Page was still hiding away reclusively, licking his wounds, it was the first encouraging glimpse Zeppelin fans would have of what the post-Zep future might actually look and sound like.

down a chance to record at Zep's old haunt, Headley Grange, choosing instead the rural surroundings of Rockfield—a farm converted into a studio complex that had played host to the likes of Queen, Rush, Judas Priest, and Motörhead.

"Rockfield was a turning point for me, personally and professionally," Plant says. "At the age of 32, when your career is finished, anything that came after that was a bonus. After all that wild stuff in Zeppelin, this place was an absolute dream. It was pastoral, funny, and had a history. I'd lived in this goldfish bowl in Led Zeppelin. All we knew about were security blokes and shadowy figures that came in the night with bags of gear. So when it all finished, it was fantastic to come here and find this whole culture around Monmouth of aspiring, failed, dismal, and elated musicians—depending on what day it was. And you could be anyone of those at any given time.

"You'd go down to the Nag's Head pub and have three pints of Wood's and come wobbling back up here to the studios." Plant's eyes glaze over as the memories of many a booze-filled night in rural Wales come flooding back.

"The first place we went to was the Old Punch House," chimes in Robbie Blunt. "The owner endeared himself to us on our first visit by asking, 'What do you scruffy buggers want?' There was also a place called The Beaufort. It was open all the time; they just used to close the curtains. We'd tap on the windows and they'd let us in."

"It had a strange mix of people," Plant adds. "You know there's that thing in some parts of Wales: there are the town folk and then there are the hill folk. And there's always a bit of friction between the two. Having that, plus musicians and a weird assortment of people passing through, made it something like the bar out of *Star Wars*. Still, I moved here and became one of those dismal, happy, sad, failed musicians that other people cross the street to avoid."

Robert Plant with new drummer, Phil Collins.

Robert Plant leans back in his chair as he pauses to remember the lighter moments of the band's time together. "We can all relate some songs to one incident or another, during recording," he says. "The song 'Horizontal Departure' is a great example. We all went to Ibiza to get in the groove of writing *The Principle of Moments*. Our bassist Paul Martinez is a lovely guy, but could come across as [stroppy]. He could be so off-hand that people would take it as an insult. One night he was in a club and someone he'd offended decked him. He flew through the door and hit the floor as he came out. We all rushed out into the street after him, and there he was on the curb, which was covered in his blood. We'd watched him come straight through the door. And that inspired the song 'Horizontal Departure.' So there were all these little innuendos, which were comical to us at the time. It's just the same for any band, I guess."

Jezz Woodroffe puts his cup of coffee on the table in front of him as he recalls another inspiring moment: "The song 'Fat Lip' was called that because Robert's son, Logan, who was six at the time, used to go round telling people he was going to give them a fat lip."

Robert Plant chuckles at that recollection, before adding, "'Burning Down One Side' was about a spliff. 'Big Log' was about a spliff as well . . . in fact it's all just one big spliff attack," he announces with a flourish, clearly warming to his theme.

Pictures at Eleven was released in June 1982, with *The Principle of Moments* coming along 13 months later. Both albums made the top five on both sides of the Atlantic. In 1984 the band returned to Rockfield, this time with Little Feat drummer Richie Hayward, to record parts of Plant's third solo album, *Shaken 'N' Stirred*.

Plant's solo catalogue has now been remastered and reissued by Warners. The program has started with a comprehensive box set called *Nine Lives*

which features all his solo albums, plus bonus live material and interviews.

"I was happy to take Warners up on their offer to remaster these albums," he says. "I was quite fearful of what it might sound like, but I think it's turned out wonderful. Some of the live versions are around eight minutes long and I thought we'd have to edit them down. But the studio staff said as they were live we should just let them run."

As it happens, for this reunion Plant brought along a CD of the some early mixes of a handful of the live tracks included in the box set, to play to his former bandmates. Recorded at the Summit Arena in Houston on September 20, 1983, the songs include "In The Mood" and "Thru' with the Two Step" from *The Principle of Moments*, "Like I've Never Been Gone" from *Pictures at Eleven*, and a rare live version of the Bob Marley song "Lively Up Yourself."

He pops the disc into a CD player, and "Like I've Never Been Gone" suddenly booms out into the room. Robert turns the volume up as we hear Robbie Blunt launch into the song's second guitar solo. Plant tells everyone to listen to how well this has come out: "That guitar solo is just storming," he beams with pride at his guitarist friend's performance from so long ago.

Once the tracks end, Plant announces he has to leave to drive to Brecon to rehearse with his new band, The Strange Sensation.

As Plant, Robbie Blunt, and Jezz Woodroffe walk outside into the courtyard, shake hands, hug, and say their farewells, they reflect on what an enjoyable experience they had together.

"I was immune to penicillin by the time I left," Plant says cheekily, to the amusement of everyone. "And I didn't get done for drinking and driving."

"I nearly did!" says Jezz.

Plant points at Robbie Blunt like he was a naughty schoolboy and laughs, "But *he* did!" ❼

THE PRINCIPLE OF MOMENTS

By: Mick Wall

The second Plant solo album, released in July 1983, was, like its predecessor, too eager to have its cake and eat it. That is, while the singer was clearly ready to try and step out from the gigantic, forbidding shadow of Zeppelin, he hadn't yet figured out a way to do that and retain his commercial appeal—still an important element in his need to prove he could live without the Zep legend.

Written, produced, and played by virtually the same team as *Pictures at Eleven*, ultimately what makes *The Principle of Moments* a better album is the quality of its best material. Still somewhat too in thrall to the past—the angular "Black Dog"-like rhythms of "Messin' with the Mekon"; the bolted-on feel of Blunt's "Kashmir"-like guitar motif in "Wreckless Love"; the synths of "Thru' with the Two Step" reminiscent of "All My Love"—it was too awash with attempts to find an "alternative" to that sound and, as a consequence, what Plant clearly saw as "experimental" then ("Other Arms," "In the Mood") now sounds firmly rooted in the dreary eighties.

What saves the day is "Big Log." A wonderfully evocative ballad with its own Latin lilt and glossy synths that owe their inspiration to no one else, even Plant's voice finds a new, snug fit, beyond the howls and moans of Zeppelin; soft and crooning, but in the best, most seductive way. It is no coincidence that "Big Log" also became Plant's first big solo hit. Here, at last, was the breakthrough he had been seeking—and that even his most ardent fans had secretly wondered whether he was capable of. The pity is, just as he and Blunt had finally found their groove, Plant was already thinking two steps ahead, to a time when he would actually make an album with no guitars at all on it. But that needlessly career-denting cul de sac was still some way off into the future. For now, at least, he could be taken seriously for the first time as a bona fide solo artist.

FIRST STEPS DOWN THE SOLO ROAD

Robert Plant's first post-Led Zeppelin interview.

By: Geoff Barton

It's a drizzly, overcast day in September 1982. I've just completed an interview with Robert Plant about his first post-Led Zeppelin solo album, *Pictures at Eleven,* and we're standing outside Blakes Hotel in South Kensington conducting an impromptu photo session with Ross Halfin. Belying his unapproachable rock god status, Plant is amenable and cooperative. He poses in this position and that, crouching low, stretching high, making my body feel brittle and stiff by comparison.

However, Plant has to apologize for not being able to straighten out an arm for one particular shot—the legacy of that car crash in Rhodes in August 1975 when he and his wife Maureen were seriously injured, which left Plant wheelchair-bound for a time and which caused an unexpected hiatus in Led Zeppelin's career. Plant rolls up his sleeve and winces as he shows me his scars.

All too soon it's over and we're saying our farewells. As a parting gesture, I present Plant with a picture I have of him performing a recent low-key gig at Dudley JB's, in the heart of his beloved Black Country.

"Dear oh dear!" he cries. "Look at the bags under the eyes. I'll tell you why that is: the show was two days after my birthday. I was just about beginning to sober up. And that hairstyle! I'd just had my hair cut. It looks like I'm wearing a soufflé."

Right on cue, Halfin whips out a copy of his photo book *The Powerage* and turns to the back page. Lo and behold, there's a photo of Plant in his classic long-haired screaming belter days, cavorting onstage with Zeppelin at Knebworth. You can't help but compare the photos of the singer at Dudley JB's and at the festival in 1979, and contrast the *now* with the *then.*

"Will you sign the book for me?" asks Halfin, impetuously. But Plant is only too willing and writes, with considerable flourish: "To Ross. It's getting better! Robert."

Plant goes to hand the book back, but he can't tear his gaze away from the snap of him onstage with Zep.

His eyes narrow, his brow creases and he says: "Oh, I don't know. Shall I grow my hair again?"

He deliberates for a moment, then exclaims: "Yeah, why not. To hell with it!"

Backtrack to a couple of hours earlier. Plant is leaning on the Blakes Hotel reception desk. Phone in hand, he's muttering something about trying to acquire a copy of Billy Fury's new single "Love or Money"—"for jimmy."

Compared to his flamboyant Led Zeppelin persona, it's a more mature, subtly changed Plant that stands before me. The hair is short, his face is lined, and his manner of dress (zippy khaki jumpsuit and tattered white baseball boots) is quite anonymous.

We adjourn to the basement restaurant. Plant leads the way to a secluded annex he's obviously had reserved for the occasion. We sit down on low, soft cushions and Plant pours tea and offers biscuits. On the table in front of him are a copy of Hunter S. Thompson's *Fear & Loathing in Las Vegas,* a Roy Harper tape, and a half-finished pack of Winston cigarettes.

It's a "lived-in" scenario, and it occurs to me that Plant must have done a whole string of interviews today; that I'm just another blurred face on the journalistic conveyor belt.

"No, you're actually the first person I've talked to," Plant reveals in a surprisingly distinctive Midlands accent.

"That's not too desperate," I comment.

"No, there's no desperation. Not really."

Edited highlights of our interview follow:

Your album *Pictures at Eleven* has received good reviews. Has that surprised you?
I was expecting to get a hammering from everybody. I don't really know why, because I'm proud of what I've done. But there's been so much slating in the past when I've tried really hard, and I thought there wasn't much chance of the album being well received.

Surely your years with Zeppelin must have rendered you immune to slag-offs?
This is different—I'm out on my own now. I could tell people were saying behind my back, "That's it, he's finished, he's not going to come up with the goods at all." All the time I was working down at Rockfield, no outsiders heard the record. But I knew what was happening, it was just getting better and better.

The most amazing thing was that so many people were pleased for me when they finally heard the record. People who I've known for years, people who run clubs in the Black Country. They heard the thing and just nodded their heads and smiled. They gave me their silent approval, and that's just great.

They've known me for such a long time they're not suddenly going to throw palm leaves at my feet.

How long ago did you start recording *Pictures at Eleven*?
Last September [1981]. Cozy [Powell, one of two drummers on the album, the other being Phil Collins] came back from wherever it was. He'd been off diving—either muffs or fish, I can't remember. But anyway, it was last September and we laid down "Slow Dancer" and "Like I've Never Been Gone."

And you released the album this July [1982]. Ten months—that's quite a quick turnaround by Zeppelin standards.
Yeah . . . in fact we did those two first two tracks I mentioned in about a day and a half. There's so much drama about "Slow Dancer." It's so brooding—and there was so much to prove, especially from my point of view. It just *had* to be right.

What exactly did you feel that you had to prove?
I just wanted to be responsible for something that was in that ilk. If I never write anything like that again . . . I just wanted it that way once more. Have a bit of *that*, then! And it worked successfully.

When exactly did you decide to go it alone and record your own album?
Well . . . obviously I was sitting on my arse after we'd lost John [Bonham]. I was thinking, "What happens next?" I had no idea at all.

Of course there was The Honeydrippers and all that, going round the clubs playing Otis Rush stuff, but that's old hat. It was obvious that something would have to come out of it that would feed my craving . . . for . . . drama if you like, for mood, to expand mood beyond singing "Stormy Monday"—which incidentally, I did very well at JB's in Dudley three weeks ago.

Yeah. A few days ago a local photographer sent us a picture of you onstage there.
In fact Bonzo's brother, Micky, videoed the gig and it's really funny. We'd hardly rehearsed . . . but it was great for Robbie [Blunt, Plant's guitarist], because since the record's been made there's been various rumors flying about, people saying, "No, he doesn't really exist; it's not Robbie, it's *Jimmy*."

Well, let me put the record straight once and for all: Robbie Blunt is a person in his own right and he is *not* Jimmy Page.

I don't really see how people can think that; I don't think Robbie plays like Jimmy at all. They're like chalk and cheese. Jimmy's very aggressive in his approach.

Did you consciously try to make *Pictures at Eleven* not sound like Led Zeppelin?
As you can imagine, I took a million pains to try and create my own individual sound. Halfway through the thing I stopped and said to Benji the engineer, a guy who was with us for years with Zeppelin, the PA man, I asked him, "Is it close? Because if it's close we stop!" And he said, "Oh no, the mood's totally different."

I was just trying to pull away as much as I could . . . but then again you can only pull away so far. I wanted to leave Zeppelin the way it was and . . . just pull those reins a little to the right.

There are similarities, of course, but that's got to be due to the fact that I'm singing and writing, and this is how I've sung and written since the beginning of time. Since we thought in black and white, really.

Just for the record, Led Zeppelin are dead and buried, aren't they?
After we lost John, we issued a statement to that effect but everybody read it as being ambiguous. I can't even remember the wording of it now. But no, there's absolutely no point. No point at all. There's certain people you don't do without in life, you don't keep things going for the sake of it. There's no functional purpose for keeping things going. For whose convenience? Nobody's, really.

No one could ever have taken over John's job. Never, ever! Impossible. I listen to Zeppelin stuff now and I realize how important John was. When he drummed he was right *there* with either my voice or whatever Pagey was doing . . . you couldn't have found anybody with the same kind of ingredient to make the band really take off like John did.

" . . . We all sort of rose out of it together going, "We don't care—take this!" And you don't start carrying on with people who weren't a part of that. Impossible.

Does all that rule out any sort of collaboration with either Jimmy Page or John Paul Jones in the future?
It was always difficult to collaborate with Jonesy because he never listened to the lyrics. I used to talk about a song and he would say, "Now, which song would that be? And I'd go, "You know, the one on *Presence*." And he'd say, "I'm sorry, I'm not familiar with the titles, what key was it in?" I'd sigh and say, "I haven't a clue, Jonesy."

But . . . I miss them. And I miss Jimmy a lot. But we've been pals for years and years, and we had a relationship that was built out of certain standards. Although we're totally dissimilar, totally unalike, we knew exactly how far to take each other. When you've been with a bloke for 14 years you naturally miss certain parts, musically and personality-wise. But there's a long way to go before I stop singing, and right now I'm having a great time with my own guys.

When you go on tour to promote *Pictures at Eleven*, what size venues will you be playing?
I can't play places like Birmingham NEC. The only group I've seen come over reasonably well there was Dire Straits, and I've seen quite a few people, including Dylan, David Bowie, and Foreigner. That size of gig is a little out of order now, in Britain at least. I mean, when Zeppelin played Earls Court in 1975 the sound was horrendous, but there was a kind of furious momentum about that whole gig that pulled us through.

I don't think I've got the kind of audience that would fill the NEC anyway. I don't know how I stand in the scheme of things, really.

> **"No one could ever have taken over [John Bonham's] job. Never, ever! Impossssible."**

In comparison to your "reclusive" Zep days, you seem to be much more open and approachable now.
That's because I'm prepared to work, I'm prepared to go out and I'm prepared to stand up and be counted. To me, everything is easy unless you make it difficult. And what's the point of being difficult when music's supposed to be a medium of expression and contact? Musically, Zeppelin wasn't safe, but we had such a following that virtually everything was accepted . . . except people always wanted "Dazed & Confused" and didn't want "Fool in the Rain."

It's great fun at the moment, very enjoyable. I'm learning new things every day, I'm meeting all kinds of new people in the business—and surprising them all, because they all thought I was some kind of demon.

Do you still like Welsh villages and all that? Bron-Y-Aur . . .
Bronnariar.

Is that how you pronounce it? I'd always wondered.
Yeah, I still like them. But I drive through them real quick. ●

ZoSo
JIMMY PAGE

How the "shattered" Led Zeppelin guitarist learned to love music all over again.

By: Mick Wall

Jimmy Page suffered most from the loss of Led Zeppelin. While Robert Plant was plainly relieved to shed the responsibility of helping to keep the Zeppelin legend alive, and John Paul Jones seemed content to retreat even further into the shadows, Page was left absolutely bereft, both musically and personally.

As he told me not long afterwards: "There was a point after [John Bonham died] where I hadn't touched a guitar for ages and I just related everything to what had happened, the tragedy. But I called up my road manager one day and said, 'Look, get the Les Paul out of storage.' He went to get it and the case was empty! I think somebody took it out and borrowed it. They shouldn't have. It eventually reappeared. But when he came back and said the guitar was missing, I said, 'That's it, forget it, I'm finished.'"

In the immediate aftermath of Zeppelin's demise, Page had been coaxed by neighbor Michael Winner into recording the soundtrack album for the director's *Death Wish II* movie. But it wasn't until he teamed up with former Free and Bad Company vocalist Paul Rodgers that Page began to discover a musical life for himself after Zeppelin. With Rodgers also "still recovering" from the loss of his own outfit, "he was one of the few people that could probably relate to what I was going through."

The result was The Firm, a four-piece also including ex-Uriah Heep drummer Chris Slade and former Roy Harper bassist Tony Franklin. Page says it "saved" him. "I was shattered at the time." The Firm allowed he and Rodgers to "get out and play and really enjoy ourselves." Both men refused to perform any material from their former bands, relying solely on the much smoother funk-tinged sound of the new outfit, although "Midnight Moonlight," the closing track on their self-titled debut album in 1984, was actually an unreleased Zeppelin number originally titled "The Swang Song." A second Firm album, *Mean Business*, was released in 1986, but neither records troubled the charts for long.

By 1988 the band had dissolved and Page was ready to release his first and only solo album, *Outrider*. Featuring Jason Bonham on drums and an array of guest vocalists, *Outrider* was a commendable collection which, like The Firm, failed to set the charts alight but did allow Page to tour Britain and America solo for the first time, the highlight of the show being an instrumental "Stairway to Heaven"—"which the audience sings for me."

The plan had been to release a second solo album, but Page's new US label, Geffen, suggested he team up with David Coverdale.

The short-lived Coverdale/Page was surprisingly invigorating. In the absence of the full-on Zeppelin reunion that Page no longer made any secret of craving, working with Coverdale was the next best thing. Certainly the eponymous album they produced in 1993 was the closest thing to Zeppelin Page had recorded since the breakup. With Coverdale inspired, too, on titanic blues-rock workouts like "Shake My Tree" and "Absolution Blues," it was not long before a publicly smug but privately piqued Plant was on the phone to Jimmy suggesting something similar—but different.

Officially, the spark had been an invitation from MTV to play in their *Unplugged* series. In truth, with Plant's solo career flagging and Page no better off left to his own devices, the chance to join forces was too good to miss. Page would have been happy for a full-on Zeppelin reformation. Plant, however, was still against the idea, arguing that the pair could enjoy the kudos of being back together without any of the problems of using the Zeppelin name by not inviting John Paul Jones along.

Despite the fact that the resulting 1994 televised concert and *No Quarter* album were built almost entirely on the Zep back catalogue, the judicious addition of an 11-piece Egyptian ensemble, plus four brand new numbers, obscured the fact that this was virtually a Zeppelin reformation in all but name. On tour, where audiences had come to hear the classics, the illusion was harder to maintain. Plant was refusing to sing "Stairway to Heaven," and a new enmity between the two was brewing. There was a second album, the good-not-great *Walking Into Clarksdale*, but the pairing ended at the start of 1999, when Plant changed his mind at the last minute about an Australian tour, claiming that he "didn't know how many more English springs I would see."

Page turned to The Black Crowes, who he successfully toured America with later that year with a set built solidly around the Zep catalogue. The resulting album, *Live at the Greek*, was not only a bigger hit than *Walking Into Clarksdale*, it was also more enjoyable.

The odd collaboration aside, Page has spent his post-Zeppelin career concentrating on keeping the flame alive, from producing the four-CD *Remasters* box set in 1990 to overseeing the ground-breaking twin release of the six-hour DVD collection and double-live CD *How the West Was Won*, in 2003. Since then, Page has made occasional recordings as collaborations, but no big solo ventures. He has been instrumental in overseeing the remastering and reissuing of Led Zeppelin's albums, making sure that new generations of listeners can have access to their music. ❶

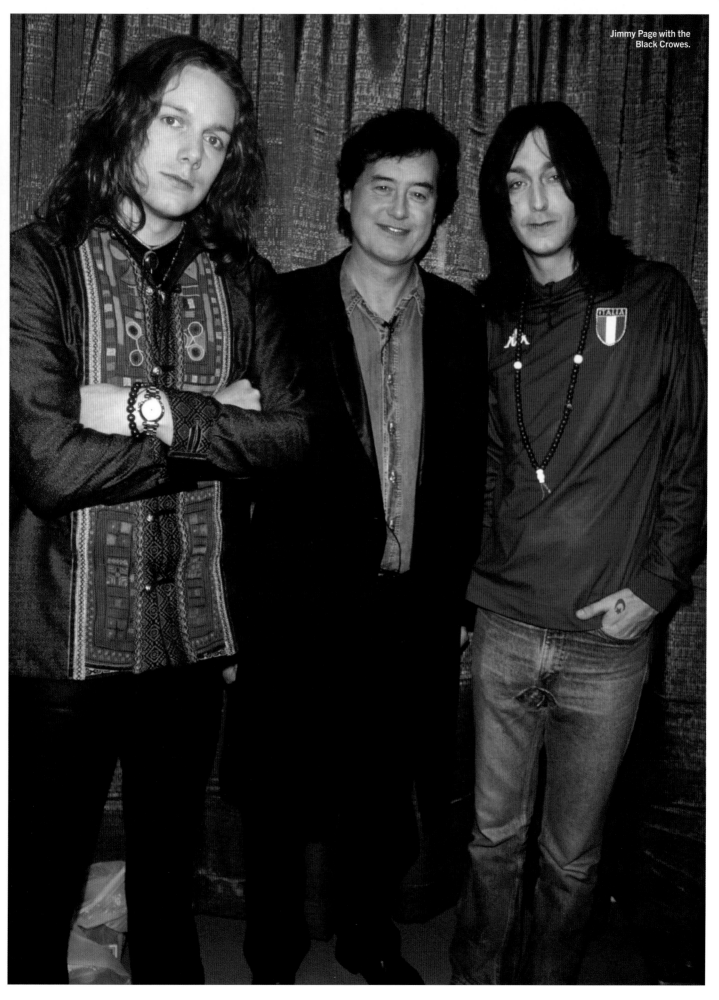
Jimmy Page with the Black Crowes.

JOHN PAUL JONES

Snubbed by his reunited bandmates, the Zep bassist hasn't stopped working or innovating.

|||||||||||||||||||||||||||||||||||||||||||||||||||||||| **By: Mick Wall** ||||||||||||||||||||||||||||||||||||||||||||||||||||||||||||||||||

According to the legend, John Paul Jones was the only member of Led Zeppelin not to have signed a pact with the Devil, which is why he was spared the personal disasters—death, divorce, drug addiction—that befell the other three. Nonsense, of course, but there's a reason the story still persists: Jones was always the "sensible one" in the band. The traditional "'quiet man" bass player, in the Bill Wyman/John Entwistle mold, seemingly happy to allow the singer and guitarist—even the drummer— hog the spotlight while he got on with the important job of holding the whole musical structure together. But while Jones may not have shared the charisma of the other Zeppelin members, he certainly didn't lack the talent. Which is why, when the group folded in 1980, his career took on a much broader, more complex musical sweep than those of the more recognizable Page and Plant—although not right away.

At first, Jones simply retreated to the Sussex farmhouse he'd owned since 1977, spending time with his family, "cooling out and just taking stock." Bonham's death, he told this writer, left him "with a sense of anger as much as loss. It was just such a waste. Especially as it looked as though we had finally gotten all the bad times behind us."

When Jones did finally emerge from his shell, his various credits as musician, producer, arranger, and songwriter began cropping up all over the place, as he began to collaborate with artists as diverse as R.E.M., Heart, Ben E. King, La Fura Dels Baus, Brian Eno, Karl Sabino, and the Butthole Surfers. He also appeared in sessions and videos for Paul McCartney, who invited him to help with the soundtrack of his semi-autobiographical musical film *Give My Regards to Broad Street*.

Perhaps Jones' most memorable moments in the eighties involved the off-the-wall soundtrack he made for director Michael Winner's 1986 film *Scream for Help*, which also had Jimmy Page on two tracks. He followed that two years later with the more conventional—and much more successful—production of *Children*, the second and best album from Sisters of Mercy offshoot The Mission, from which came the band's biggest hit, "Tower of Strength." "We couldn't believe our luck, getting John as our producer," recalled Mission frontman Wayne Hussey. "We kept muttering under our breath, 'Look out, Led Zeppelin guy! Led Zeppelin guy!'" In 1990, Jones also produced an album for his eldest daughter, singer Jacinda Jones—a less successful but "even more wonderful" collaboration.

Jones was "very hurt" to be overlooked for the Page and Plant reformation in the mid-nineties. "I read that Robert said they'd lost my phone number," he sniffed disdainfully. In retrospect, it could be argued that it was Jones who was making the greater musical contribution at this point.

In 1994, he recorded—and received co-billing on—the excellent Diamanda Galás album *The Sporting Life*, where his multi-instrumental embellishments on tracks like "Devil's Rodeo" added luster to the poet diva's songs of lust and decay, and later also joined her for a spectacularly well-received world tour. Playing with the feisty songstress was "the most fun I'd had since Zeppelin."

Jones also set up his own recording studio, where he recorded his first solo album, *Zooma*, released in 1999. An instrumental tour de force, on tracks like "Tidal" and the thunderous title track, Jones created tumultuous pieces full of avalanching rhythms and eerie, sonic soundscapes, using a battery of four-, 10-, and 12-string basses. Other tracks, like "Bass 'N' Drums" (inspired by Jacinda introducing him to drum 'n' bass), showed his sense of humor and willingness to explore new musical territory. "The Smile of Your Shadow" demonstrated he had not lost his ability for conjuring up suitably dry iced atmospherics, either.

Two years later he was back with the follow-up, the adventurous but even more accessible *The Thunderthief*, on which he played just about everything except the drums—from bass, guitars, and keyboards to autoharp and koto. It also included his debut as a solo vocalist on the witty, punk-derived "Angry Angry" and the more traditional-sounding folk ditty "Freedom Song." Mostly, though, it was the driving rhythms of tracks like "Down the River to Pray" that impressed.

Emboldened, he put together a touring band and gave concerts based on his solo work in the UK, US, and Japan. In 2004, he also toured as part of the group Mutual Admiration Society, along with singer Glen Phillips and various members of the band Nickel Creek.

Jones played on Foo Fighters' *In Your Honor* album, (mandolin on "Another Round," piano on "Miracle," both included on the "acoustic disc"). Foos frontman Dave Grohl described working with Jones as the "second greatest thing to happen to me in my life."

He's also made a return to production, not least on such titanic latter-day recordings as The Datsuns' "old-school heavy rock" album *Outta Sight, Outta Mind* in 2004 and, a year later, on Uncle Earl's neo-country collection *She Waits For Night*. He's completed more soundtrack work, too, including the theme to *The Secret Adventures of Tom Thumb*.

Would he still consider striding the boards under the Led Zeppelin banner, though? Of course he would. As he told me in 2003, "There's definitely the feeling of unfinished business about the band. Even though it's unimaginable, in one sense, to try it without Bonzo, we had hoped to do to the eighties what we did to the seventies.

"I still very much regret that we never got that chance." ❂

The piece opposite was written before JPJ joined Them Crooked Vultures in 2009, one of the most satisfying post-Zep outings.

29 PSALMS
THE BEST OF PAGE, PLANT, AND JONES

The 29 tracks every fan should buy and burn for the perfect double album of post-Zeppelin manic nirvana.

By: Hugh Fielder & Mick Wall

SHAKE MY TREE
Coverdale/Page
Coverdale/ Page, 1993

When word got out that the former Zep maestro was working with the ex-Whitesnake charmer, most critics nearly gagged on their tea and digestives. And yet what should, on paper at least, have been a disaster turned out to be the best thing either man had done since their respective seventies heydays. And here was the proof right from the off. Built on a bastardized version of Zep's "Nobody's Fault But Mine" riff, such was its appeal, it wasn't long before Robert Plant was on the blower persuading Page he should come back and do the real thing.

BURNING DOWN ONE SIDE
Robert Plant
Pictures at Eleven, 1982

First solo album, track one—some kind of statement needed here? It's irrelevant now, but back in '82 the weight of expectation upon Plant's first steps outside the comfort zone provided by Messrs Page, Jones, and Bonham was daunting. But Percy needn't have worried. A clever, succinct blend of the new and the familiar, "Burning Down One Side" sends out a simple, straightforward statement: this is life beyond Led Zeppelin.

MIDNIGHT MOONLIGHT
The Firm
The Firm, 1985

"This isn't the sort of thing where you sign five-album contracts at the age of 41," said Jimmy Page when it was first announced he had formed a band called The Firm with Paul Rodgers. "I might not even live to 46." In fact, it lasted for two albums—and might have lasted even longer if the secret plan for a post-Live Aid reformation of Zeppelin hadn't put paid to the group. Of the two Firm albums, though, only a handful of tracks lived up to the band's promise. This was the best of them. The most Zep-like of all the Firm numbers—indeed, some claimed it was reworked from an old Zeppelin tune called "The Swan Song"—"Midnight Moonlight" was first performed on the 1983 American leg of the ARMS tour, and was initially known as "Bird on the Wing."

CRACKBACK
John Paul Jones
Scream for Help, 1986

Taken from the soundtrack album John Paul Jones made for director Michael Winner's 1986 film *Scream for Help*, which was the bassist's first real work of note as

an artist in his own right since the collapse of Zeppelin. The album also featured Jimmy Page on two tracks, of which "Crackback," an urgent if somewhat eerie-sounding instrumental, was easily the best. "It was a horrible film," Jones later reflected. "A bit of a disaster all round really." Of the "couple of good tracks" on the album, "Crackback" was "good fun to record" and his own personal favorite.

WONDERFUL ONE
Page and Plant
No Quarter, 1994

The best of the new songs to emerge from *No Quarter*, "Wonderful One" is a ballad that draws on Zeppelin's acoustic heritage but with a slow, haunting heartbeat that they would never have got away with back then. Having said that, the song has echoes of "The Rain Song" from *Houses of the Holy* as Page and Plant slip back into a telepathic communication.

BIG LOG
Robert Plant
The Principle of Moments, 1983

By the end of his second album we should be getting a strong sense of Plant's solo persona. "Big Log" is moody, mellow, and restless, which isn't far wide of the mark. Don't speculate too deeply on the title which never actually appears in the lyrics. There are those who would have you believe that Plant is having a conversation with his late buddy Bonham, but the words are too abstract for that. Actually he's just gazing at a log burning on the fire. Or more likely inhaling it.

TALL COOL ONE
Robert Plant
Now and Zen, 1988

After putting as much distance as possible between himself and Zep, Plant decides he can now confront the ghosts of his past. Some confrontation. The tempo of "Tall Cool One" is alarmingly (deliberately?) similar to "Rock and Roll." But the pace is even more relentless, driven by a fierce, robotic beat, just to remind you how times are different now. That's just the start. The dive-bombing guitar that intermittently flashes across the song, taking your head with it each time, comes to you courtesy of Jimmy Page who has joined Plant for the bracing nostalgia trip. That subliminal "Hey hey mama" is Plant sampling himself from "Black Dog." And before you know it, Zeppelin samples are flying thick and fast: "Dazed and Confused," "Whole Lotta Love," "Custard Pie," "The Ocean." Well, everyone else is sampling Zeppelin, why can't they?

Robert Plant & The Honeydrippers on *Saturday Night Live*, 1984

ROCKIN' AT MIDNIGHT
The Honeydrippers
The Honeydrippers Volume One, 1984

The standout good-time track from an album seemingly featuring nothing else but, this glorious reworking of the Roy Brown tune was especially fun for Zep aficionados as it featured the unholy trinity of Plant, Page, and Jeff Beck. It was also, quite simply, a great track. Indeed, a version of The Honeydrippers—featuring Plant, guitarist Robbie Blunt, and former Stray Cats frontman Brian Setzer on guitar—performed it live on *Saturday Night Live* in December 1984 (along with an impromptu "Santa Claus is Coming to Town"). As this issue went to press, Plant was due to reform The Honeydrippers for a special one-off charity show on December 23 at Kidderminster Town Hall.

THE ONLY ONE
Jimmy Page
Outrider, 1988

An uptempo rocker and one of the highlights from Jimmy Page's debut solo album, featuring lyrics and lead vocals from Robert Plant. "Well, I played on a couple of tracks on his album [*Now and Zen*]," said Page, "and when I had the [music for the] track, I thought it would be perfect for Robert if he wanted to do it, and he really enthused about it. I gave him a cassette copy of the tape and he came down with reams of lyrics and we had a great time." How similar was it to the way they had worked in Zeppelin, though? "I guess it's bound to be different. But we still get on in that sort of working environment, as far as sparking off each other."

SHIP OF FOOLS
Robert Plant
Now and Zen, 1988

A serene ballad that glides on a sea of ethereal strings and delicate guitars, gently steered by a resonant bass—at least until midway through when the drums kick in and prod guitarist Doug Boyle into a masterful solo. Tailor-made for Plant's mystical inclinations to take flight once again, you'd think. But you'd be wrong. Instead his voice is close-up and reflective as he muses on some of the practical

problems since the ship set sail. It's an aspect Plant has scarcely explored before and a warning not to take him for granted again.

HURTING KIND (I'VE GOT MY EYES ON YOU)
Robert Plant
Manic Nirvana, 1990

An exhilarating fifties rock 'n' roll pastiche "delivered through the barrel of a machine gun." according to Plant, who claims the song was inspired by the late, great Gene Vincent. "As a kid listening to Radio Luxembourg I wanted to be Gene," he remembers. "He was kind of slinky. There was a lot of sex in his voice." Plant may not have acquired the former, but he has the latter in spades.

IN MY TIME OF DYING
Jimmy Page & The Black Crowes
Live at the Greek 2000

If ever you needed proof that all that stuff about Zeppelin not being able to reform without John Bonham was simply not true, *Live at the Greek* is most definitely it. Either that or The Black Crowes were a much, much better band than anyone ever gave them credit for, because together with Page they sure knock the bejayzus out of the material on this. We have chosen just two tracks from it, but the fact is we could have gone for any of the 13 Zeppelin covers therein. That said, "In My Time of Dying," with its slow-fast, light-and-shade is perfect at showcasing just how tremendous the old songs sound with Page and a hot band—any hot band—in full-force behind them.

ZOOMA
John Paul Jones
Zooma, 1999

Recorded at his Sunday School home studio in the mid-1990s, this was the title track of the first Jones solo album. A driving instrumental that sums up the album as a whole, mainly blues-rock oriented, built around the use of his famous four-, 10-, and 12-string basses, yet incorporating an array of computerized processes meshed over a live rhythm section; a method of working which, he said, was "something that came out of working on the Diamanda Galás project. I enjoy that sound very much." So do we.

Jimmy Page in his days with The Firm.

GALLOWS POLE
Page and Plant

No Quarter, 1994

As the song that established Led Zeppelin's folk-rock credentials back in 1970, "Gallows Pole" was an ideal choice for Plant and Page's ethnic excursions on *No Quarter*. Although the song gathers pace in much the same way as the original, the varied instruments bring a different kind of intensity—less electricity but just as frantic.

LIAR'S DANCE
Robert Plant

Manic Nirvana, 1990

This short, melancholic acoustic call-and-response number finds Plant in a refreshingly cliché-free zone. The folk-style guitar harks back to sixties vintage Bert Jansch (the same period that Jimmy Page appropriated for Zep's "Black Mountain Side") and Plant takes another opportunity to explore the more intimate side of his vocal style. Intriguingly, he also offers a glimpse of a direction he would pursue more productively on his next album.

SEA OF LOVE
The Honeydrippers

The Honeydrippers Volume One, 1984

The Honeydrippers was a good-time R&B band fronted by guitarist Robbie Blunt that Robert Plant became involved in, playing gigs around the north of England in the early 1980s. By the time they came to make their one-off mini-album of R&B and rockabilly covers, recorded without fuss and performed as-live in the studio, they also featured Jimmy Page and Jeff Beck, playing together for the first time since The Yardbirds. "Sea of Love," their remake of the Phil Phillips tune, was released as a single and actually made the Top 10. It was, said Plant, "the most fun I've had onstage for about 10 years."

CITY DON'T CRY
Page and Plant

No Quarter, 1994

Built around a single-chord riff and a basic rhythm, "City Don't Cry" is a deliberately risk-free excursion for Page, Plant, and the Egyptian musicians they've recruited. Once Page has set up the riff and rhythm the other musicians pick it up, savoring the essence and holding back from needless complexities. Likewise, Plant's melody is little more than a three-note refrain that he refuses to elaborate, allowing the other singers to express the melody in their own fashion.

NOBODY'S FAULT BUT MINE
Jimmy Page & The Black Crowes

Live at the Greek, 2000

Another absolutely humongous track from the most awesomely humongous album Page—or indeed anyone else from Zeppelin—has recorded since the original band expired. No, it's not Bonzo on drums, nor even Planty on vocals, but it doesn't really matter.

29 PALMS
Robert Plant

Fate of Nations, 1993

Often dismissed as Plant's paean to pop by the rock 'n' roll taste police, "29 Palms" is a deceptively whimsical ride across the Mojave Desert in Southern California en route to the town of the title.

Plant's relaxed vocals, the bittersweet lyrics, and Doug Boyle's sublime melodic guitar riff that gradually pervades the song combine to create an atmosphere that shimmers like a heat haze in the desert. But according to Plant, "It's not a poetic, charming story. It's about a female's arrogance and need to be the big wheel, the insecurity of a beautiful woman who has just taken the world by storm." Some people have speculated that "29 Palms" is about Alannah Myles, the Canadian rock singer who had a worldwide smash hit with "Black Velvet" in 1989 and is rumored to have had a relationship with Plant around the time she toured America with him at the start of the nineties.

SHINE IT ALL AROUND
Robert Plant & The Strange Sensation

Mighty Rearranger, 2005

"Shine It All Around" burns with a ferocity that would be enviable in anyone half Plant's age. But as he says, "It's pointless for me to do anything in half measures at this time in my life." Plant's features may have become more craggy of late, but his voice remains gloriously intact. In fact it was potent enough to earn "Shine It All Around" a Grammy nomination for Best Solo Rock Vocal in 2006.

ABSOLUTION BLUES
Coverdale Page
Coverdale Page, 1993

One of the other breakout choices from the *Coverdale Page* album, "Absolution Blues"—strident, haunting, moving—would have held its own on any of the early Zeppelin albums, which makes it even more remarkable that it was David Coverdale who brought it out of Jimmy Page, not Robert Plant.

TIDAL
John Paul Jones
Zooma, 1999

Listening to Jones' solo instrumentals and imagining Plant's voice layered on top, or Page's guitar bursting through, can give you a tantalizing glimpse of what could have been if Zep's surviving members had worked together in the nineties. *Zooma* provided several such moments, from the folksy fingerpicking on "The Smile of Your Shadow" to the cool riffage on "Nosumi Blue"—but in 1999 the album's thunderous closer "Tidal" sounded as relevant as anything by the Chemical Brothers, while still sounding like it could have been an unfinished track from *Presence*. This is the man who wrote the riff for "Black Dog," remember.

NIRVANA
Robert Plant
Manic Nirvana, 1990

For 20 seconds it's as if Plant is trying to recreate "Communication Breakdown" with knobs on, but then he suddenly tips over a bubbling cauldron of influences he's been brewing up and finds himself assailed by jangling psychobilly guitars, tribal beats, hardcore funk metal, and various jagged noises that swerve by like a rally driver on acid. We have been here before of course, somewhere around the demented middle section of "Whole Lotta Love." But that was then and this is now, and Plant uses the latest studio technology to bind it together.

DEVIL'S RODEO
Diamanda Galás & John Paul Jones
The Sporting Life, 1994

The standout track from Jones' collaborative album with the American-born avant-garde performance artist, vocalist, keyboardist, and esoteric composer known for her operatic voice, with its distinctive three-and-a-half octave range, it made the Page and Plant collaboration of the same year look like what it was: a rehash of old tunes, and nothing so original or startling as this. "I learned so much from working with her," said Jones, who also toured the world with Galás that year. "It taught me about how to be a musician again."

SATISFACTION GUARANTEED
The Firm
The Firm, 1985

The other "keeper" from the first Firm album, a smoldering funk workout featuring slinky slide guitar (played by Page using an empty beer bottle in the video) and suitably thunder-rolling drums from Chris Slade, creating a bubbling brew of atmospherics which made even Rodgers' saccharine lyrics sound like they meant something deep. "It was a good one to play live, too," said Page. "We used to really steam into it."

HEY JOE
Robert Plant
Dreamland, 2002

Sensibly steering clear of the classic Hendrix version by restoring the first verse of the original folk ballad, before veering off into a psychedelic maelstrom, at seven minutes plus, this is such a total reinvention. In fact, were it not for the deliberate reference to the Jimi classic in some of the extended guitar breaks at the finale, you might actually think it was a completely different song. "I viewed it like a folk song," said Plant. "The whole thing is like a miasma. At some points you think, where the hell is this thing going to? It's an adventure and I have no problem with it being considered to be anything else but that. Truly, it's an adventure and it's a lot of fun."

John Paul Jones performing onstage with Them Crooked Vultures in 2009.

SHINING IN THE LIGHT
Page and Plant
Walking Into Clarksdale, 1998

A stripped-back, mid-tempo rocker that harks back to *Led Zeppelin III*. The secret lies in Charlie Jones and Michael Lee's impeccable rhythm section that adds strength to Page's acoustic guitar and allows Plant the freedom to roam. Brief slashes of electric guitar are the only other adornment the song needs, and the repeated three-note riff at the end leaves you with a memorable hook.

BLUE TRAIN
Page and Plant
Walking Into Clarksdale, 1998

Perhaps the best example of how Page and Plant learned to use power without excess. The opening bass line and Plant's whispered vocals draw you in, and although Page adds some jangling guitar lines it's Plant's voice, gradually getting louder, that becomes the focus of the song's buildup. Once the power shifts to the drums, "Blue Train" takes on another dimension and Page responds with a vintage solo to complete the transformation. If you were trying to convince a hardcore Zeppelin fan of the merits of Page and Plant, this would be the song to do it with.

TIN PAN ALLEY
Robert Plant & The Strange Sensation
Mighty Rearranger, 2005

"Tin Pan Valley" finds Plant at his most lyrically scathing—and vocally sublime. Attacking those who "flirt with cabaret" (is that the sound of Rod Stewart shifting uncomfortably in his seat?) or "fake the rebel yell" (come in, Sir Mick?), this is proof positive that passion still stirs in the old lion's loins. ❷

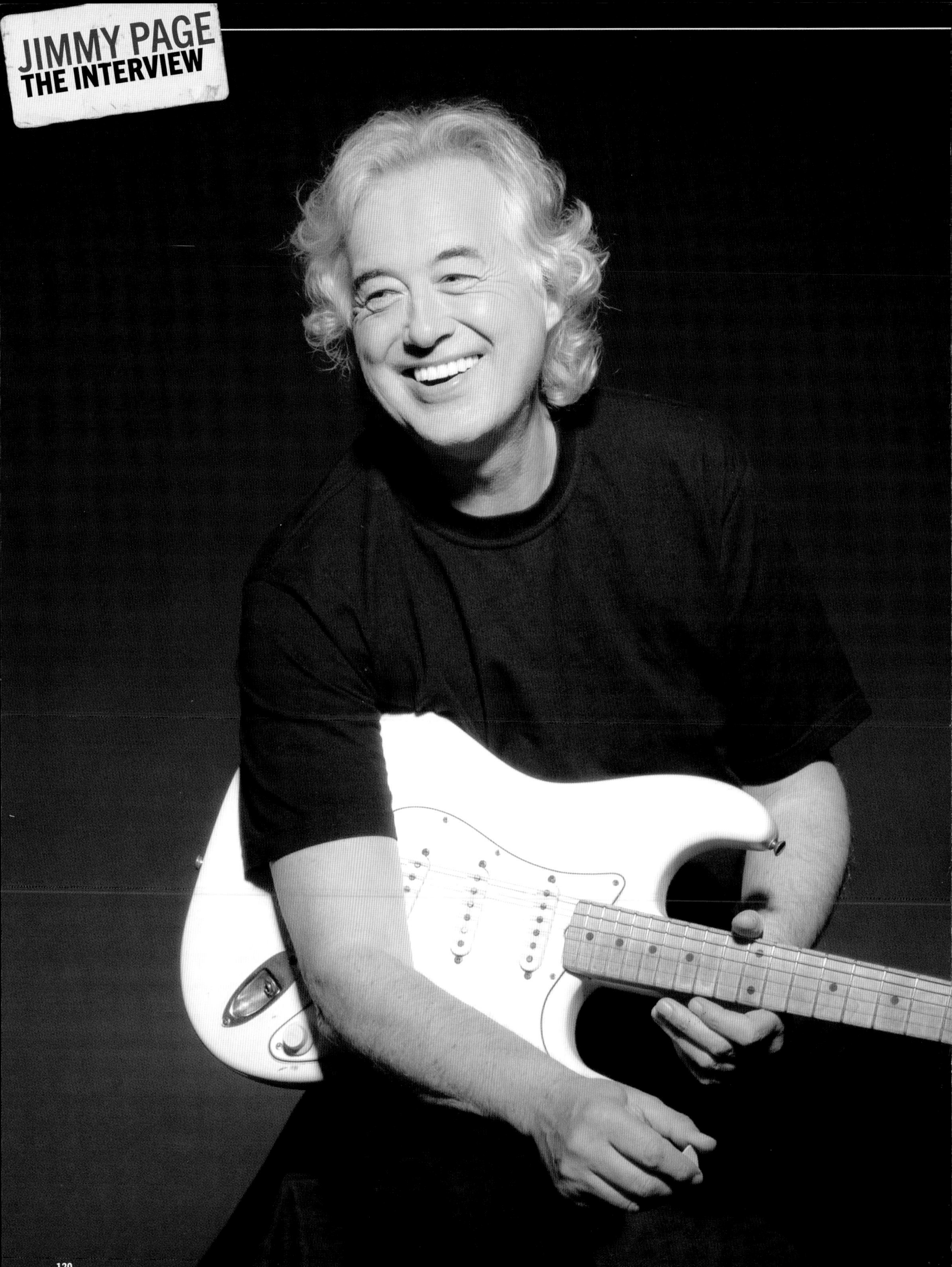

Jimmy Page:
The Interview

On November 26, 2007, Led Zeppelin took to the stage at London's O2 Arena for one night only. Jimmy Page explains how they got there.

INTERVIEW: PETER MAKOWSKI **PORTRAITS:** ROSS HALFIN

ADDITIONAL MATERIAL: DAVE LING

> "The purpose of the first rehearsal was to see how we would all get on. There is that camaraderie, but there's also been a lot of water under the bridge..."

I n what can only be described as the reunion of the decade, it seemed that everyone from Stephen Fry to Paul McCartney and Sigur Rós came out of the closet to declare their unconditional love for Led Zeppelin at the O2 Arena.

Apart from the obvious, what made this monumental get-together so special is that it hadn't been pulled together by the lure of filthy lucre or some condescending, world-saving crusade. The reasons were twofold. First and foremost it was a nod of respect to Atlantic's founding father Ahmet Ertegün (monies raised went to a school foundation set up by his wife). Secondly, and equally as importantly, it was a chance for Zep's surviving members to show a new generation of music fans what the fuss was all about.

As Robert Plant declared, "We need to play one last great show." In an exclusive interview—ahead of the now-legendary gig—Jimmy Page spoke to *Classic Rock* about the reunion, rehearsals, John Bonham, Live Aid, and more.

The obvious question is, why did you decide to have the Led Zeppelin reunion now?

Why now? Mmm, I guess there was the clarion call with the tribute to Ahmet and for the charity that has been set up. Really it was a question of anytime, any place.

Originally there was talk of doing it at the Albert Hall. Then we thought we'd get together, in a clandestine location, to see how we all got along playing together. That was really good, but before we even got in there it was leaked that we were going to do the O2 whether we were any good or not! [Laughs.] But we had a really good time during that initial rehearsal with Jason. And then we had another get-together to pick over the numbers that we'd do relative to a set. Originally it was proposed that we would do an hour, but there was no way that we'd do only an hour. So that stretched to 75 minutes, then 90 minutes and beyond. By that point we were going to make a joint statement, then it got leaked again. So the expectations are accelerating, but it's okay. We'll be rehearsing all the way up to O2.

How are the rehearsals going?

With attitude! One of the things we agreed on was that if we were going to play together then we'd put as much into it as we possibly could. There had been a couple of previous get-togethers like Live Aid, which involved a couple of hours' rehearsal in one of the dressing rooms with a drummer we'd never played with before, and then getting onstage with another drummer we hadn't played with. It was totally shambolic. So this time it's important that we are well prepared.

Led Zeppelin factoid
Zep's debut album cost £1,782 to make. It was recorded in less than 30 hours, over three weeks.

Live Aid was quite a risky venture for you to undertake. You had no control over the environment and a short set.

I think we came together in the spirit of Live Aid. At the time Robert was out on a solo tour and I was probably out with The Firm and it was a bit of a wing and a prayer. Sometimes those things can be a glorious success or it can be a glorious shambles [laughs]. You have to understand other people had taken it on properly, rehearsed and it showed.

Was it easy or difficult to pull this reunion together?

Well, the key to it was actually getting in a room together, playing together, going through a number, and just getting the feel of the whole thing. That was the purpose of the first rehearsal, to see how we would all get on. There is that camaraderie, if you like, that we had but there's been a lot of water under the bridge. It was really important to see how we would all get on. But the key to it is the music, because the music is so powerful. You have to throw yourself into it, the way you might throw yourself naked into a bed of stinging nettles. It's a commitment.

What would John Bonham think of this reunion?

He would be absolutely so proud of Jason. In rehearsals Jason has such an infectious enthusiasm that it's undeniable. The most important thing that you must never forget is that John Bonham loved Led Zeppelin's music.

There have been on various petitions on fan websites for a selection of drummers including Dave Grohl. Did you ever consider anyone else for the job other than Jason?

The thing is that Jason's more than proved himself as a musician in his own right. We played together before. He was on my solo album and toured with me in the eighties. He's come into the situation as Jason the man as opposed to Jason the kid and he's certainly playing in that capacity. Don't forget Jason appears on *Song Remains the Same* and he appeared with us at the Atlantic 40th bash and he played remarkably well. So within the framework of Led Zeppelin material there's no other choice.

In fact it would be insulting not to do it with Jason. He more than measures up.

Is this the only show you will be doing? Is it too early to say what you will be doing next?

The current target is the gig. I mean, of course, everybody's projecting this, that or the other and there was a massive demand for the O2 show.

Were you surprised by that?

I knew it was going to be big, but it was more overwhelming than any of us could have guessed.

Were you surprised by the general warm response from musicians and the media?

No, because the music was always well crafted from the first album. The albums and the live shows are two different aspects and facets of Led Zeppelin. But it's the albums that people are more aware of because when was it we did our last proper show, 1980? So there's certainly a young audience out there who like Led Zeppelin and want to experience the band in a live setting.

Has it been difficult picking material for the show?

Not really. Not at all, actually. But I'm not going to tell you what the set list is [laughs].

There are a lot of people who really want to see you perform but aren't going to get the opportunity. Are you going to at least film or record the show?

I'm not sure about that. The most important thing at the moment is to do this gig with the spirit that it deserves.

It seems to the outsider that while John and Robert have been pursuing solo careers, you seem to have concentrated on working on and protecting the Zeppelin legacy with a series of remastered albums, compilations and *The Song Remains the Same*.

Absolutely right! As far as Led Zeppelin is concerned, I've been very keen on making sure that things are right; taking care of the legacy, making sure that the live material came out, like *How the West Was Won*, and pushing to get *The Song Remains the Same* out on a DVD of a high standard. ⚡

Jimmy Page, London, July 2007
The white Strat was used to record Zep's "Ten Years Gone." John Paul Jones had just returned it to Jimmy.

"As far as Led Zeppelin is concerned, I've been very keen on . . . taking care of the legacy.**"**

I t's Friday, November 2, 2007, three days before the third-ever *Classic Rock* Roll of Honour, and Jimmy Page has broken a finger. Zep's comeback gig will have to be postponed, and Jimmy might not be able to make it to the awards.

Steven Tyler has already flown in from Boston. At Gibson HQ there's a Les Paul specially signed by Les Paul himself, waiting for Jimmy. Somewhere in Luton, an editing team is beavering away on the short film covering Page's enormous career that will be shown to the room before Tyler presents Jimmy with his award. Somewhere in America, Aerosmith's right-hand man John Bionelli is making the six-hour drive from his house to Joe Perry's ranch to video some congratulatory words from Joe and email the footage to the guys in Luton.

Is it all going to be in vain?

Within hours the panic is over. Of course Jimmy's coming—he just won't be shaking too many hands.

So how's the finger?
It's mending really, really well. I don't want to jinx it but the specialist says it's healing as nicely as could be expected in the space of a week. At least it looks like a finger again [laughs]. But it's had a fracture, which is a bloody awful thing to happen to a guitarist—especially given the timing.

The Zoso knitwear range failed to capture the public's imagination.

Page onstage in Chicago, 1977.

Jimmy Page and his broken finger.

There were entire years when it wouldn't have made any difference, and then I have to fall over right before the gig at the O2. It's such a shame it ended up inconveniencing so many people that were traveling to the show. I hope they'll still come.

Your house presumably has an entire wing to accommodate the many awards you've received down the years. Is this one for *Classic Rock*'s Living Legend just another to add to the mantelpiece?
Good Lord, no. I've never attended an awards ceremony like it [laughs]. Good Lord, it was so heartfelt. It also meant a lot for so many of my peers to have been here. And we were able to have a bit of a laugh through seeing all that [video] stuff from when I was an enthusiastic 13-year-old. We all start off that way, don't we, but not everyone ends up with all that stuff haunting them on *YouTube*. Then of course there were [messages from] Scotty Moore [Elvis Presley guitarist] and Les Paul . . . Heaven help us.

Was it emotional?
To be honest, I was choked when Steven [Tyler] did such an excellent speech. Then there was that whole wonderful tableau of images and it made me think, "Gosh, it is quite some career, isn't it?"

Were you surprised by the fact that 20 million people wanted tickets for the gig at the O2?
Well, we knew that if the band ever did something that we could prepare for properly that it would be very popular, that it would sell out overnight. But nobody thought for a moment that there would be such an intense and overwhelming response.

Does that reaction make you a little nervous?
[Instantaneously:] Oh, no. Don't forget that right up until the point of the finger intervention, we had some rehearsals. And we were right on—it was sounding incredibly good.

You must've received ticket requests from the milkman to passers-by in the street. Do you have a standard rebuffal?
[Laughs] It's been difficult, you're right. For so many people, Zeppelin was the high point of their musical lives. After so many years of not doing this, I've got many, many

friends that I'd like to come and see the show. But it's not a Led Zeppelin show, it's a charity performance. I only had 20 tickets for my own family. Luckily, most people seem to understand that.

At the awards, Alice Cooper made an astute comment about market forces. He believes that because 20 million people tried to buy tickets to see Led Zeppelin, there will have to be some sort of tour.
That's a crafty little question. But let me put it this way, our only existing target is the O2. Momentum is really strong, but I really can't say what will happen afterwards.

This award recognizes your achievements as a musician, songwriter, and producer. Which role do you identify with the most?
All of it! Definitely all of it. I don't think there's one role that's more important than the other.

Going back to the beginning, what inspired you to pick up a guitar and form a band?

> ## "I've never attended an awards ceremony like it. Good Lord, it was so heartfelt. It also meant a lot for so many of my peers to have been here."

I was seduced by the music I heard—because at that point in time it was so dynamic. It was of the youth and it was pulling me in. And I made every effort to follow what was going on at the time. I was a fan. We had a guitar at our house, but I had no idea what to do on it 'til someone showed me some chords, and it went on from there.

Your first television appearance was on a show called *All Your Own* with a skiffle band—how did that come about?
I think somebody wrote off on our behalf to go on the audition. I remember being in the hall with loads of other kids and the presenter, Huw Wheldon, came in looking worse for wear and shouted, "Alright—where are those

bloody kids?!" The parents were horrified—they were putting their hands over their children's ears [laughs].

Did you have any aspirations to eventually become a full-time musician?
No! We were grammar school boys from Epsom. One hadn't put two and two together to realize that you could make a living out of your passion. At that time everyone was still genuinely a fan. It was exactly the same when I eventually got to meet people like Jeff [Beck] and Eric [Clapton]—they had been the only guitarists in their neighborhood too.

In the early days what was the most unusual gig you've ever did?
Holloway Prison, when I was playing with Neil Christian and the Crusaders. Heaven knows how that happened. I remember we had to go to the warders' office beforehand and we were put on a vow of secrecy not to reveal who we saw on the inside. The women in there had cotton-print dresses in four different colors which were washed out. It was very interesting and quite erotic. After we left, there was a riot. It was probably because Neil Christian had wound the girls up. It was a terrific experience—though not quite like Johnny Cash at San Quentin.

Oh, I don't know, I'd rather play Holloway than San Quentin.
Yeah, I suppose it did have its plusses.

When did you start doing sessions?
Well, I was in various bands before that, but I got into doing sessions when I played in an interval band at the Marquee with a guy called Andy Wren, who was the pianist with Screaming Lord Sutch and the Savages. We never had rehearsals, we just used to go in there and play. Actually, I can tell you a story about Andy. One night when he was in the Savages, he came along with a flying-boot covered in bandages. Sutch would make references to it during the course of the show and say how fortunate we were to have Andy playing with us tonight, because he broke his leg and was in considerable pain. Then halfway through the show, Sutch came on with this huge mallet and started beating Andy's foot with it. Some of the audience jumped up onstage to try and stop

Plant's Salute

Robert Plant couldn't make the *Classic Rock* awards, but he sent a video salute. Here's what he said in full.

Your vision and resolve knows no boundaries, extending beyond the music, inspired and propelled by the great ones. Everything and anything has been probable and often possible in your work, always free from the chains of repetition and mediocrity. The challenge for me was how to complement your whirlwind contrasts, so many radical twists and turns with such colorful complementary construction, always pushing the limits from the comfort of the bosom to the naked raw edge. You dug deep and deeper, driven by emotion, art, and literature towards the one light of invention and excitement.

On the first day we met I realize the breadth of influence: the ideas we exchanged were vast: from William Blake to Skip James, from Kaleidoscope to Christina Rossetti, from Otis Rush to Dylan Thomas. To make music inspired by these influences you created music from beyond music. Our travels through India, Thailand, and Morocco in the early seventies, brought shared experiences mirrored in some of the most illuminating, and intensively inventive guitar performances of our genre.

Your delivery and poise mirrored and extended the visceral experiences from the physical to the musical form. The limitless creations you shared with John Paul and Bonzo remain unequalled. I was always amazed if I could find lyric and melody to complement the roaring "Achilles Last Stand" or the caressingly beautiful muse that is "The Rain Song." Just examples of the contrasts we experienced. The terrain—often bleak, sometimes remote, and sometimes immersed in love has been spectacular. Best wishes to you and congratulations tonight.

It's been a whirlwind career for James Patrick Page.

"We had a guitar at our house, but I had no idea what to do on it 'til someone showed me the chords, and it went on from there."

him—of course, it was all a set up.

So, anyway, I was doing these interval shows and got headhunted at the Marquee. Someone came up and asked me if I would like to play on a record.

So what was your first official session?
It was "Diamonds" by Jet Harris and Tony Meehan—I played an acoustic on it. And the B-side was a written part and I just didn't have a clue what it was all about. I could read chord sheets but not dots [musical notation] at the time.

During the sixties, you did literally hundreds of sessions, and you have been credited with appearing on some of the most influential records of that decade. There are a lot of rumors and myths surrounding what tracks you actually appeared on. Is it true you played on The Kinks' "You Really Got Me"?
No, I wasn't on that. I played on some of the Kinks' records but definitely not that one.

The Who—"Can't Explain"?
I played on that but I wasn't needed in the end [laughs]. Pete's doing all the lead parts. I mean, there might be a couple of phrases on the B-side that you can hear me. But, to be honest, I don't really know why I was there, except to just play along. Townshend's doing all the important stuff. You wouldn't have noticed if I wasn't on it.

Them—"Baby Please Don't Go"?
Yeah, I played on that.

Joe Cocker—"With a Little Help from My Friends"?
Yeah.

The Rolling Stones—"Heart of Stone"?
I played on a version of that eventually surfaced. Also more recently I played on "One Hit to the Body."

How about the iconic James Bond theme, "Goldfinger," with John Barry?
That was a phenomenal session. John Barry had been rehearsing this massive orchestra and they were waiting for Shirley Bassey. When she arrived, she just took off her coat and went straight into the studio. John Barry counted it in, she sang, and then at the end she just collapsed on to the floor. And, I'll tell you what, for a 17-year-old kid playing with an orchestra and watching all that happen was quite astonishing.

I've read that you were called in on some sessions just in case group members didn't turn up or couldn't deliver.
Yeah, I was a bit of an insurance policy. I was a hired gun, and certainly in the early days a lot of the time you weren't told who you were working with. But I was doing about three sessions a day, five days a week, and sometimes at the weekend. And there was a constant change of venues

as well—from Decca to Pye, EMI, and Phillips. So there was a hell of a lot of stuff and I can't remember everything I've done, but I think if I heard it I could recognize the guitar. And there's a lot of stuff I did that I won't tell you about.

Will we ever find out?
Yes, when my book comes out! [*Jimmy Page by Jimmy Page* was published in 2014]

Do you feel that your session work prepared you for Zeppelin?
It was like an apprenticeship and I treated it like that. Because as I've already said, I didn't read the dots when I went in. Initially it was a more a question of "play what you want and if you could come up with a riff that would be fantastic." But it came to the point where they started giving out the musical charts, and it was going to be essential to be able to read them. So as I was learning to read music, they would give me my charts first to give me a chance to become familiar with them by the time it came to rehearsals. Over the forthcoming months, I really became quite a reasonable reader, and if you can read music then you can write it, and I ended up doing arrangements. You've got to remember that in those days a session musician was brought in to do everything across the board. It wasn't like I was a specialist, although I was being pulled in on purpose to come up with invention, if ➤➤

you like. Because I had eclectic tastes, I was pulled in on a variety of sessions.

What made you stop doing session work?
It was a muzak session. I can't name what muzak I did or what lift it was being played in [laughs], but let's just say it became hard work because you were just given a ream of musical notation and you just had to read, turn up, and make no mistakes, no re-runs. So looking back on it as far as the discipline in the studios was concerned, that aspect really served me well in my apprenticeship. And the fact that I was intrigued by the record production employed in the fifties, let alone the sixties. I was pulled in by it and I absorbed everything around me. Recording techniques were something that I paid a lot of attention to. I saw how to do it and how not to do it. I was an established musician, but I needed to step aside—I wanted to play live again.

Moving forward to Zep, let's talk about the debut album. Did you know it would work out so well?
Yeah, quite a while before it was recorded I knew exactly what it was going to be. When the album came out, it had so many ideas on it that were pretty unique [compared] to anything else at that period of time. It touched so many different areas that people hadn't quite got to. The blues is on it, there was a bit of a reference to world music, there was folk music that had been taken out of any sort of sphere that had ever been approached prior to that. And there was some really fine songwriting from members of the band. It was a classic debut album, which is what it should be. It was a new band saying, "This is what we've got."

When you recorded it, were you fearlessly confident of what you were doing or were there any doubts?
Well, obviously, we didn't just walk into the studios and pull it all together in a few hours. There had been a writing process running up to that and we had done some touring in Scandinavia as well. So we were playing very well together as a band. But it was still early days. By the time we got to the second album, we had the benefit of having played together. In fact, some of the second album was done in England and the rest of it was done on the road.

It's difficult to believe that *Led Zeppelin II* was done on the hop.
Well, it sort of was and it wasn't. We were in LA and Mirasound studios was still there, and to my ears there wasn't too much wrong with the recordings they produced for Del-Fi records [an influential label from the early sixties whose roster included Richie Valens and Bobby Fuller]. I didn't realize how good it was until we got in there and that's where we recorded "The Lemon Song" and "Moby Dick." We did "Bring It on Home" at the Atlantic studios. Anyway, without going into to each location with great detail, the fact was that we did bits here and there, all over the place. The final mixes were done in New York.

Is it true that you would have liked to have recorded at Sun Studios?
Oh yeah, I would have liked to have recorded there when I was 13 years old! But by the time we were recording *II*, it wasn't the original Sun Studios.

The production work on *II* was astonishing; most noticeably on "Whole Lotta Love."
Curiously enough, that was the first song we did and it

was recorded in London at Olympic studios. "Whole Lotta Love" definitely captures the attitude and swagger of the band at the time.

And then came Led Zeppelin *III*.
By the third album, we had been touring and we had our foot in the door of America. Because it's such a massive continent, between the first and the third album we spent a lot of time over there. So by the time we got to the third album, we were having our first proper lengthy break. We couldn't spend any more time in America, because in those days there was the threat of getting drafted into the Vietnam war if you stayed over six months, so we thought it would be better to go home and do an album.

It seemed to confuse the critics and received mixed reviews—how did you feel about that?
Well, what was it that confused the critics? I mean, it's got "Immigrant Song" on it, that's a classic rock riff track. It's got "Since I've Been Loving You." It's got some really strong material on it. People really didn't fully understand what a kaleidoscopic talent there was within Led Zeppelin. So they had already made up their minds after the first album and second album what we were about. And with the third album they were saying, "Where's 'Whole Lotta Love'?" and we weren't doing format, nor should we have done.

The thing is that you could tell what was working from the response of the audiences. In those days, Led Zeppelin was traveling word of mouth, by people's ears, not by reviewers' copy. As I've said in the past, I'll give it the benefit of doubt and say that maybe that the reviewers only had a short amount of time to review the album, because it totally went over their heads. Nobody else at the time was moving with that kind of rapidity, if you like—many bands were happy to stick to a formula. Also there were definite hatchet jobs. The *Rolling Stone* review was a definite hatchet job, we were told that. But it didn't matter because we had a bigger circulation than *Rolling Stone* [laughs]. The fact is that we were pretty well established after the first two records, so if there's someone who's into the band and the music, they're just going to get the product as it

Robert Plant and Jimmy Page onstage together.

NEIL ZLOZOWER

"To be honest, I will only really do something if I really enjoy it."

comes out and then they're going to take it home and absorb it. It was unquestionably good music and as long as you believe in it yourself or yourselves, collectively, that's what matters.

The last album, *In Through the Out Door,* is the one that seems to have received the most criticism.
Well, I'm not going to add to it. That's my answer to that. I don't want to add any more fuel to any fires.

When Zeppelin ended, did you feel any immediate pressure to produce music?
The first thing that came along was the soundtrack for *Death Wish [II],* which was great because I really got into the process of writing for film—the syncopation of it and the mood of it. And I wrote it in the studio, I didn't go in there with anything. It was fascinating. I learned a lot doing that—I learned a lot about myself. I surprised myself with what I could actually do under those sort of circumstances.

Would you want to do something like that again?
Probably not. But I did enjoy it. It came to me at the right time, because obviously one was really shattered having lost John [Bonham], a real dear friend and the most incredible musician. So it was really good because it was something that kept me focused, creating 45 minutes of music for a 90-minute film.

The only thing that was a bit of a shock was when I'd finished, I was told that I was supposed to do an album for it as well. I had no idea that there was

supposed to be an album, which was interesting.

With The Firm and Coverdale/Page, did you feel any pressure to create something as monumental as Zeppelin?
No, the collaboration with Paul [Rodgers] was an offshoot from the ARMS tour. Originally Steve Winwood sang in London, and then there was a proposal asking if we would like to take it to America. And Steve didn't want to go to the States. Joe Cocker went instead, and I asked Paul would he like to come along as well and he said yes. And that's when we started getting some material together. "Midnight Moonlight" was one of the songs that came out of that. And you don't go out playing something like that unless you have real confidence about yourself. Paul's whole application to the lyrics and the melodies was fantastic and I really enjoyed working with him—what a vocalist. And when the ARMS thing finished, I said, "What about it? Let's go do something else." Which is how The Firm came about.

And then there was your solo album, *Outrider.*
Yeah. Y'know, I thought it was time to do a solo album. It gave me a chance to go out on tour and just play all the music that I enjoyed. So I went out and did some Yardbirds material, some blues, some Zeppelin, some stuff from *Outrider,* The Firm, and the *Death Wish* soundtrack. I really enjoyed doing that—it was fun. And then I did the Coverdale/Page thing, and I really enjoyed that too. Actually, to be honest, I will only really do something if I really enjoy it. I enjoyed working with David Coverdale; he was really together and professional

to work with. I think we did some really good material with Coverdale/Page.

It seems you've done pretty much what you've wanted since leaving Zeppelin.
Well, I have. I've been really lucky to have worked with some fine vocalists. I mean, the best.

What draws you to a vocalist?
Singers that can deliver a vocal performance and have the range and confidence to deliver. Because that's what they would and should expect from a guitarist.

In the past you've praised Chris Cornell.
Yeah, I particularly like Chris Cornell's writing. I think "Black Hole Sun" is an amazing piece of work.

How about your stint with the Black Crowes?
The only unfortunate thing with the Black Crowes project was that live there was a balance between their material and the Led Zeppelin stuff. And the whole set was recorded live at The Greek Theatre, but when it got to releasing an album, they came unstuck because of contractual problems and could only use the Zeppelin material. This was a shame because I really enjoyed doing their songs. The Black Crowes were then and still are a fine, fine rock band.

Let's talk about your collaboration with P. Diddy.
There was a communication that came through the office that he wanted to do a track with me and would I talk to him. So I called him up, and he said that he'd been asked to do this music for *Godzilla* and he couldn't get this idea of using "Kashmir" out of his mind because of this huge beast—he wanted something epic musically. So he really wanted to do something around "Kashmir," but said he didn't want to sample it because he wanted to do something different. So I said, "When do you want to do it?" He said Saturday, and it was already Tuesday! So I went into a studio in Wembley where they set up a link, so I could see him on a screen, but I'm basically playing everything down a telephone line over the internet. It was interesting because he was in LA and there was this massive time lapse in our conversation and the audio. When we finished, he said, "Right, I'm going to put an orchestra on top of this." I was told that he ended up using two orchestras simultaneously.

When I went to New York on other business, he invited me up to the studio when he had mixed it. It was absolutely epic—and he played it really loud too! Superb! And then I had a chance to play with him on *Saturday Night Live* and that was terrific.

We did the run-through and he did something different for each performance as far as body language and his physical approach went. But his vocal timing was spot-on with every take. It was an interesting time because I was suddenly getting asked to do autographs by Black people, which hadn't happened for quite a while!

These days are you more comfortable onstage or in the recording studio?
I think it's equal. It's two different worlds, and my approach is different to both.

What are your solo plans for the future?
I've got a variety of material which I've written and have been working on that I hope will surface. And that's a mixture of things that have been around for a while and other things that are more current. That's it, really. I've always done projects along the way as they've come along and enjoyed them. ✖

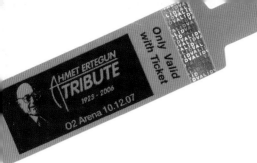

THE REUNION, REVIEWED

By: Scott Rowley

In the days before The Gig, *Classic Rock* is interviewed by Sky News, Canadian television, the *Los Angeles Times*. They all ask the same question: why is everyone so excited about the return of Led Zeppelin?

Classic Rock whitters on about how Zeppelin masterfully mixed the blues with folk and rock and soul and Eastern music, about how they're up there with The Beatles and the Stones, about how this is as big as it gets.

You can see it in the guest list. Kate and Naomi, Noel and Liam, Marilyn Manson, Joe Elliott, Dave Mustaine, and Julliette Lewis. Somewhere in the building, Paul McCartney, Mick Jagger, Priscilla Presley, and Lulu are fighting over the vol-au-vents. Saxon at Butlins it most definitely isn't.

A seventies TV screen appears out of the darkness and an American news report reminds us that the band outsold The Beatles. Seconds later, the defiant opening chords of "Good Times, Bad Times" explode from the stage.

As an opener, it's perfect: not just the first song on their first album, but a short, ballsy, feedback-strewn statement of intent, Plant kicking his mic stand into the air, Page suited and booted, legs akimbo—still the ultimate guitar hero. There was speculation that Zep would lean on a spectacular light show to carry the show; they do exactly the very opposite. The house lights stay on most of the night (annoyingly so to anyone who wants to get lost in the darkness). The stage is bathed in white light, the band gathered around the drum riser for much of the gig—not Plant on a pedestal at the front, not Page in a spotlight every time he does a solo. The message is clear: this isn't some showbiz act. This isn't the Stones and their traveling jukebox. This is a *band*. Led Zeppelin. Three old guys (and their sorcerors' apprentice), sure, but three old guys who can still perform with dignity.

"Ramble On" serves notice that there's going

to be some surprises; by our reckoning it's never been played live in its entirety before and the fact that Plant has in the past admitted embarrassment at its Tolkien-referencing lyrics suggests that, far from being the reluctant party, the singer has thrown himself into this and is giving it his all.

"Black Dog" gets the crowd singing. Then, just when you think it's going to be all crowd pleasers, there's worthy epic "In My Time of Dying," followed by the live debut of "For Your Life" from *Presence*. (Followed immediately by the sound of around 19,000 people turning to each other and saying under their breath: "Which one is this again?") "Trampled Under Foot" gets the funk out and the supermodels dancing. Plant introduces "Nobody's Fault but Mine" with references to the Staple Singers and Blind Willie Johnson versions and joking that, "We musta first heard this in a church in Mississippi in 1932 . . ." His harmonica solo is suitably ear-rattling, and he finishes by spinning the harp high in the air and catching it.

For "No Quarter," dry ice floods the stage as John Paul Jones lays on the atmospherics and Jimmy hits the wah-wah. On "Dazed and Confused," Page starts pulling his hands off the strings like the guitar is stinging him, before getting the violin bow out for some alchemy. The video screens get more and more trippy, mashing up the spectacle right before our eyes.

Next thing you know, he's holding a double-necked SG and we're climbing a "Stairway to Heaven." The notes that would get you kicked out of guitar shops across the country ring out, distortion saving the song from the recorded version's twee excesses. Plant sings, "And the forests will echo with laughter," and the stadium echoes instead with his ad-lib from "The Song Remains the Same": "Does anybody remember laughter?" The solo—you know, the one that's been voted the greatest guitar solo of all time—is great; not slavishly recreating the original, but referencing it enough to acknowledge

the respect it's held in.

"Hey Ahmet, we did it!" Plant shouts at the end. Some people sit for "The Song Remains the Same"—one of the night's few unremarkable moments—but they're not down for long. "There are people from 50 countries here tonight," says Plant. "This is the 51st country . . ."

And then "Kashmir" starts.

At once, everyone's on their feet. We're plunged into welcome darkness as lights strafe the crowd and grown men are (literally) seen to weep. You can keep your Grand Canyon, and your Niagara Falls; this is the eighth wonder of the world.

Is it the Zeppelin of old? Of course not. These days there are Thermos flasks and tea mugs on the right-hand side of the drum riser. (On the left are Jimmy's bottles of Kaliber). These days, JPJ needs just one keyboard, not banks of them. These days, half of the audience seem to view the entire gig through their mobile phones (on the rare occasions that the house lights go off, the floor of the arena twinkles like a star-filled sky). And these days, on the drums is the son of the guy who used to be on drums. Ironically, he's the only one with no hair.

("Jason was f****** great," says Dave Grohl, who knows about these things, in an email to photographer Ross Halfin the following day. "Face it; he had people like me, Chad Smith, and [Black Crowes drummer] Steve Gorman watching his every move, all night long, and afterwards we all agreed that he played great.")

By the end of the show, Jason isn't just copying his father's parts, but also adding his own fills, flailing away, knocking hell out of the kit (look at the picture, right, to see the delight in the older three's faces). When they take a final bow, Jason gets on his knees before them in a "we're not worthy" pose, then leaves the stage, clearly emotional, rubbing his head like someone who's just had his mind blown. Considering that we have too, and we're *just watching*, you can only imagine how he must feel.

Tellingly, there are no emotional goodbyes, no "Thanks for coming to see us one last time" speeches, just props to Ahmet and the sight of The World's Greatest Rock Band *reborn* walking off the stage.

There's an old saying: "Buy land, because God's not making any more of it." He's not making bands like this any more, either.

Set List

Good Times, Bad Times
Ramble On
Black Dog
In My Time of Dying
For Your Life
Trampled Under Foot
Nobody's Fault but Mine
No Quarter
Since I've Been Loving You
Dazed and Confused
Stairway to Heaven
The Song Remains the Same
Misty Mountain Hop
Kashmir

Encore 1
Whole Lotta Love

Encore 2
Rock and Roll

Plant, Page, and JPJ face Jason Bonham at the band's reunion at the 02 in 2007.

"You can keep your Grand Canyons and your Niagara Falls; this is the eighth wonder of the world."

Rock's Sonic Architect

As well as being the guitar hero and co-songwriter in Led Zeppelin, Jimmy Page was also the man behind the mixing desk, the guy who produced every single one of their albums. And in doing so, say his engineers and contemporaries, he shaped the very sound of rock music.

ANDY JOHNS ENGINEER ON *LED ZEPPELIN IV*

As a producer, Jimmy was very innovative. Also, he was very thorough. He knew what he wanted, which is a very important thing for a producer. As a producer, you don't always know how you're gonna get there but you know where you need to go. And that's pretty much what I saw in him. Of course, when I was working with Jimmy I was just a young engineer. This was in 1973, and I hadn't produced anything at that point in my career. I was pretty much in awe of the whole thing. I contributed as much as I could.

Whenever you're working with a member of a band who's a producer, like a Jimmy Page or Pete Townshend, there's nobody in the booth with you. You're there by yourself and they rely on your feedback: "How was that?" Jimmy was one of the few people as a musician who could take an objective overview. Most musicians get too involved and they get lost. That's why you have such things as producers. It took me a few years to figure out why geniuses like the Stones or Jimi Hendrix would need someone there to tell them where it was at. Jimmy didn't need anybody.

He had a vision for what the songs should be. He had his tricks that he'd worked out over the years. He was also a brilliant arranger. He was always looking for new sounds, but it was mostly his talent as an arranger. If you listen to those Zeppelin records, there's not a lot of overdubs. Even on "Stairway to Heaven," there aren't that many overdubs. It's just bass, drums, a little bit of piano, an acoustic guitar, electric rhythm now and again, and bits coming in and out. It's not like we do now, with four rhythm guitars and double-tracking everything else and you've got this bloody great wall of sound.

When recording those albums, Jimmy would be in the control room with me and we'd be doing all kinds of things. The other guys either weren't there or they'd be milling around in the studio. They knew that he was the producer. He was in charge.

ACE FREHLEY OF KISS

Jimmy did it all, and that's what was so amazing about it. When you think about Jimmy Page today, nobody was really doing what he was doing. I mean, Jimi Hendrix had producers, Eric Clapton had producers. Clapton didn't do as much writing in the early days as Jimmy Page did. But Page wrote the stuff, he phelayed it fabulously, and he produced it. He was a triple threat. I can't think of anybody else that was doing what Page was doing at the time.

BILLY GIBBONS OF ZZ TOP

Jimmy's a really fine player, from a number of angles; he's got tone, he's got style. He can manage a single-string lead guitar solo with speed and elegance. Massive! Jimmy's ability to cover so many points of delivery is astounding. His background in the studio launched a complete understanding of how things work: writing, then getting it recorded, followed with the gift of taking it to the stage. Superb showman all around.

As for Jimmy as a producer, take the range of tempo and tone covered in so many different songs. There's a real challenge in coming off an all-out thrash and dialling it down to "Stairway to Heaven," all with purpose and great delivery. That's a Page speciality.

Led Zeppelin is pure, out-and-out rock 'n' roll. Booming percussion, low-down bottom" Jimmy's ability to cover so many points of delivery is astounding." It'll always remain a value.

RON NEVISON ENGINEER ON *PHYSICAL GRAFFITI*

Working with Led Zeppelin was very similar to The Who, except that Robert [Plant] wrote the lyrics and Jimmy Page was the producer. In terms of The Who, Pete [Townshend] pretty much wrote everything. It was all scripted out beforehand. But in Zeppelin's case, there was more of a collaboration between Robert and Jimmy. But the thing that struck me working with them was that John Bonham played to the guitar. A lot of drummers are stuck with the bass player. Whatever riff Jimmy would come up with, Bonham would accent where the riff was on drums. That was very interesting. I'd never noticed anyone doing that before.

DANNY GOLDBERG FORMER LED ZEPPELIN PR

I feel to this day that most of the heavy metal groups were influenced by either Jimi Hendrix or Jimmy Page. I don't think anyone else comes close. Jimmy was much more than a guitar player. Jimmy was an incredible writer: the structure of the Zeppelin songs

Ace Frehley
"Page wrote the stuff, he played it fabulously, and produced it. He was a triple threat."

Billy Gibbons
"Jimmy's ability to cover so many points of delivery is astounding."

Nancy Wilson
"Jimmy is so underrated as a producer. When he pulls out instruments like the hurdy gurdy . . . it's really inventive stuff."

where he used acoustic and went into hard rock; the unusual and idiosyncratic Wagnerian stature of the songwriting totally influenced all other groups. And as a producer, although now the technology has evolved far beyond that, the sound he got on the drums at that time has changed the sound of drums on rock records.

I always thought his true and greatest genius was as a writer and producer. And he was also an excellent guitarist. I think he's one of many excellent guitarists, but he stands alone as a conceptualizer of what a rock band should sound like. And the greatness of Zeppelin comes from him as a writer and a producer.

EDDIE KRAMER ENGINEER ON FIVE LED ZEPPELIN ALBUMS

Page's ability as a producer was his clear vision of what the final product should be, and his deep knowledge of music. He knew instinctively what will work and what won't work. I tell stories about Jimmy Page and Jimi Hendrix because there are interesting parallels I find with these two guys. They were both very clear about what they wanted in the studio. They were very clearheaded and had a focus on the end product. When they wrote a song, they knew in their head that this is the way it's supposed to sound. They also had a very clear vision and laser-like concentration in the studio. Absolute laser-like concentration. It was amazing.

Jimmy was a real hard worker in the studio. Total focus. He was also a lot of fun. It was a tremendous challenge to work with him because you really had to have your s*** together. The same with Hendrix. You had to be on top of it and try to interpret what they wanted. It's the artist who has given us this wonderful music, and then it's up to us as engineers and producers to reinterpret and try to help them realize their vision. That's what we do. If we don't do that, then we haven't done our jobs.

In the studio, Jimmy knew what he wanted but he was very open to experimentation. He was always looking for new sounds. Any time I came up with a wacky sound, he would go, "Yeah!" or "No, sorry, that doesn't work." He was very receptive. We were always trying to push the envelope with Zeppelin because the music was so inspiring. The music just sort of kicked you in the butt.

ELLIOT EASTON OF THE CARS

During his days as a studio musician Jimmy appears to have learned a great deal about the mechanics of record production. He's a master of mic-ing techniques. He was really into ambient sounds, backwards reverb, and distance mic-ing. They set Bonham's drums at the end of a hallway and put the mics at the other end of the hallway. He'd get these really great sounds. He'd also use smaller amps to get a huge guitar sound. That was all part of Page's repertoire of studio techniques.

I love Jimmy's solo on "Heartbreaker," the little break where everybody stops and he plays. It's so weird and crazy. He just goes haywire. It always made me giggle [laughs].

Those Zeppelin records sound as huge today as they did when they were first released, and the music has aged really well.

JAMES "JY" YOUNG OF STYX

Jimmy Page's songwriting and production notions still resonate as strong today as they did when Zeppelin began. Apart from The Beatles and The Rolling Stones, Led Zeppelin are right there with The Who as rock's greatest bands. And Jimmy Page is the reason for that. Certainly everyone else in Led Zeppelin was a great contributor, but Page always appeared to be the ultimate arbiter of what went on in that group.

LUKE MORLEY OF THUNDER

As an arranger and producer, Pagey really excelled himself on *Physical Graffiti*. "Ten Years Gone" is a classic example of that. It's one of my favorite Zeppelin songs. The multi-tracked guitars are amazing. As always, when Pagey was multi-tracking, it had a purpose. In the eighties, a lot of bands multi-tracked to get a bigger sound, but Pagey did it to add harmonies and create a mood. It sounds a bit pretentious—and I'm risking sounding like Nigel Tufnell here—but Page was painting with sound textures, lots of little brush strokes.

RICKY PHILLIPS OF THE BABYS, STYX, AND COVERDALE/PAGE

Any great producer knows what he wants and knows how to get it out of the musicians he's working with. Jimmy certainly knows that and does the job with ease. ⇛➙

NANCY WILSON OF HEART

Jimmy is so underrated as a producer. When he pulls out instruments like the hurdy gurd . . . and all kinds of strange Eastern-sounding things, and things that you don't know *what* it is, it's really inventive stuff. Jimmy's such a musician—capable of reading music, writing music, making string charts, writing out actual notation. There's a lot of actual theory going on in their musicianship. But that's part of the reason why Zeppelin's sound is a standout.

RIK EMMETT OF TRIUMPH

I think his talent as a producer was maybe his greatest gift, and that he had enough intelligence and vision to draw out the best from Plant, and Bonham, as Led Zeppelin matured. He also gave John Paul Jones room to grow the progressive side of the band, with Mellotron parts and clever use of keyboards. And it does a bit of a disservice to John Paul Jones to overlook his feel. Bonham's style and sound always gets kudos, plus he's one of those legendary rock stars who died young. But Jones was every bit the musical equal of the others. He had taste and feel and knew his role, and played it perfectly.

One of the legacies of Led Zeppelin was that they had a unique, uncompromised approach and follow-through, like Frank Sinatra or the Sex Pistols—they did it their way.

I think Jimmy Page found great minds that thought alike when he eventually formed the quartet. Their personalities were a huge part of their sounds and textures. As an ensemble, they had an uncompromised sound like no other band, and I suspect it was Page who had the overriding vision.

PAUL STANLEY OF KISS

What was interesting about the guitar players in The Yardbirds is how they all took their love of the blues and took it in different directions, particularly when you listen to Jeff Beck and Jimmy Page, who seemed less purist and more adventurous. It's interesting to note that both The Jeff Beck Group, which he formed after his stint in The Yardbirds, and Led Zeppelin came about at virtually the same time. Led Zeppelin's first show as Led Zeppelin was October of 1968, and they were rehearsing before that. The Jeff Beck [*Truth*] album came out in August '68. So both in a sense were incubating at the same time.

It's interesting to see how much broader and wider Jimmy Page's vision was of what was possible. Jimmy understood the complexities and subtleties of producing and arranging and brought that to his band. As brilliant as Jeff Beck was, that's something he couldn't do, whether it was the limitations of the people he played with, which he himself has said he found frustrating, or just the fact that consistently Jimmy Page turned out to be a visionary. Jeff Beck had to use his phenomenal guitar talents to try and compensate for a lack of interesting or original material.

The great thing about somebody like Jimmy Page is he brought a lot of influences and flavors to the pot. He was able to realize that for something to be heavy didn't mean that it had to be crude; that part of what makes something heavy was the depth and the intricacy or the lightness. Here's a guy who knew Celtic music, rockabilly, American folk, and international music forms, besides the obvious admiration for Robert Johnson and everyone who followed in his footsteps. They [Zeppelin] were all fans of Sandy Denny and Fairport Convention. He understood that for something to be truly bombastic it had to have depth, and depth doesn't come just from cranking up an amplifier.

The idea of being able to paint sonically, to paint with light and dark and to see things cinematically, almost so that your canvas is large and your color choices—you're not afraid to use the whole palette. That's what makes those songs so dramatic. If "How Many More Times" was just one guitar cranked, it wouldn't have anywhere near the drama that it has. To a listener who doesn't really understand what they're listening to, that's what it might sound like. But in fact it's so much more. And that becomes evident when you hear somebody trying to emulate it by just taking a guitar and cranking it up through an amplifier.

STEVE LUKATHER OF TOTO

Jimmy was a master producer. Look at the musicians he had to work with in Zeppelin—everybody was a giant. Jimmy had that old-school background with John Paul Jones as a studio guy. The experience he had in London working with all the best engineers and

producers was put to good use in the studio when he produced all those Zeppelin records. He had a sound in his head that he was able to translate from his brain and soul. He knew exactly what he wanted his band to sound like. As a producer, he brought ambient recording to rock 'n' roll.

Also, Jimmy would orchestrate his guitar parts with layering and overdubs and it would create this wall of sound. Sonically, he came up with some of the most amazing guitar tones that still hold up to this day.

You gotta remember that at that time everybody was wanting to one-up everybody else. It was a great time for rock music. Everybody was listening to everybody else. It made the music better for everyone. It was healthy competition and everybody respected each other.

JOE SATRIANI

We can all go out and get ourselves a Les Paul and a Marshall, but how Jimmy gets that sound, no one knows. It's in his fingertips. The other great thing about Jimmy Page is probably the biggest thing, and that's as a writer, producer, arranger, and band member, he's almost in the field all by himself. He's just on the mountaintop for being so creative in so many aspects of rock music. Just look at those great Led Zeppelin records and how he chose to play and record himself. It's just amazing. He created a style and a genre, and we all kind of follow it.

TOM HAMILTON OF AEROSMITH

Jimmy's production ideas back then went far beyond what anybody else was doing. He was a visionary. He had this thing in his head of having music that would be lush and juicy but much more powerful. The drums would speak. They'd be much more up-front. Back then, the proper recording techniques for drums were to dampen them down as much as possible to control the frequencies that were coming out so it didn't interfere with other instruments. But Jimmy knew how to open it up and give it more space, to the point where you could hear the kick-drum pedal squeaking or the hi-hat rattling back and forth.

Jimmy's talents as a producer and songwriter are almost beyond his technical prowess as a shredder. There are other people who might have even smoother or faster technique than him, but he was the whole package. He had as much understanding of the studio as he did of music. He created a whole new way of making records, and to this day people are still trying to make records that have the power of those old Zeppelin records.

JOE BONAMASSA

It's amazing how good he was in the studio. I don't think Jimmy gets the credit for being an extraordinarily gifted producer. We all walk into the studio with a blank tape, and it all depends what we walk out with. And Jimmy walked out with some insanely good music. And you can hear that as Zeppelin became more successful, he became more confident, because he knew their fans would follow them wherever they went. That kind of freedom is just awesome.

The thing I always got from hearing early Led Zeppelin stuff was a feeling of "I'll show them." They were trying out new sounds that had never been recorded before. The fact is that you'd have a hard time today getting many of those sounds in the studio. I don't know what they were doing or how they were doing it, but the effect is hauntingly beautiful. Especially the violin-bow stuff. That's just incredible. You listen to it today and you still go, "Wow!" It's so stark and frighteningly original that you just can't help but take notice.

I remember watching the violin-bow sequence on *The Song Remains the Same*—that Madison Square Garden concert—when I was a kid and thinking, "I didn't know you could do that with a guitar." And then there's that bit where he using the Echoplex and it's like he's throwing the notes off the end of the bow. For all the kids in the audience, it must have been like a surreal, out-of-body experience. And that's what it is, entertainment. I mean, we are still in the entertainment business.

RITCHIE BLACKMORE

As I've said before, Jimmy Page has an incredible overview of what's going on within the context of a band. He doesn't just play a solo as most guitar players do. He hears the whole arrangement of the song and incorporates a lot of color with a producer-like awareness. So with Led Zeppelin, he is a producer as well as a songwriter as well as a stage performer—and as well as a guitarist.

I'm glad to see that Jimmy Page has made a big name for himself, as he is one of the greatest talents around.

Joe Satriani
"[Jimmy Page] created a style and a genre, and we all kind of follow it."

Steve Lukather
"Sonically, [Page] came up with some of the most amazing guitar tones that still hold up to this day."

Ritchie Blackmore
"I'm glad to see that Jimmy Page has made a big name for himself, as he is one of the greatest talents around."

"YOU NEVER SAY NEVER"

By: Marcel Anders/Rob Hughes

Portraits:
Ross Halfin

With Led Zeppelin's film out and the "What next?" rumors in full swing, Jimmy Page and John Paul Jones look back and forwards.

At one point, it looked like it may never happen. But finally, despite Jimmy Page's initial concerns about it being "a massive job to embark on", the DVD film of Led Zeppelin's 2007 comeback show was released November 19, 2012. *Celebration Day* captures their performance at the Ahmet Ertegun Tribute Concert at London's O2 Arena in all its dazzling pomp. With Jason Bonham on drums in place of his late father John, it was the band's first headline show in 27 years.

The DVD follows a worldwide theater release, and a series of press conferences in which the three remaining founder members fielded inquiries about a further Zeppelin reunion with a mixture of tolerance and irritation. The whole thing, true to the band's gilded history, felt like an event.

Rock 'n' roll maestros Jimmy Page and John Paul Jones took time out to give *Classic Rock* the real inside story in 2012.

Celebration Day:
"You can't just do a quick cut and push it out. If it's art, it's got to be right."

How did it feel watching the O2 show five years on?
Jimmy Page: I knew we'd performed a pretty incredible concert. That's what we had in our sights—to go out there and knock everybody's socks off. Beforehand, I said, "We've got to rehearse for this properly." Because in the past there was Live Aid, where we had no rehearsal really, and the Atlantic 40th show [1988] wasn't what it could have been. So it was imperative that we were going to show people why we were so revered. There was such a respect and such a reputation for Led Zeppelin. Within the first of the rehearsals we were really

already good, but we needed to be extra special. It was an opportunity for us to stand up and be counted. I actually had an accident on the way through. I broke my finger in three places, and we had to postpone. We didn't want to cancel. Even a broken finger wasn't going to get in the way of this.

Why has it taken five years for this project to get released?
John Paul Jones: Five years is like five minutes in Zeppelin time. I'm amazed it's come out so quickly, actually. It's always the thing with big bands, everything moves at a glacial speed. Then when we decided to put it out, we went backwards and forwards, and that sort of thing just takes forever. Plus, you can't just do a quick cut and push it out. If it's going to be art, it's got to be right.

Did you feel the pressure of knowing that 20 million people had applied for 18,000 tickets for that one concert?
Jones: Pressure and expectations are the same for 10 people or 10,000 people. There's no difference for me. I just always try to do my best, even if I'm playing to three people on the sofa. Because it's the music you're trying to serve. Yes, you want to get it right, because you know there are a lot of people who've traveled from all over the world to see you and you don't want to let them down, but you wouldn't want to let anybody down that you're playing to.

Given the huge demand, you could have easily done a lot more shows. What happened?
Page: You have to be really brutally honest

about it. It'll be five years in December. And from a concert like that you would have thought there might have been some sort of whisper or hint about another gig over here or over there. For maybe very good reasons, charitable causes or whatever. But there wasn't. That's all I can tell you. So if there's a five-year span, I wouldn't expect there would be any more concerts, really.

I've got to look at it in an objective way, and just forget about broken fingers and all the rest of it, and go in with a really positive attitude of knowing that we did a really great show. And that Jason had played marvellously. His father would have been so proud of him.
Jones: It must have been the most nerve-racking thing in the world to be in Jason's position, but he pulled it off amazingly. And he took chances, which was great because that's what Zeppelin was always about.

Were there plans to form another band with a different singer and maybe tour?
Page: Certainly for Jason, myself and John Paul Jones; Robert had his Alison Krauss project to promote. It seemed the right thing to go in and start playing new material. I thought that really we should play to our strengths here, which was the music. But there were a lot of movements to bring in singers and do this, that and the other. And that would've changed the character too early from what we were doing. I won't say there was pressure, but there was a lot of hinting about this singer ➡➡

"Pressure and expectations are the same for 10 people or 10,000 people . . . I just always try to do my best, even if I'm playing to three people on the sofa."

John Paul Jones

and that singer. For me it was more a question of, let's see what we can really do. And I don't think we really got a chance to do that. Of course we would've played Led Zeppelin material, but you want to be playing some really, really good new material.

Jones: There wasn't a plan beforehand, we just really wanted to do the gig—get it done and get it done well. And I suppose afterwards we didn't all agree that we all wanted to do it again. Robert didn't want to do it. So, as me, Jim, and Jason had worked so hard together, I thought, let's start a different band, a totally different band.

So we're not actually talking about Led Zeppelin here?
Jones: Not at all. That's a total misunderstanding. I said, "Of course, if we go out we're going to have to do some Zeppelin numbers." And there's nothing wrong with that. In fact I think we rehearsed "Carouselambra" [from *In Through the Out Door*], which we've never done live before. And we had a whole bunch of new material done. But Jimmy and I couldn't agree on singers. We got a few people in but, looking back on it, I suppose it would have been hard to have made it a different band in everybody's eyes. I quite liked Myles Kennedy. He's got the range, but his voice is completely different to Robert's. Which was fine by me, because it's going to be a completely different band. But it

didn't work out and we all moved on.

So it's definitely not going to happen?
Page: I don't think so. Let's put it this way: this time last year, I intended to be actually playing by now, in a live outfit. So that will have to be postponed now into the tail end of next year. But I definitely want to be doing that. There are some other things going on too, like the sort of remastering of the catalogue.
Jones: It's pretty unlikely that [Zeppelin] will do anything. You never say never, but I can't really see it happening. It would've been awful if Robert didn't want to do it and then we went out. And if he was unhappy with it, that would've been worse. I mean, I haven't done it since 1980, when the band finished, if you think about it. Okay, Page and Plant did a bit of it, so you know what I mean.

You mean they never called you?
Jones: No! I was probably more pissed off then than I was this time. But you move on. And I've got plenty to do.

Does Led Zeppelin still occupy most of your time these days?
Page: Absolutely. But providing the things that you're involved with, on a Led Zeppelin

> "We had a whole bunch of new material done . . . but Jimmy and I couldn't agree on singers."
> John Paul Jones

Above: the power of three. There's still an extraordinary chemistry between Jones, Page, and Plant.

front, are really honorable things. And they're things everyone in the band can be proud of. If they're things that the fans are really looking forward to hearing, then it's worth doing. It's essential, really.

How does it feel knowing that Led Zeppelin is still massively popular even after all these years?
Page: When the first Zeppelin album was done, it was definitely one hope. I'm sure everyone else in the band felt the same way—that they wanted other musicians to come up and say, "Hey, that's a really good album and that's a really good band." But the chemistry of Led Zeppelin means that you've got four incredible musicians—and I'm going to count Robert as a musician individually. The thing was that we could play as a band. That was the difference between us and all of the others. We were all on top of our game, and that element of us playing together was just something else. If you want to play guitar, if you want to play bass, or harmony, or whatever you want to do, there's a wonderful textbook there in Led Zeppelin.
Jones: I'm very proud of it all. And it was a really good band. It's very gratifying, and I suppose it is very surprising that it's lasted so long. But I don't feel we've cheated anybody, ever. I know we've ◆▶ always worked hard on our shows and always worked hard on our music. So I think it's deserving.

The opening sequence of *Celebration Day* is footage of Led Zeppelin arriving in Atlanta on a private jet, having a police escort and two limousines in tow, and 76,000 fans setting a new ticket record. How did it feel to make that transition to superstardom?

Jones: The private jet and the police escort was just something you finally got to do. I mean, we first toured America in a car. It was awful! Then I think we graduated to a Greyhound bus, then we did scheduled airlines. We've done it all the wrong way—the hard way. So when we finally figured it out—or could afford it—we did it with a private plane. And yes, it got bigger and bigger and bigger. It turns more into an event than a musical experience.

Page: When I first went to America with The Yardbirds, they were still screaming in those days of The Beatles. And we played in an ice rink. This was when Jeff Beck was still in the band. And I remember they mobbed the stage. We had to run away. There was only this little bit of carpet to take you from the dressing room area, and you were slipping over and having your clothes ripped off. That's the sort of mania that I can remember, having been through all of that as well. And The Yardbirds were playing in stadiums as a support band, too. So I definitely paid my dues along the way. I had a really good idea about Led Zeppelin. And at the time, FM radio stations were playing whole sides of albums, which was really quite refreshing.

How much credit does Peter Grant, your late manager, deserve for Led Zeppelin's successes?

Jones: Well, he was the fifth member. He was just very smart. He could be aggressive verbally and he could be physical, but he always used to use his brain and his mouth first. And it wouldn't have been anywhere near the same without him. He was an architect of how we were presented. He never said anything about the music, except, "I like it. I know nothing about music, that's your department." He basically kept everybody away from us while we were doing stuff, working on our records.

And he talked you, John, into staying with the band in 1973, when you told him you'd decided to quit.

Jones: I'd temporarily had enough. We were touring so much. And I just thought about it and it seemed silly.

Does Led Zeppelin sometimes seem like a monster you created, or is it the best thing that could've happened to you?

Page: I'm really proud of my Led Zeppelin heritage. And I'm sure everybody else is. It was such a wonderful band to be in—it was a privilege to be in a band like that. But we didn't waste our time. We really made the most of what we had of that creative flow. Looking at all of that work, I can see a whole sort of movement and change.

It must have been a particularly intense 11 years. After the band ceased, did you need to get away from it all?

Page: The first thing I actually did after we lost John, was I played with Alan White and Chris Squire from Yes. Because I had my own studio at that point, it was suggested that I play with them. And I thought, "That's really going to be testy." Because Yes' music is

Page stands and delivers.

really good and I love them. Then after that, I got the chance to do the soundtrack for *Death Wish II* [1982], which was really a challenge. I had to come up with a lot of stuff and make all of it up on the spot. I had the opportunity to do more soundtracks, but after that I got together with Paul Rodgers [in The Firm]. We did a couple of albums and quite a bit of touring. Then I had a solo album in 1988 [*Outrider*]. So I guess now it's time to do another solo album. We'll see what I manage to pull together under those circumstances. I had some really ambitious ideas.

Earlier this year, Jimmy, you released a vinyl version of 1972's *Lucifer Rising*, the soundtrack to Kenneth Anger's cult film of that name.

Page: I'm pleased that came out, because that's really flirting with the avant-garde. It's the sort of stuff that I couldn't have done with Led Zeppelin. But I was thinking that way as much as I was thinking rock 'n' roll. It's sort of like the mad scientist at home in his laboratory.

> "I'm really proud of my Led Zeppelin heritage . . . It was such a wonderful band to be in."
> Jimmy Page

John, what's the latest on the proposed second album from Them Crooked Vultures, your band with Dave Grohl and Josh Homme?

Jones: I hope it can still happen, though I don't want to spend a lot of time doing big tours again. I've got a lot of other stuff to do. I'm writing a classical opera at the moment. It's based on a play by Strindberg, *The Ghost Sonata*, so it's going to be very dark and mysterious. And I also work with [avant-garde jazz combo] Supersilent, Seasick Steve and have my own little duo, Minibus Pimps, which is me and Helge Sten; it's pretty hardcore electronics. So there's lots of stuff. But maybe if we can do a quick album somewhere and a few dates, then I'm up for it, because it was great fun doing the Vultures. It was very easy, too.

I just like to play and make music. That's all I've ever been interested in. I was never one to be famous or be on the television. My ambition was never to have a real job, to try to play music all day. That's all I ever wanted to do. ❼

Celebration Day is available now on DVD and Blu-ray via Atlantic.